Apropos of Nothing

Apropos of Nothing

Woody Allen

ARCADE PUBLISHING,
an imprint of Skyhorse Publishing, Inc.

Arcade Publishing books may be purchased in bulk at special discounts for sales promotion, corporate gifts, fund-raising, or educational purposes. Special editions can also be created to specifications. For details, contact the Special Sales Department, Arcade Publishing, 307 West 36th Street, 11th Floor, New York, NY 10018 or arcade@skyhorsepublishing.com.

Arcade Publishing® is a registered trademark of Skyhorse Publishing, Inc.®, a Delaware corporation.

Visit our website at www.arcadepub.com.

10 9 8 7 6 5 4 3 2 1

Library of Congress Cataloging-in-Publication Data is available on file.

Cover design by Albert Tang and Brian Peterson

Hardcover ISBN: 978-1-951627-34-8
Large Print Edition ISBN: 978-1-951627-35-5
Audio Book ISBN: 978-1-951627-36-2
Ebook ISBN: 978-1-951627-37-9

Printed in the United States of America

For Soon-Yi, the best.
I had her eating out of
my hand and then I noticed my arm was missing.

Like Holden, I don't feel like going into all that David Copperfield kind of crap, although in my case, a little about my parents you may find more interesting than reading about me. Like my father, born in Brooklyn when it was all farms, ball boy for the early Brooklyn Dodgers, a pool hustler, a bookmaker, a small man but a tough Jew in fancy shirts with slicked-back patent leather hair a la George Raft. No high school, the Navy at sixteen, on a firing squad in France when they killed an American sailor for raping a local girl. A medal-winning marksman, always loved pulling a trigger and carried a pistol till the day he died with a full head of silver hair and twenty-twenty eyesight at a hundred. One night during World War I his boat got hit by a shell somewhere off the coast in the icy waters of Europe. It sank. Everyone drowned except for three guys who made the miles-long swim to shore. He was one of the three that could handle the Atlantic. But that's how close I came to never being born. The war ends. His father who's made some dough always spoiled him, favoring him shamelessly over his two dim-witted siblings. And I mean dim-witted. As a kid, I always thought his sister reminded me of a circus

1

pinhead. His brother, weak, wan, and degenerate looking, drifted around the Flatbush streets peddling newspapers till he dissolved like a pale wafer. White, whiter, gone. So Dad's dad buys his favorite sailor boy a real fancy car in which my father tools around post–World War I Europe. When he comes home, the old man, my grandfather, has added a few zeroes to his bank account and smokes Corona Coronas. He's the only Jew working as the traveling rep for a big coffee company. My father runs errands for him, and one day lugging some coffee sacks around he passes a court-house, and down the steps strolls Kid Dropper, a thug of the times. The Kid gets into a car and some nonentity named Louie Cohen jumps on the car and puts four slugs through the window while my dad stands there staring. The old man told me this tale many times as a bedtime story, which was a lot more exciting than Flopsy, Mopsy, Cotton-tail, and Peter.

Meanwhile, my father's father, looking to become an industry, buys a string of taxicabs and a number of movie houses including the Midwood Theater, where I would spend so much of my childhood in flight from reality, but that came later. I first had to be born. Unfortunately, prior to that little cosmic long shot, Dad's dad, in a burst of manic euphoria, bet more and more on Wall Street, and you can see where this is going. On a certain Thursday the stock market did a big Brodie, and my grandfather, high roller that he was, was reduced to instant abject poverty. The cabs go, the movie houses go, the coffee company bosses jump out windows. My father, suddenly responsible for his own caloric intake, is forced to go on the hustle; he drives a cab, runs a poolroom, strikes out with assorted scams and makes book. Summers he is paid to go to Saratoga to attend to questionable horse-racing business for Albert Anastasia. Summers upstate were another series of bedtime stories. How he loved that life. Fancy clothes, a big per diem, sexy women, and then somehow he meets my mother. Tilt. How he wound up with Nettie is a mystery on a par with dark matter. Two characters as mismatched as Hannah Arendt and Nathan Detroit, they disagreed on every single issue except Hitler and my report cards. And yet with all the verbal carnage, they stayed married for seventy years— out of spite, I suspect. Still, I'm sure they loved each other in their own way, a way known perhaps only to a few headhunting tribes in Borneo.

In Mom's defense I have to say Nettie Cherry was a wonderful woman; bright, hardworking, sacrificing. She was faithful and loving and decent but not, let us say, physically prepossessing. When I said years later my mother looked like Groucho Marx, people thought I was kidding. In her last years, she suffered from dementia and died at ninety-six. Delusional as she was, at the end she never lost her ability to kvetch, which she had raised to an art form. Dad, spry into his midnineties, never a worry nor a care ever disturbed his sleep. Nor a single thought his waking hours. His philosophy amounted to "If you don't have your health you got nothing," wisdom deeper than all the complexity of Western thought, succinct as a fortune cookie. And he kept his health. "Nothing bothers me," he would brag. "You're too stupid for anything to bother you," Mom would patiently try to explain. Mom had five sisters, one homelier than the next, with Mom arguably the homeliest of the swarm. Let me put it this way: Freud's Oedipal theory that all us men unconsciously want to kill our fathers and marry our mothers hits a brick wall when it comes to my mother.

Sadly, even though my mother was a much better parent, much more responsible, more honest, and more mature than my not-so-moral, philandering father, I loved him more. Everybody did. I guess because he was a sweet guy, warmer, more demonstrably affectionate, while she took no prisoners. She was the one who kept the family from going under. She worked as a bookkeeper in a flower shop. She ran the household, cooked the meals, paid the bills, made sure there was fresh cheese in the traps while my father peeled off twenties he couldn't afford and stuffed them into my pocket while I slept.

On those rare occasions over the years when he hit his number, we all got cut in big-time. Dad played the numbers every single day rain or shine. It was the closest thing in his life to religious observance. And whether he left the house with one dollar or one hundred dollars, he spent it all before returning home. On what? Well, clothes and other essential items, like tricky golf balls that rolled funny and he could use to cheat his pals. And he spent it on me and my sister, Letty. He spoiled us with the same generous freedom with which his father had spoiled him. Example: at one point, Dad was a waiter on the Bowery working nights for no salary, only tips. Yet every morning I woke up—I was going to high school at the time—there on my night table was five bucks. The other kids I knew were getting fifty cents or maybe one dollar allowance a week. I was getting five bucks a day! What did I do with it? Ate out, bought magic tricks, used it to bankroll my card or crap games.

See, I had become this amateur magician because I loved

everything about magic. I always took to anything that required solitude, like practicing sleight of hand or playing a horn or writing, as it kept me from having to deal with other humans who, for no explainable reason, I didn't like nor trust. I say "no reason" because I came from a large, loving, extended family who were all nice to me. It's like I was a genetically born louse. Meanwhile, I'd sit all alone and practice card moves and coin moves, manipulating the deck, false shuffles, false cuts, bottom dealing, palming. Anyhow, it was a short jump for a born louse, from pulling a rabbit from a hat to realizing I could cheat at cards. Having inherited my father's DNA for dishonesty, I was soon hustling at poker, cleaning out the unsuspecting, dealing seconds, hopping the cut, and pocketing everyone's allowance.

But enough about me and what a lowlife I started out as. I was filling you in on my parents and still haven't come to the part where Mom gives birth to her little miscreant. My father led a charmed life and my mother—who by necessity had to handle all the serious problems of daily survival—was all business and not fun or interesting. She was intelligent but not book smart, which she'd be the first to tell you, proud of her "common sense." I frankly found her too strict and pushy, but it was because she wanted me to "amount to something." She glimpsed the results of an IQ test I took at five or six, and while I won't tell you the figure, it impressed my mother. It was recommended that I be sent off to Hunter College special school for sharp kids, but the long train ride every day from Brooklyn into Manhattan was too grueling for my mother or my aunt, who alternated taking me on the subway. So they plopped me back into P.S. 99, a school for backward teachers. I hated all schools and probably would've gotten little or nothing out of Hunter had I stayed. My mother was forever browbeating me, telling me I had such a high IQ, how could I be so complete an idiot in school? Example of my scholastic idiocy: In high school I had two years of Spanish. Upon entering New York University, I hustled my way into being allowed to take freshman Spanish—like it was totally new to me. Can you believe I failed it?

Anyhow, my mother's smarts did not extend to culture, and so neither she nor my father, who never rose academically above baseball, pinochle, or Hopalong Cassidy movies, never once, not one single time, ever took me to a show or a museum. I first saw a Broadway show when I was seventeen, and I discovered paintings on my own playing hooky and needing a warm place to hang out, and the museums were free or cheap. I can safely say my father and mother never saw a play or visited a gallery or read a book. My father owned one book, *The Gangs of New York*. It was the only book I browsed growing up, and it imbued in me a fascination with gangsters, criminals, and crime. I knew gangsters like most boys knew ball players. I knew baseball players, too, but not like I knew Gyp the Blood, Greasy Thumb Jake Guzik, and Tick-Tock Tannenbaum. Oh, I also knew movie stars, thanks to my cousin Rita, who papered her walls with color portraits from *Modern Screen*. I'm saving writing about her as she was one of the true bright spots of my growing up and deserves some special space. But in addition to Bogart and Betty Grable and how many wins Cy Young had and how many RBIs Hack Wilson hit in one season and who pitched two consecutive no-hitters for Cincinnati, I knew Abe Reles could sing but not fly—

plus where Owney Madden wound up and why an icepick was the weapon of choice for Pittsburgh Phil Strauss.

In addition to *The Gangs of New York*, my entire library consisted of comic books. I read only comic books until I was in my later teens. My literary heroes were not Julien Sorel, Raskolnikov, or the local yokels of Yoknapatawpha County; they were Batman, Superman, the Flash, the Sub-Mariner, Hawkman. Yes, and Donald Duck and Bugs Bunny and Archie Andrews. Folks, you are reading the autobiography of a misanthropic gangster-loving illiterate; an uncultivated loner who sat in front of a three-way mirror practicing with a deck of cards so he could palm off an ace of spades, render it invisible from any angle, and hustle some pots. Yes, I eventually got blown away by Cezanne's heavy apples and Pissarro's rainy Parisian boulevards, but as I said, only because I would cut school and needed succor on those snowy winter mornings. There I was at fifteen, on the hook, confronted by Matisse and Chagall, by Nolde, Kirchner, and Schmidt-Rotluff, by *Guernica* and the frantic wall-sized Jackson Pollock, by the Beckmann triptych and Louise Nevelson's dark black sculpture. Then lunch in the MOMA cafeteria, followed by a vintage movie downstairs in the screening room. Carole Lombard, William Powell, Spencer Tracy. Doesn't it sound like more fun than Miss Schwab's obnoxious picklepuss demanding the date of the Stamp Act or the capital of Wyoming? Then the lies at home, the excuses next day at school, the hustling, the tap dancing, the forged notes, caught again, parental exasperation. "But you have such a high IQ." And by the way, reader, it's not so high, but you'd think from my mother's cri de cœur I could explain string theory. You can tell from my movies; while some are entertaining, no idea I ever had is going to start any new religion.

Plus—I'm not ashamed to admit it—I didn't like reading. Unlike my sister, who enjoyed it, I was a lazy boy who found no joy in cracking a book. And why would I have? The radio and movies were so much more exciting. They were less demanding and more vivid. In school, they never knew how to introduce you to reading so you'd learn to enjoy it. The books and stories they chose were dull, witless, antiseptic. No one in those carefully chosen stories for young boys and girls compared to Plastic Man or Captain Marvel. You think a hot-to-trot kid (again, defying Freud, I never had a latency period) who likes gangster movies with Bogart and Cagney and cheap, sexy blondes is going to go a hundred over "The Gift of the Magi"? So she sells her hair to buy him a watch fob and he sells his watch to buy combs for her hair. The moral I drew was you're always safer giving cash. I liked comic books, sparse as the prose might have been, and when school later introduced me to Shakespeare they managed to force-feed it in such a way that when it was over you never wanted to hear another *hark*, *prithee*, or *but soft* as long as you lived.

Anyhow, I didn't read until I was at the tail end of high school and my hormones had really kicked in and I first noticed those young women with the long, straight hair, who wore no lipstick, little makeup, dressed in black turtlenecks and skirts with black tights, and carried big leather bags holding copies of *The Metamorphosis*, which they had annotated themselves in the margins with things like "Yes, very true," or "See Kierkegaard." For whatever irrational carnal singularity, those were the ones who captured my heart, and when I called for a date and asked if they'd like to go to a movie or a baseball game and they wanted rather to hear Segovia or catch the Ionesco play off Broadway, there'd be a long awkward pause before I said, "Let me get back to you," then scrambled to look up who Segovia and Ionesco were. It's fair to say these women were not eagerly awaiting the next issue of *Captain America* or even the next Mickey Spillane, the sole poet I could quote.

When I did finally date one of these delectable bohemian little kumquats, it was brutal for both of us. For her, because early on in the evening she would realize she was stuck with an illiterate imbecile who didn't seem to know what position Stephen Daedalus played, and brutal for me because I became aware that I was indeed a submental and if I ever hoped to kiss those unlipsticked lips or see her a second time I was going to have to actually delve into literature deeper than *Kiss Me Deadly*. I couldn't get by just on anecdotes about Lucky Luciano or Rube Waddell. I was going to have to grab a look at Balzac, and Tolstoy, and Eliot so I could hold up my end of the conversation and not have to take the young lady home, as she claimed suddenly to be stricken with a case of Bronze John. Meanwhile, I would wind up at Dubrow's Cafeteria to commiserate with the other strikeout victims of Saturday night.

But those fiascos lay in the future. Now that you have some idea of my parents I'll mention my only sibling, my sister. Then I'll double back and get born so the tale can really take flight.

Letty is eight years younger than me. Naturally, when she was about to come into the world my parents prepared me in the consummately wrong way: "When your sister is born you will no longer be the center of attention. You won't be getting the presents anymore, she will. We'll all have to shift our attention to her and her needs, so don't expect to be the main attraction ever again." Another boy of eight might have been a bit shaken by the prospect of suddenly being cast aside in favor of the new arrival. But while I loved my parents dearly, I was aware they were a couple of rank amateurs who had no flair for child rearing and their dire predictions were dopey and empty, which they proved to be. I guess it's a tribute to them that they loved me in such an unequivocal way that I knew while they came on like Cassandras, they would never abandon me and their devotion to my happiness and well-being, and they did not.

The second I set eyes on my sister in the crib I was totally taken with her, loved her, and helped raise her, shielding her from the friction between my parents, which could escalate exponentially over trivial concerns. I mean, who could believe a disagreement over gefilte fish could morph into a battle worthy of Homer? I played with Letty, took her with me many times when I went out with friends. They all found her cute and smart, and she and I always got along swimmingly. It reminded me of an exchange of letters I had with Groucho, whom I had gotten friendly with over the years thanks to Dick Cavett, whom I'll tell you about later. I wrote Groucho when Harpo died, and he wrote me and said he and Harpo never had exchanged a serious argument or bad words, and that's how it's been with my sister, who today produces my movies.

But now, I'm ready to be born. Finally, I enter the world. A world I will never feel comfortable in, never understand, and never approve of or forgive. Allan Stewart Konigsberg, born on December 1, 1935. Actually, I was born on the thirtieth of November very close to midnight, and my parents pushed the date so I could start off on a day one. This has given me zero advantage in life, and I would have much preferred they left me an enormous trust fund. I mention it only because in a meaningless bit of irony, my sister was born eight years later on the exact same day. This remarkable coincidence and fifteen cents will get you on the subway. I was delivered in a Bronx hospital though the folks lived in Brooklyn. Don't ask me why my mother schlepped all the way up to the Bronx to produce me. Maybe that hospital was giving away free dishes. Anyhow, my mother didn't schlep back from the Bronx hospital. Instead, she nearly died up there. In fact, it was touch and go for a few weeks, but as she tells it, constant hydrating pulled her through. That's all I would've needed, to be raised only by my father. I would probably have a rap sheet by now the length of the Torah. As it is, having two loving parents I grew up surprisingly neurotic. Why, I don't know.

I was the cynosure of my mother's five sisters, the only male child, the darling of these sweet yentas who fussed over me. I never missed a meal, nor wanted for clothing or shelter, never fell prey to any serious illness like polio, which was rampant. I didn't have Down syndrome like one kid in my class, nor was I hunchback like little Jenny or afflicted with alopecia like the Schwartz kid. I was healthy, popular, very athletic, always chosen first for teams, a ball player, a runner, and yet somehow I managed to turn out nervous, fearful, an emotional wreck, hanging on by a thread to my composure, misanthropic, claustrophobic, isolated, embittered, impeccably pessimistic. Some people see the glass half empty, some see it half full. I always saw the coffin half full. Of the thousand natural shocks the flesh was heir to, I managed to avoid most except number six eighty-two— no denial mechanism. My mother said she couldn't figure it out. She always claimed I was a nice, sweet, cheerful boy till around five, and then I changed into a sour, nasty, disgruntled, rotten kid.

And yet there was no trauma in my life, no awful thing that occurred and turned me from a smiling, freckle-faced lad with a fishing pole and pantaloons into a chronically dissatisfied lout. My own speculation centers around the fact that at five or so, I became aware of mortality and figured, uh-oh, this is not what I signed on for. I had never agreed to be finite. If you don't mind, I'd like my money back. As I got older, not just extinction but the meaning-lessness of existence became clearer to me. I ran into the same question that bugged the former prince of Denmark: Why suffer the slings and arrows when I can just wet my nose, insert it into the light socket, and never have to deal with anxiety, heartache, or my mother's boiled chicken ever again? Hamlet chose not to because he feared what might happen in an afterlife, but I didn't believe in an afterlife, so given my utterly dismal appraisal of the human condition and its painful absurdity, why go on with it? In the end, I couldn't come up with a logical reason why and finally came to the conclusion that as humans, we are simply hardwired to resist death. The blood trumps the brain. No logical reason to cling to life, but who cares what the head says— the heart says: Have you seen Lola in a miniskirt? As much as we whine and moan and insist, often quite persuasively, that life is a pointless nightmare of suffering and tears, if a man suddenly entered the room with a knife to kill us, we instantly react. We grab him and fight with every ounce of our energy to disarm him and survive. (Personally, I run.) This, I submit, is a property strictly of our molecules. By now you've probably figured out not only I'm no intellectual but also no fun at parties.

Incidentally, it is amazing how often I am described as "an intellectual." This is a notion as phony as the Loch Ness Monster as I don't have an intellectual neuron in my head. Illiterate and uninterested in things scholarly, I grew up the prototype of the slug who sits in front of the TV, beer in hand, football game going full blast, *Playboy* centerfold Scotch-taped to the wall, a barbarian sporting the tweeds and elbow patches of the Oxford don. I have no insights, no lofty thoughts, no understanding of most poems that do not begin, "Roses are red, violets are blue." What I do have, however, is a pair of black-rimmed glasses, and I propose that it is these specs, combined with a flair for appropriating snippets from erudite sources too deep for me to grasp but which can be utilized in my work to give the deceptive impression of knowing more than I do that keeps this fairy tale afloat.

Okay, so I'm raised in a bubble by many doting women, mom, my aunts, and four loving grandparents. Try and keep track: Dad's dad, once rich, a man who sailed to London merely to go to the horse races, who owned a box at the opera, now impoverished, earning a pittance God knows how. His wife, also an immigrant he married so they could both enter the country. She was fleeing Russian pogroms and he compulsory military service. She was a raisin of an old woman, diabetic, living with her spouse and brood in a cheesy hovel with an upright piano that no one played. But she loved me, slipping me dough on the QT, sugar cubes from the yellow Domino box, asking for nothing in return except occasional visits, and forever generous despite their poverty.

My maternal grandparents also loved me. Mom's mom, fat and deaf, just sitting by the window all day, every day (from her looks, she'd have been more at home on a lily pad). Grandpa, active, virile, always in shul, and here's the way a louse like me repaid his kindness. Me and my friends came into possession of a counterfeit nickel. Pure lead. We were scared to try and pass it at the candy store lest we wind up on Riker's, so I volunteered to slip it past my grandfather who was old and would never catch wise, and he didn't, and I exchanged it with him for five pennies from his snap-open purse, and it wasn't like in the movies where the old guy chuckles and knows what I'm up to but humors me with a sly twinkle in his eye. Nope. He was conned, and I took him to the cleaners for his five pennies and stuck him with the lead nickel and went off to buy Goobers.

Finally, there was the true rainbow of my childhood, my cousin Rita. Five years older than me, blond, zaftig, her companionship had perhaps the most significant influence on my life. Rita Wishnick, her father yet another fleeing Russian Jew named Vishnetski, anglicized to Wishnick. She was an attractive girl, a polio victim who had a slight limp, who took a liking to me and took me everywhere—to the movies, the beach, Chinese restaurants, miniature golf, pizza joints—who played cards with me, who played checkers with me, who played Monopoly with me. She introduced me to all her friends, boys and girls who were older than me, and whatever precociousness I had seemed to delight them, so I ran with them and became very sophisticated for a little boy, and my childhood took a big step forward.

I had friends my own age, too, but I spent a lot of time with Rita and the boys and girls of her set. They were bright, middle-class Jewish kids getting educated to teach, to become journalists, professors, doctors, and lawyers.

But let me get back to the movies, Rita's passion. Now remember, I'm five, she's ten. Apart from papering her walls with color photos of every star in Hollywood, she went to the movies regularly, which meant every Saturday at noon to the double feature, usually at the Midwood, and while she went with friends, she always took me. I saw everything Hollywood put out. Every feature, every B picture. I knew who was in the pictures, recognized them, got to know the smaller players, the character actors, recognized the music as I knew all of popular music because Rita and I sat and listened to the radio together endlessly. The *Make Believe Ballroom, Your Hit Parade.* In those days, the radio was on from the minute you woke up till you went to sleep. Music, news, and what music.

The pop music of the day was Cole Porter, Rodgers and Hart, Irving Berlin, Jerome Kern, George Gershwin, Benny Goodman, Billie Holiday, Artie Shaw, Tommy Dorsey. So here I am inundated with such beautiful music and movies. First, a double feature every week, then as the years pass, I go more and more. Such excitement to enter the Midwood Saturday morning while the house lights were still on and a small crowd bought their candy and filed in as some pop record played to keep the seat takers from mutinying till the lights dimmed. Harry James—"I'll Get By." The sconce shades were red, the fixtures gold brass, the carpets red. At last the lights go down and the curtains part and the silver screen lights up with a logo that makes the heart salivate, if I may mix my metaphors, with Pavlovian anticipation. I saw them all, every comedy, any cowboy movie, love story, pirate picture, war film. Many decades later when I stood with Dick Cavett on a street where a once-grand theater had been and was now an empty lot, we both stared at the blank real estate plot and remembered how in the middle of that lot we once sat, transported to foreign cities full of intrigue, to deserts surrounded by romantic Bedouins, on ships, in trenches, to palaces and Indian reservations. Soon a condo would be there with Rick's Café long demolished.

As a young boy my favorite films were what I've dubbed champagne comedies. I loved stories that took place in penthouses where the elevator opened into the apartment and corks popped, where suave men who spoke witty dialogue romanced beautiful women who lounged around the house in what someone now might wear to a wedding at Buckingham Palace.

These apartments were big, usually duplexes, with much white space. Upon entering, one or one's guest almost always headed directly to a small, accessible bar to pour decantered drinks. Everybody drank all the time and nobody vomited. And nobody had cancer and the penthouse didn't leak and when the phone rang in the middle of the night, the people high above Park or Fifth Avenue didn't have to, like my mother, drag ass out of bed and bang her knees in the dark groping for the one black instrument and hear maybe a relative just dropped dead. No. Hepburn or Tracy or Cary Grant or Myrna Loy would just reach for a phone on their night table inches from where they slept, and the phone was usually white and the news did not revolve around the metastasizing of cells or a coronary thrombosis from years of deadly brisket, but more likely solvable conundrums like "What? What do you mean we're not legally married!?"

Just imagine a scorching summer day in Flatbush. The mercury hits ninety-five and the humidity is suffocating. There was no air-conditioning, that is, unless you went inside a movie house. You eat your morning soft-boiled eggs in a coffee cup in a tiny kitchen on a linoleum-covered floor and a table draped with oilcloth. The radio is playing "Milkman Keep Those Bottles Quiet" or "Tess's Torch Song." Your parents are in yet another stupid "discussion," as my mother called them, which stopped just short of exchanging gunfire. Either she spilled sour cream on his new shirt or he embarrassed her by parking his taxicab in front of the house. God forbid the neighbors should discover she married a cabdriver instead of a Supreme Court justice. My father never tired of telling me that he once picked up Babe Ruth. "Gave me a lousy tip," was all he could remember about the Sultan of Swat. I thought of it years later when I was a comic working at the Blue Angel and Sonny, the doorman, gave me his character rundown of Billy Rose, the wealthy Broadway sport who loved playing big shot. "A quarter man," Sonny sneered, having learned to categorize all humans by the square footage of their gratuities. I tease my parents in this account of my life, but each imparted knowledge to me that has served me well over the decades. From my father: When buying a newspaper from a newsstand, never take the top one. From Mom: The label always goes in the back.

So it's a hot summer day and you kill the morning returning deposit bottles to the market to earn two cents per bottle
so you can ante up at the Midwood or the Vogue or the Elm,
our nearest local three movie houses. Three thousand miles
away in Europe, Jews are being shot and gassed for no good
reason by ordinary Germans who do it with great relish and
have no trouble finding coat holders all over the continent.
You sweat your way down Coney Island Avenue, an ugly
avenue replete with used car lots, funeral homes, hardware
stores, till the exciting marquee comes into view. The sun
is now high and brutal. The trolley makes noise, cars are
honking, two men are locked in the moronic choreography
of road rage and are screaming and starting to swing at each
other. The shorter, weaker one is running to secure his tire
iron. You buy your ticket, walk in, and suddenly the harsh
heat and sunlight vanished and you are in a cool, dark, alternate reality. OK, so they're only images—but what images!
The matron, an elderly lady in white, guides you to your seat
with her flashlight. You've spent your last nickel on some
blissful confection fancifully christened Jujubes or Chuckles.
And now you look up at the screen and to the music of Cole
Porter or Irving Berlin's unspeakably beautiful melodies,
there appears the Manhattan skyline. I'm in good hands.
I'm not going to see a story about guys in overalls on a farm
who rise early to milk cows and whose goal in life is to win
a ribbon at the state fair or train their horse to transcend
a series of equine tribulations and place first in the local
harness race. And mercifully, no dog will save anyone and
no character with a twang will hook his finger into a jug's
ear to suck out the contents, and no string will be attached
to any boy's toe as he dozes at the old fishing hole.

To this day, if the opening shot of a movie is a close-up of a flag being thrown and the flag is on the meter of a yellow cab, I stay. If it's on a mailbox, I'm out of there. No, my characters will awaken and the curtains to their bedroom will part, revealing New York City with its tall buildings and every bit of its thrilling possibilities out there, and my cast will either dine in bed with a bed tray complete with a holder for the morning paper—or at a table with linen and silver and this guy's egg will come to the table in an egg cup so he just has to tap the shell to get to the yolk and there will be no news of extermination camps, only maybe a front page showing some beautiful babe with another guy that sets Fred Astaire off since he loves her. Or, if it's breakfast for a married couple, they actually care about each other after years of being together and she doesn't dwell on his failures, and he doesn't call her a douchebag. And when the movie ends, the second feature is a detective thriller where some hard-boiled private eye solves all life's problems with a sock in the jaw and goes off with a stacked tomato the likes of which did not exist in any of my classes or any of the weddings, funerals, or bar mitzvahs I attended. And by the way, I never attended a funeral: I was always spared reality. The first and only dead body I ever saw was that of Thelonious Monk, when I stopped off en route for dinner at Elaine's to view him out of respect as he lay in state in a funeral home on Third Avenue. I took Mia Farrow with me; it was very early in our dating, and she was polite but dismayed and should have known then she was beginning a relationship with the wrong dreamer, but that whole mishigas comes later.

So now the double feature is over and I leave the

comfortable, dark magic of the movie house and reenter Coney Island Avenue, the sun, the traffic, back to the wretched apartment on Avenue K. Back into the clutches of my archenemy, reality. In my movie *Sleeper*, as part of one comic sequence, by some kind of mind-bending process I imagine I'm Blanche Du Bois from *Streetcar Named Desire*. I speak in a feminine, southern accent trying to make the sequence funny while Diane Keaton does a perfect Brando. Keaton's the type who complains, "Oh I can't do this, I can't imitate Marlon Brando." Like the girls in class who tell you how lousy they did on the test and the results come back and they're straight As. Naturally, her Brando is better than my Blanche, but my point is, in real life I am Blanche. Blanche says, "I don't want reality, I want magic." And I have always despised reality and lusted after magic. I tried to be a magician, but found I could only manipulate cards and coins and not the universe.

And so, because of cousin Rita, I was introduced to movies, movie stars, Hollywood with its patriotic morality and miraculous endings; and while I brushed off everything everyone tried to teach me, from my parents to my Spanish teachers when I'd already had the two years of Spanish, Hollywood took. *Modern Screen. Photoplay.* Bogart, Cagney, Edward G. Robinson, Rita Hayworth— their celluloid world was what I learned. The larger-than-life, the superficial, the falsely glamorous, but I do not regret a frame of it. When asked which character in my films is most like me on the screen, you only have to look at Cecilia in *Purple Rose of Cairo*.

So where was I? Oh, I was born. I was definitely born, and I put it that way because there were three close calls for me not having a life. The first was when my father was one of only three swimmers who made the long swim to shore when his boat sank. The second also involved him, but not so heroically. He was at a family party of some sort with my mother, his fiancée. It was all my mother's side of the family. They were a bunch of decent, noisy Jews with their makeshift lifestyles. Example of their style: we had a relative named Phil Wasserman, whom I will return to soon, as he was a major contributor to my career in later years. But there was also another relative named Phil Wasserman, equally as important a member of the family and he was always referred to as "the other Phil Wasserman." So in conversations about either Phil Wasserman, one always had to specify and one did by saying, "I was walking in Manhattan and I ran into the other Phil Wasserman." Or "I have to buy a gift for the other Phil Wasserman." As a child I wondered if when he phoned he opened with, "Hi, it's the other Phil Wasserman." Or did his wife say, "This is my husband, the other Phil Wasserman"? Or, on his tombstone, does it say, "Here lies the other Phil Wasserman"? Jerry-built as the system was, it worked.

Anyhow, here's this party and one cousin shows off her new diamond ring. Many oohs and ahhs over its size and beauty, although I'm sure it didn't approximate the Hope Diamond. Meanwhile, an hour later it's missing and panic ensues. No one can find the precious jewel. I don't know how the mystery got solved, but it was discovered my father had stolen it. Well, you can imagine the stunned disbelief. Eyes widened, hands were clapped to heads in the manner of the Yiddish theater, there was a collective "Oy vey" as glasses of sweet wine were put down and chicken legs were abandoned in mid-mastication. Naturally, my mother keeled over and that night the wedding was called off. My birth is now in peril yet again. It was only the charm and smooth talking of my father's father having a sit-down with my mother's father that eventually ameliorated this crisis. My father's father made the promise that his dopey gonif son would never do such a thing again and that he would also get out of the rackets, stop booking bets for the mob, and go straight. With that, he somehow helped my father buy a failing grocery store on Flatbush Avenue, and with some careful planning and hard work, my father managed to double its losses in record time. By now, you realize Dad had no flair for supporting a family, a topic of much stimulating conversation over the years, causing my father many times to angrily pack all his clothes in a valise before unpacking the valise and going back to bed.

My third brush with nonexistence came shortly after birth. At least I was up and running. My mother, who I told you was always forced to work to supplement my father's many unprofitable enterprises, had to leave me with maids. These were unknown young women, often different from day to day depending on who the agency would send over. My mother would instruct them where the cod liver oil was, that I only drank chocolate milk, and that no matter how cute I looked, not to trust the little momza. I was in a high chair, usually upset when she left although to this day, I don't know why because she was such a pill, not a fun mother like Billie Burke or Spring Byington. Anyhow, being alone with a stranger every day could prove fatal, and one maid closed me up inside a blanket explaining how simple it would be for her to smother me and then she would put the blanket with me dead in it, in the trash can. Things got pretty warm and airless, bundled up in that blanket. Luckily for me the maid belonged to the variety of crazies who do not act out, rather than the kind who wind up on Page Six in an orange jumpsuit having skipped their clozapine.

As I say, I was lucky, and this good luck has followed me all the days of my life, so far. Its potency cannot be over-estimated. People will point to my career and say it can't be all luck, but they don't realize how much of it has been the roll of the dice and nothing more.

So while my entrance into the world was threatened and my early existence precarious, I made it alive to Fourteenth Street right off Avenue J in Brooklyn. And while I don't have many memories of those early years except for drinking a glass of milk directly squeezed from a cow's udder (which was supposed to thrill me, but I found it warm and disgusting), and breaking away from my mother at some Disney film to try and run down the aisle to touch the screen, there are no other dull anecdotes worth mentioning. Oh yes, I seemed to have been a born paranoid. I can recall my first dwelling, an apartment which my parents shared with Uncle Abe and Aunt Ceil, my mother's sister. I remember thinking that all the other people in the world, including my mother and father and aunt and uncle, were aliens from another planet who would at some moment remove their masks, revealing the monster faces they really owned, and hack me to pieces. Why such a terrible fantasy, I don't know. My parents and aunts and uncle, as I said, were good and loving to me.

We first lived in a wonderful neighborhood I came to really appreciate only after it was gone. This was Avenue J, a commercial street, which was no big deal then but now seems to me like a paradise. It had wonderful candy stores, delicatessens with succulent meats, toy stores, a hardware store, delicious Chinese restaurants, a poolroom, a library. There were myriad small stores selling clothing and freshly baked cakes and bread and, of course, the lady who sold pickles, a fearful creature who just sat like the minotaur next to a big barrel of pickles. She was a lump dressed in many sweaters, the layered look in spades. And for five cents, she would dip her hand into the barrel and find a nickel-sized pickle and give it to you, and after decades of dipping that hand into the brine all day, every day, her hand had become pickled. I wondered as a kid, how many gallons of Jergens lotion it would take to get it back to normal. Then there was the Midwood, the movie house I practically lived in. How nice, in those days, in my dinky little neighborhood, there were countless movie houses within walking distance, all showing double features. The poorer ones showed two films, five cartoons, a weekly serial like Batman, and a funny short if it was Robert Benchley and not Joe McDoakes.

Unfortunately, sometimes a travelogue would pop on, where Mister Fitzgerald would take us to places like Ceylon and Java, the land that time forgot, whether we wanted to go or not. And sometimes you'd get a door prize, perhaps a paper gun that made a loud noise when you snapped it forward, but here's the killer—for all that, the price of admission was twelve cents. That was when I was little. Though not so little I couldn't go to a movie. The price in the classy cinemas was twenty cents, then a quarter, then thirty-five cents. When it hit fifty-five cents, the neighborhood rose up like the crew of the *Potemkin*. Someone told me a ticket now can be twenty dollars. You know how many deposit bottles I would have had to return to get twenty dollars?

There were movie houses around every corner and not a day passed when there wasn't something worth going to— if you're okay with *Crime Doctor* or *The Whistler*. I loved them all. And one day my life changed when my father took me to Manhattan for what today would be called some quality time, although he was probably going into the city to pay off some bookies. I was about seven years old and till then had only seen Brooklyn.

We rode the subway, got off at Times Square, and walked upstairs, emerging at Broadway and Forty-Second Street. I was flabbergasted. Here's the kid's view: a million people, many soldiers and sailors, marines. Endless movie houses all up Broadway and lining both sides of Forty-Second Street. Dance halls. Stylish women, or so I thought. Guys playing instruments for money. The Bond clothing sign, the Camel cigarette sign with the guy blowing the large smoke rings. Desiccated types screaming to a gathered group about the end of the world coming Thursday. (Does this guy know something?) And just how did those paper dolls dance in the air with no strings? On Forty-Second Street was the Laugh Movie, with its distorting mirrors outside (which I must say failed to amuse me even at seven) and then Hubert's Flea Museum boasting a hermaphrodite, whatever the hell that was. We paused there only so my father could shoot the .22-caliber rifles and put out the candles, and he went for about five bucks on bullets.

My dad never saw a gun he didn't like. He could never resist a shooting gallery, which then had rifles and live ammunition. In later life he got a pistol permit, rationalizing that he needed to pack heat because he carried around jewelry. In those years he hustled jewelry and came home late because he also waited on tables nights. He didn't need a gun and pulled the pistol only twice: once, he marched a trouble-maker off a city bus; once, alone in the subway at three a.m. and confronted by four young men, he took it out and fired a shot into the black of the tunnel. They turned on their heels and ran. Not that they attacked him, but he sensed they were going to, although for all he knew they were a barbershop quartet—in which case he was right in scaring them off.

And so we walked up Broadway past one movie house after another and the restaurants; McGinnis's, Roth's, Jack Dempsey's, the Turf, and finally Lindy's. We hit the various penny arcades, ate frankfurters, and drank pina coladas, maybe saw a movie. I was so young I can't recall, except that I experienced instant passion for Manhattan, and over the years I returned every chance I got. There are no more blissful memories for me than playing hooky, getting on the train at Avenue J in Brooklyn, riding into the city, buying a paper, ducking into the Automat, scarfing up some cherry pie and coffee, and reading Jimmy Cannon. By then, the Paramount would open and I'd catch the movie and the stage show, always loving the comic. I recall going to the Roxy when the Duke Ellington band was there, and when the film ended and the orchestra rose out of the pit playing "Take the A Train," the top of my head blew off. From then on, any movie that was set in New York had me. How many times did I sit enthralled watching some leggy tootsie come home from a nightclub montage in Manhattan, toting an extortionate pelt over her shoulder as she entered a Fifth Avenue lobby, pressed the elevator button and rode up to her apartment, not turning in till dawn was coming up to the slow strains of "Out of Nowhere"?

Every time I returned to Brooklyn it was the city across the river that I wanted to live in. I longed for the day I could go into a Manhattan bar and say, "The usual." Years later Mort Sahl had a brilliant idea about starting a class action suit against the movies for ruining all our lives. But I digress.

In our story I'm still on Avenue J in Brooklyn, sunsuit togged by day and finally going from my crib to a single bed. I do recall that little rite of passage. So fearful a kid was I, that from night one in my new bed, I formed what I called my "sleeping position," a position on my right side that enabled me to push myself up in a flash and react should a werewolf emerge from the closet. I slept prepared to vault out of bed, but to do what? Good question. Jiu-jitsu was rather popular in those war years, but you had to get the werewolf to shake hands with you before you threw him over your shoulder. Anyhow, I will say with age has come maturity and I can see now how silly it all was and how much wiser it is to simply sleep with a Louisville Slugger at arm's reach.

Commensurate with the escapist fantasies of a chic Manhattan life—and I say *chic* because while other boys saw movies and came out wanting to be John Wayne, Gary Cooper, Alan Ladd, I identified more with Reginald Gardiner, Clifton Webb, and the more effete characters. Oh, and Bob Hope to a fault; I never missed him in the movies or on the radio. I loved the radio. It was another version of bliss, being sick or feigning illness so I could stay home from school. Pretending to be sick was hard. If I had no temperature I had to go to school, and since my mother always sat there after she stuck the thermometer in my mouth, it was almost impossible to find a radiator or light bulb to jack up the mercury without getting coldcocked. But to be home sick: my spot in bed, the radio next to me. The *Breakfast Club, Helen Trent, Luncheon at Sardi's, Queen for a Day,* Lorenzo Jones and his wife Belle, and yes, André Baruch *was* married to Bea Wain. Finally late afternoon, *Hop Harrigan, Tom Mix, Captain Midnight*; and later at night *The Answer Man, Baby Snooks, The Lone Ranger.* Meals in bed. My father coming home from work with ten new comic books, a buck's worth. Radio was a huge part of everyone's life in those days, and in retrospect I've found it interesting that my father, brawler that he was, preferred the comedy programs and never missed Jack Benny or Charlie McCarthy, or later Groucho. I would've thought *Gangbusters* or *David Harding, Counterspy,* but no, it was *The Life of Riley* and *Fibber McGee and Molly.*

I lapped them all up but was never allowed by our family doctor to listen to *Inner Sanctum* or anything deemed too scary. Dr. Cohen advised my mother never to let me see any Frankenstein movies or Dracula because I was a tense kid who'd have nightmares. My mother drew all her child-rearing advice from our local GP, who listened to my heart with his stethoscope, thumped my chest, hit my knee with a rubber hammer, heard Mom regale him with stories of what a rotten kid I was, psychoanalyzed me, prescribed Cocillana and a couple of mustard plasters, and all done with the convenience of a house call, for a deuce. My mother would take his diagnosis as if Avicenna had made it. She sought medical advice both physical and mental from any doctor or anyone with any sort of tenuous connection to the world of medicine. Often, she sought counsel from our local dentist above the bakery, and not just on matters relating to molars and gums. Also from the local druggist. If you could fill a prescription or sell corn plasters, she'd let you perform brain surgery. If you were an actual doctor, you were God. A doctor's name was pronounced with the same reverence accorded a rabbi.

So I loved being sick and luxuriating in my bed, radio, comic books, and chicken soup. Here I should note part of the serendipitous delight of coming down with a hundred-and-one fever was something I mentioned before; I hated, loathed, and despised school. There was nothing about P.S. 99, with its dumb, prejudiced, backward teachers, to commend it. I'm talking about the early 1940s. After the war, it got some teachers who were better. Let me put this delicately. The staff were blue-haired Irish women like what a casting director would think of for strict, abusive nuns. I was dragged up a flight of stairs by my ear by Miss Reid, the assistant principal, may she rot in the "serl." That's how she pronounced it while I cringed—"The worm is good for the serl." It's *soil*, fatso, I wanted to say and then shovel her under it.

The few male teachers were more relaxed liberal Jews. One of the best was fired because his ideas were too liberal. At something called Sing, where each class would choose a song, sing it, and stage it in the assembly hall, he chose a turn-of-the-century number called "Boops-a-Daisy," which went, "hands" (dancers touch hands), "knees" (dancers slap their knees) and "Boops-a-Daisy" (couples turn away from each other and bump their backsides together). Well, the biddies stood there aghast as if he had staged a gangbang in the auditorium. This was not the usual antiseptic rendition of "You're a Grand Old Flag" or "Bicycle Built for Two."

To these frigid anti-Semites it reeked of lewdness. Today it would be called "inappropriate" by the Appropriate Police. Needless to say, this errant Hebrew pedagogue was out on his rear end at the soonest possible moment. The fact that he had pronounced leftist leanings politically didn't endear him to Miss Fletcher, the principal, and her grubby minions.

But it was not just the coven of teachers, it was the whole regulated routine, designed to see that no one ever learned anything. You had to get there on time and line up in the basement or in the yard if weather permitted. You lined up and couldn't talk—what the hell was that? You marched to class. You sat "feet flat on the floor, eyes straight ahead," and there was no talking, joking, note passing, nothing that made the grim business of human existence bearable. You learned by rote, except you never learned. Once a week there was an assembly period. First the Pledge of Allegiance, hand over your heart. They wanted to be sure we weren't siding with the Axis. Then a bullshit prayer. Never answered, none of them. Not even, I'll get back to you on that. God is silent, I used to say, now if we can only get the teachers to shut up.

Then came the music. Could they have picked anything duller? All that Cole Porter and Rodgers and Hart on the radio; there were so many beautiful Gershwin tunes. Songs with pretty melodies and exciting rhythm. "Anything Goes," "Lady Be Good," "Mountain Greenery"; so many to have a nice time with, to learn to really enjoy music. But no, first our class recites "In Flanders fields where poppies blow..." I guess to put us in an up mood. Then we get to sing "Recessional." Or "Abide with Me." At that point, I thought maybe if I faked an epileptic fit they'd send me home. I just wanted out. Let me hold the thermometer over the radiator or let me play hooky and ride to Manhattan, knock off some clams at McGinnis's and go watch Esther Williams do the backstroke south of the border. I still cringe thinking back on the school lines in the basement, indoors because it was raining or snowing; the stink of wet wool from our sweaters that got soaked, and getting caught doing something innocuous like whispering to a friend or stealing a kiss in the wardrobe closet and having your mother sent for.

"He's always flirting with the girls," one of the sterile drones said to my mother. Yes, I liked the girls. What am I supposed to like, the multiplication tables? Should I like your soul-deadening spiel on the first Thanksgiving? Should I like clapping the erasers together to beat the chalk dust out of them? A privilege some of the more sluggish kids vied for. No, I liked the girls. From kindergarten on, I was not interested in "Do You Know the Muffin Man" or playing musical chairs. I wanted to get on the subway with Barbara Westlake, ride into Manhattan, take her up to my penthouse on Fifth, drink dry martinis (whatever dry meant), go out on the terrace and kiss her in the moonlight. You can imagine this idea was not appreciated by the teaching staff at P.S. 99, my mother, or even Barbara Westlake, who was six, not into dry martinis, and sobbed hysterically when Bambi's mother got whacked. Hence, no matter how often I proposed the Astor Bar, I could not get faded. Please note, I was only talking the talk. While I knew the score, I could not have traveled to Manhattan by myself, found the Astor Bar, been admitted or served anything stronger than an egg cream. Not to mention I would have had trouble raising the nickel subway fare, much less a dime to take a dame.

My mother was called to see the teacher so many times, she became a familiar face. All the kids said hello to her on the street long after they were grown up and married. They knew her from that dreadful ritual when the class would be learning some useless thing like "the correct word for the numeral zero is *aught*." (I'm fine with *zero*.) Meanwhile the door opens and it's my mother. Class is halted for five minutes while the azure-haired crone chats with my mother in the hall telling her how incorrigible a son she has and how I floated a billet-doux to Judy Dors suggesting we have cocktails. "There's something wrong with him," my mother says, instantly taking the side of anyone who hates me. Yes, there was something wrong with me. I liked girls. I liked everything about girls. I enjoyed their company, I liked the sound of their laughter, I liked their anatomy and I wanted to be at the Stork Club with them and not in the shop class with the local male troglodytes making a lopsided tie rack.

Some of the teachers would keep kids after school as punishment but it was always the Jewish kids. Why? Because we're shifty little usurers and in keeping us after school, we'd be late or couldn't attend Hebrew school. Now unbeknownst to them, this punishment to me, if I may use a Yiddish word, was a mitzvah. I hated Hebrew school as much as public school and now I'm going to tell you why. First of all, I never bought into the whole religious thing. I thought it was all a big hustle. Didn't ever think there was a God; didn't think he'd conveniently favor the Jews if there was one. Loved pork. Hated beards. The Hebrew language was too guttural for my taste. Plus it was written backwards. Who needed that? I had enough trouble in school where things were written left to right. And why should I fast for my sins? What were my sins? Kissing Barbara West-lake when I should've been hanging up my coat? Fobbing a plug nickel off on my grandpa? I say live with it, God, there's much worse. The Nazis are putting us in ovens. First attend to that. But as I said, I didn't believe in God. And why did the women have to sit upstairs in the synagogue? They were prettier and smarter than the men. Those hirsute zealots who wrapped themselves in prayer shawls on the premier level, nodding up and down like bobbleheads and kissing a string up to some imaginary power who, if he did exist, despite all their begging and flattery, rewarded them with diabetes and acid reflux.

Not worth my time, and my time was the great rub here. I couldn't wait till the three o'clock bell rang and I was freed from public school so I could hit the streets and the school-yard and play ball but oh no, to have to pack that in and go sit in a Hebrew class reading words, the meaning of which were never taught to us, and learning how the Jews had made a special covenant with God, but unfortunately failed to get anything in writing. But I went. Parental pressure, my allowance, the threat of no radio, not to mention I'd get hit. My mother hit me every day at least once. Hitting was very de rigueur in those days, though my father only did once, when I told him to fuck off and he made his displeasure known with a gentle tap across my face that gave me an un-impeded view of the Aurora Borealis. But mom whacked me every day and it was the old Sam Levenson joke—"Maybe I don't know what you did to deserve it, but you do." And so it came to pass that I was eventually bar mitzvahed and so had to take special bar mitzvah lessons and sing in

Hebrew—and let me tell you, as they say in the Old Testament, there was much wailing and gnashing of teeth.

My mother was the observant one. Because of her, we kept a kosher home. She was pretty strict about dietary laws that forbid pork, bacon, ham, lobster, and many delectable treats available to lucky infidels. To keep my mother placated, Dad faked being observant, but he couldn't hide his addiction to tasty contraband and gobbled pig meat and shellfish like the Assyrians fell upon the fold. Hence, once in a while at a restaurant, I got to knock off a meal Yahweh, as his friends call him, hadn't signed off on. I remember what a treat it was when at eight, my father first took me to Lundy's, the legendary seafood restaurant in Brooklyn where I could pig out on clams, oysters, and shellfish, confident God was nowhere near Sheepshead Bay that day. Lundy's was the first time I was ever given a finger bowl. I'd never heard of anything so astonishing as finger bowls, and it was a thoroughly exhilarating experience using one. Like having your own swimming pool. So impressed was I that two years later, when my aunt took me there for a shore dinner, all I could think of was, this joint has finger bowls. Consequently, when we ordered steamers and the clam broth was served with them, I was convinced this must be the finger bowl. Intensely excited, my certainty overrode Aunt Ann's muddled skepticism, and the two of us sat there washing our hands in the clam broth. It was not until the actual finger bowls arrived at the end of the meal did my aunt realize she'd been right and struck me affectionately a number of times, perhaps twelve or fourteen, on the head with her purse.

OK, so I'm still a small boy, loving movies, loving women,

loving sports, hating school, longing for a dry martini. Oh, while I admit I'm a terrible student, one thing I could always do was write. I could write before I could read. I didn't learn how to read until first grade, but in kindergarten I could come home and write—that is, make up fictions. Write without the ability to write down. The oral tradition. Like the ballads. While *Beowulf* and *Lord Randall* were on the brutal side, my narratives took place at scintillating dinner parties and foreshadowed a future never besmirched by an honest day's work.

For a while, I dreamed of being a scientist and was gifted a microscope. I will outgrow this noble ambition, seduced by a lifestyle ignited by MGM. I suffered rejection after rejection from the cute girls with their high marks and lovely handwriting. "Oh God, no. My mother would never let me go out on a date." "The subway to New York? I'm not allowed." And later, "Sorry, I never go out with boys my own age."

Anyhow, the bar mitzvah comes. Today, they have theme bar mitzvahs: *Star Wars*, King Arthur, the Wild West. My theme was Gorky's *Lower Depths*. My initiation into manhood is not held at some fancy place but at our house near the railroad tracks. Uncles and other men on their feet, smoking two packs a day despite a medley of massive heart attacks and strokes, wink and smugly shake my hand with a ten spot in theirs. Big deal. Like they're duking me with a G. My aunts, cousins, Rita, her older sister Phyllis the nurse, hallowed by her profession like Eve Curie, Phil Wasserman, and of course the other Phil Wasserman. Phil (the original) is a very amusing character who works as a press agent. In a few years when I try writing my first jokes, I will bring them to him and he will encourage me to mail them in to the various Broadway newspaper columnists who run gags usually attributed to celebrities. I am going to follow his advice, and my feeble quips will open up the entire world to me.

But at thirteen I was still an obnoxious youth, a wise guy full of wisecracks with a growing feeling for show business. Speaking of show business, let me describe the entertainment that ensued at this little Ashkenazi luau, wherein a young Jew is supposed to become a man, although I remained a mouse. My father was then a waiter, one of his myriad occupations, which included a surefire get-rich scheme to sell by mail "beautifully boxed pearl necklaces," a venture that couldn't find a single human who wanted even one pearl, so our house was inundated with beautifully boxed necklaces for many months. The stock was finally liquidated for about fifteen cents on the dollar. But now he was a waiter at Sammy's Bowery Follies, where he toiled from 6 p.m. to 5 a.m. every night.

Sammy's was a Gay Nineties joint on the Bowery complete with sawdust on the floor and where buxom, Sophie Tucker–type dames would sing turn-of-the-century favorites, in floozy gowns while wearing big hats. Mabel Sidney was such a blousy singer, sister of the actress Sylvia Sidney, her brother was George Sidney, a successful Hollywood director. I knew none of Mabel's pedigree, only that she could belt out "Who's Sorry Now" and "You Tell Me Your Dream," among many other vintage gems. As a favor to my father she came to my thirteenth birthday party and put a little oomph into an event otherwise indistinguishable from laying my uncle Abe to rest at Riverside Chapel. In those years, the family always benefited from my father's working on the Bowery, with its enormous drunkard population crowding every street, bar, and flophouse under the El. Example: We needed the house painted. Among many of the inebriants, one could find any profession from carpenter to archeologist, from stockbroker to merchant seaman, from actor to housepainter. Men whose dreams had run out of steam and were now hopeless alcoholics. All these poor souls wanted was the price of a single drink. And so for a few bucks, our house would be transformed by a squad of rummies with paintbrushes who would work cheaply— if they'd show up. The job might take longer because of an interrupting bender but it got done, by God. Mom always fed them well, but they had to drink out of a special glass cordoned off for strangers, which I believe was then shipped off to the Marshall Islands, where our government buried toxic waste.

Another perk of working among the sad dipso populous of the Bowery was that many of them stole. Their clearcut goal was money to buy the next whiskey, and so if anyone left anything around it would vanish in seconds. John Bananas, as they were sometimes called, would walk into a bar like the one my father worked at, or they might accost my father while he was on the street and offer stolen merchandise: an overcoat, a tape recorder, a bag of steaks. All the thief wanted in return was enough for a single shot. My father, always open to a proposition, would oblige. It was in this fashion we had an Underwood typewriter for a dollar fifty, a Mixmaster, and a fur coat for my mother, just to name a few hot items. I typed my first one-liners on a stolen typewriter and made my first malted on a purloined Hamilton Beach machine. And so, Mabel Sidney made my bar mitzvah livable doing her mugient rendition of "My Man" for a farrago of scraggly Hebrews.

It was at said fete that I received among all the other swag a book on magic. This book, with its photos of exciting equipment, Chinese boxes, a vanishing bird cage, billiard balls and silks, a guillotine, and myriad other paraphernalia whetted an interest in me that grew into an obsession, and it wasn't long before I was spending all my spare time practicing and like the John Bananas, using any penny I could beg, borrow, or steal not for bourbon but on magic tricks. I had all the standard stuff: the linking rings, cups and balls, a red velvet changing bag, Passé Passé bottles—all startling effects you don't know by name but have enjoyed many times. The Miser's Dream means nothing to you, but there I was plucking coins from the air and tossing them into the bottom of a pail. As times went on, I matured beyond the allure of flashy-looking apparatuses with rhinestones and tassels and fake bottom chests.

I began to see that it was magic books that counted, and they were among the first books I read, if not *the* first. I understood that to buy a piece of equipment that anyone could purchase and learn to perform was not worth my time or the lunch money I saved by going hungry in school. The real deal was learning the secrets of sleight of hand from books and practice, endless practice, to palm coins or steal from the bottom of the deck, cut and restore ropes and manipulate silk handkerchiefs, billiard balls, and cigarettes. And that was what I practiced, digital dexterity. I thought

I got pretty good, but when I see the level of sleight of hand today, one's breath is taken away. Practicing as much as Jascha Heifetz or Glenn Gould, there are any number of artists who are their equal in dedication to this other demanding field of exotic art. But I'm not one of them, and this is my story, so let me get on with it.

Simultaneous with being bitten by the magic bug and already a movie addict who longed to live on Fifth Avenue, shake my own cocktails, and have a sharp bantering relationship with a beautiful woman on loan from Paramount who would share my penthouse, I experienced another apocalyptic event. A few years earlier, at eleven, I had developed the practice of taking the subway to my beloved city across the river, and spending my allowance on a day in Manhattan. This was unheard of for a kid of that age, but I had plenty of freedom, or else my parents didn't care if I was kidnapped. While I could never get a date to go with me, sometimes my friend Andrew would go along. Andrew also had a little letch for show business and was a good-looking kid whose parents had some dough and spoiled him much worse than I was spoiled, so much so that he ended up jumping out a window in his twenties when real life made its grinning appearance. Poor Andrew. Narcotics to escape, then the open window in the hospital. But these two precocious dreamers rode sporadically to Times Square, walked around, picked a movie to see, ate at Roth's or McGinnis's, and did the town till our stash played out. I loved walking on Park and Fifth Avenue and into Central Park. It was the Manhattan of the Hollywood movies I grew up escaping into.

One such Saturday we couldn't find a movie we wanted to see, and searching the newspaper we noticed on Flatbush

Avenue in Brooklyn a movie house called the Flatbush Theatre. They were playing some low-grade comedy by the Ritz
Brothers or Olsen and Johnson that we wanted to see. We
grabbed the subway back to Brooklyn, found the Flatbush
Theatre on Flatbush and Church Avenues, and discovered
that in addition to the movies there were five acts of live
vaudeville. So the film ends, the curtains part, and onstage
there's a full orchestra, Al Goodman with drummer Willie
Krieger. I then see five acts of vaudeville: a singer, a tap
dancer, acrobats, another singer, a comedian. I'm blown
apart. I thrilled to every moment of those second raters
crooning their rendition of "Sorrento" or clicking their tap
shoes to "Tea for Two." And the corny jokes and spot-on
impressions of Cagney and Gable, of Bing Crosby and Bette
Davis. I'm so taken with vaudeville, I return every weekend
for years, never missing a single Saturday until the theater
closes and reopens as a legit house with *Three Men on a
Horse.* It was comedians I loved most, and soon, by bringing
a pencil and writing down their acts on the torn-up inside
of the Good and Plenty box I could do every routine, every
impersonation, of every Hollywood star, and I was certain
that somewhere between comedy and magic, I was going to
wind up performing.

By fourteen, this would happen and here's how: My stage
debut was at a local social club, and a nice man named Abe
Stern booked me with no audition out of sheer generosity,
paying me two dollars, which was probably a legitimate fee
given what his budget must've been. I did a few uninspired
magic tricks using my sister as a stooge. Her job was to sit in
the audience and scream, "I saw him put the egg under his
arm!" Of course, I had faked putting it there. And the crowd

reacted like a lynch mob, demanding I raise my arm so they could catch me hiding the egg and humiliate me, but it was somewhere else. I would then lift my arm and show it empty. I had vanished it into the trick bag. There were a half dozen other effects just as thrilling as the egg bag, and as the audience fought the onset of narcolepsy, I exited and hoped the boss got his two bucks worth. I also remember auditioning for the *Magic Clown* TV show, a Sunday morning show for little kids, and I chose for my audition trick, the Passé Passé bottles, a trick using two whiskey bottles. Needless to say, I didn't get the job. But I noticed that whenever I inflicted my fatal prestidigitation on audiences, my spontaneous patter, as I marched around the stage quacking nervously, would always break up the crowd. It never crossed my mind afterward that I had some potential as a comic, but only that I was a failed magician. Not to waste all the hours I spent practicing sleight of hand before a mirror, I decided I should use my technical ability with cards to cheat people, take their money and, as Max Shulman—a very funny writer who, along with Mickey Spillane accounted for any reading I might be caught doing—said, "Get rich, sleep till noon, and screw 'em all."

It was announced there was to be a talent show at school. I thought I might do some impressions. Impersonations, they were called then. I don't know when they magically changed into impressions. I did Cagney, Gable, Peter Lorre. As I was waiting my turn to audition, I watched another boy perform. He auditioned as a comic but not with some jokes cribbed from the *Reader's Digest* or *1000 Jokes*. He didn't begin like some of those square, cringe-inducing teachers who tried to leaven an assembly with wit: "It seems these two dentists..." No, Jerry Epstein did a professional routine with opening remarks, funny one-liners, material about war movies and gangster films. His act was the real article. After school, I sidled up to him near the huge snow mound on the street near P.S. 99. (I neglected to tell you that it was winter, a very snowy one.) We talked and hit it off, not just about comedy but also baseball. We'd go on to play for the same PAL baseball team. He was a good left-handed first baseman. I played second base.

That's the other misconception about me, other than I'm an intellectual; people think because I'm on the smaller side and I wear those glasses, I couldn't have been much of an athlete. But they're wrong. I was track medal fast, a very fine baseball player with fantasies of pursuing that as a career, which only faded when I was suddenly hired as a gag writer. I was a schoolyard basketball player who could catch a football and throw it a mile. I do not expect you to take my word for this, but if any of you readers ever run into guys from the old neighborhood, ask them. When I happen to run into one of them, they always get on the subject of my skill as a ball player and, for some reason, never my movies. Many will also tell you about my ability at a poker table. In my thirties, I used to play night after night from about nine till the sun came up and made enough to live well and buy a Nolde watercolor and a Kokoschka drawing. I only stopped because David Merrick said he had been a player, too, but he one day realized what a time waster it was. It rang a bell, so I quit.

Same abrupt quitting of baseball. When I was older, I still played softball in the Broadway Show League, a game I never loved. As I walked toward my outfield position one day, a younger player said to me, "Mr. Allen, don't worry. If there's anything you can't get, I'll help you." I looked at him and thought, Are you kidding me? Any ball hit to the outfield I can chase down, autograph, and then catch. Moments later, a line drive got past me, a drive I would've caught behind my back in my earlier days. I put down my glove, walked off the field, asked to be replaced, and never went near a bat, ball, or glove again. The humiliation was so intense; I can feel the shame as I write this.

I was also shamed in a celebrity vs. all-stars game at Dodger Stadium. I and a group of schlemiel actors—I mean they're great actors but schlemiel ball players—played against the likes of Willie Mays, Willie McCovey, Boog Powell, Jimmy Piersall, Roberto Clemente. For some reason, the oddsmakers had them as the favorites. I only had one at bat against Don Drysdale and flied out. I did have the distinction of Willie Mays flying out to me. A year later when I ran into a kid I grew up and played with, he said, "I saw your softball game on TV. I couldn't believe you didn't hit Drysdale." Yes, I should've held my feet a tad closer and really gotten the wood on the ball, and God forbid I wake in the middle of the night and the game comes back to me and I become remorseful, drowned in regret, filled with rage, self-loathing, and I should have hit Drysdale. I need another at bat. Next time, I'll hold my feet closer. I can definitely hit this guy. Soon, I'm hyperoxygenating, and the room is spinning. Christ, the day I can't hit Drysdale—I need another at bat—I'm eighty-four—is it too late? Where am I? Where were we?

Ah—yes—back to the snow bank. Jerry tells me he has an older brother Sandy who is the real comedian in the family.

He emcees college shows and I should meet him. And off we go to meet a very big early influence on me. Sandy Epstein of Avenue J and Dickinson College. When he performed he looked and sounded like a professional stand-up comedian. "Sorry I'm a little late, folks, I just got out of a sick bed. My girlfriend had the measles." And while this is not Wilde or Shaw, it was pretty much the kind of routines professional comics were doing. He taught me a number of routines and bits and gags, and as public school passed and Midwood High School became my alma mater, the classrooms were the only venues to use this material, which I did to the irritation of the teachers. It wasn't long before my mother was a frequent visitor, embarrassed as I tried to explain to the dean what I meant by the line, "She had an hourglass figure and all I wanted to do was play in the sand." Things were very prissy in those days and the Appropriate Police were everywhere. I did some routines at a local Jewish club to great success, and by junior year I was a wannabe comic, wannabe magician, wannabe baseball player, but in the end just a lousy student. I was the wise guy in the movie house who threw in a joke during an intense or romantic moment on the screen and broke up anyone who heard it. I got as many shut-ups as laughs. My friend Jerry bought a tape recorder and proudly demonstrated it for me.

"What is that music?" I asked.

"It's a jazz concert I recorded," he said, "off the radio. *Ted Husing's Bandstand.*"

"It's great," I said, tossing my schoolbooks aside in the direction of the garbage pail.

"A concert in France."

"Who is that?"

"Sidney Bechet."

"Who's that?"

"A New Orleans soprano saxophonist."

It was the first New Orleans jazz I heard. Why it clicked so deeply I'll never know. Here I was, a Brooklyn Jew, never out of New York, with kind of cosmopolitan taste, a great appreciation for Gershwin, Porter, Kern, very sophisticated popular composers, and here were these African-Americans in the Deep South, having nothing in common with me and yet they quickly became an obsession, and soon I was a wannabe comic, wannabe magician, wannabe baseball player, and wannabe African-American jazz musician. I bought a soprano sax, I learned to play it; I bought a clarinet and learned to play it. I bought a Victrola. That I could play with no lessons. I bought records, books on the birth of jazz, the life of Louis Armstrong. My three friends, Jack, Jerry, Elliot, and I must have seemed like a strange quartet. While all the other kids were submerged in pop commercial music of the day, Patti Page, Frankie Laine, The Four Aces, we sat at our record players playing jazz music hour after hour, day after day.

We listened to all kinds of jazz, but our favorites were the primitive New Orleans records. Bunk Johnson, Jelly Roll Morton, Louis Armstrong, and of course Sidney Bechet, whom I worshipped and modeled my playing after (and if that doesn't give you a laugh, nothing will). I sat in my bedroom alone playing along to Bechet and later with George Lewis recordings. He was another idol of mine; with him and Johnny Dodds, yet another clarinet genius, I felt I had finally found myself. The pleasure was so intense I decided I would devote my life to jazz. Little did I realize that

Bechet, Armstrong, George Lewis, Johnny Dodds, Jelly Roll Morton, and Jimmie Noone were musical geniuses. Their idiom was primitive, but within the parameters of New Orleans jazz, they had something truly magical inside them that oozed out of every note they blew. I, naïve clod that I was, did not understand that I did not have that genius, that I was destined, for all my enthusiasm and love of the music, to never amount to more than a musical nonentity who would be listened to and tolerated on the basis of a movie career and not for anything worth a damn as far as jazz is concerned.

Practice though, I did, and still do. I practice every day and with such dedication that to make sure I get it in I've practiced on freezing beaches, in churches while my film crew lit, in hotel rooms after work, at midnight, getting into bed and pulling the quilts over my head so as not to wake the other guests. Yet listen to the music as I have, read the stimulating tales of the musicians' lives, and blow, blow, blow with different mouthpieces and reeds, always searching for that combination that will make me sound better, I still stink. I remain like a weekend tennis player among Federer and Nadal. Sorry to say, I just don't have it: the ear, the tone, the rhythm, the feeling. And yet I've played publicly in clubs and on concert stages, in opera houses all over Europe, in packed auditoriums in the U.S. I've played in parades in New Orleans and bars there, at the Jazz Heritage festival and at Preservation Hall, and all because I can cash in on my movie career. Years ago, Dotson Rader, a witty man, asked me over dinner, "Have you no shame?"

Between my love for the music and my limits as a player, if I want to play I can't afford shame. I tried explaining to him

I used to play only at home with a few other musicians. It was for fun, like a weekly poker game. Then they suggested we do it at a bar or a restaurant—so there would be some small audience. I had years of nightclub experience and did not crave another audience but they did, so I said OK. It started small and grungy and wound up decades later that we're regular fixtures at the Carlyle Hotel in Manhattan and we've always sold out concert halls in Europe, with audiences as large as eight thousand people who have stood in the rain to hear us. So here I am, a boy in Brooklyn, smitten with jazz, struggling with a clarinet. I call a great jazz musician, Gene Sedric, the clarinetist with Fats Waller, and say, I am that young guy who sits at the front table every week listening to you play the jazz concerts with the Conrad Janis band. Would you consider helping me with my clarinet? Expecting a rejection, I hear him say I'd have to charge you two dollars. So for a couple of rugs he rides every week from Harlem to Flatbush, and since I can't read music, he puts his horn together, blows a phrase, and says, "Say this."

I try and blow it but, having no ear nor any discernable talent, I fail. Patiently, week after week, he works with me and I get better—but always within the limits of "no real flair for it." We became great friends, and till he died he remained a constant source of encouragement, although if you hear me play you might call him an enabler.

What got me playing with others, because I played only with records for years, was when I was a comic working the Hungry I in San Francisco. Between sets I'd walk around the block to a joint called Earthquake McGoon's where Turk Murphy, a great jazz trombonist, led a band. I sat outside and listened night after night until one of the guys in the band said, Why don't you come in and listen? Shy wretch, jazz lover that I saw myself as, I said, That's okay, I'm happy in the alley pressed against the exit door trying to filch a smidgen of pleasure from the music inside. Turk, however, wouldn't hear of it. I was the starring comic at the Hungry I, and he insisted I come in and enjoy the band.

I did and he got me talking, and he could tell I knew a huge amount about jazz, and it came out I was a clarinetist. Not knowing what he was letting himself in for, he insisted I bring my instrument and sit in. After many demands, I did one night, and I must say I knew all the tunes. Turk insisted I come back as often as I wanted. The guys in the band were very polite and encouraging, clapping their hands to their ears with the utmost discretion when I blew. When I returned to New York, having played with the Turk Murphy Band, I was no longer satisfied playing alone and got together some guys to play at our houses once a week. The rest is history—but so is the Holocaust.

Years later, on a visit to New York, I invited Turk to sit in with my band playing at Michael's Pub. He did, and I couldn't help reflecting on the irony that I had begun sitting in nervously with his band, and now years later he was sitting in, surprisingly nervous, with my band. Then, realizing the vacuous little irony meant nothing, I moved on to another subject. Nowadays as I step forward to take my solo I can only think somewhere two great jazz musicians, Gene Sedric and Turk Murphy, are spinning in their graves.

So I'm about fifteen, a multiple wannabe, failing in school, and as my hormones reach a critical mass I began my love life, or as one might have called it, Theater of the Absurd. Adrift in a sea of testosterone, looking for sex but more pointedly searching for that combination of Rita Hayworth's sensuality, June Allyson's supportive devotion, and Eve Arden's sarcastic wit. This was a difficult package to locate anywhere on the planet Earth much less among the local fifteen-year-olds whose idea of a date was a movie, a soda, and home, getting the key out six blocks from their house lest they shouldn't be ready to open the door and rocket inside before you could kiss them. There were a few winners I dated, though, those simple, lovely girls, smart, literate, cultivated, fetchingly neurotic, and bored stiff by a bumbling wimp like me who couldn't hold a conversation on any subject more complex than the Road pictures or how to hit a slider. One girl asked me to take her to the film *O. Henry's Full House*. The only O. Henry I knew was a candy bar. Another brought up *Swann's Way*, but I was too busy demonstrating how funny it was when Milton Berle walked on the sides of his feet. These girls read and spoke French, and one had been to Europe and had seen Michaelangelo's David.

"Yes," I would say, anxious to get on to a subject I can handle, "but when Cuddles Szakáll wiggles his jowls..." There was something about these women; the fact that they were beautiful naturally, that they always seemed to be dramatically and flatteringly in black with silver earrings. They were not commercial. And their smarts were seductive. They were political liberals. Besides the fact that Lincoln had freed the slaves, my knowledge of politics was slim. They could hum the Brandenburg Concertos, and rumor had it they were sexually advanced, although I'd never find out, as dates would often cut the evening short, unconvincingly remembering a pressing appointment in Hindia Belanda or having to feed a pet emu. I took one little amuse-bouche on her request to Greenwich Village. As I recall, she dragged me to a production of *Macbeth* performed by Thai puppets. Fortunately I awoke before the curtain came down. After, in a snug little drop over candlelight she waxed euphoric over Czeslaw Milosz and the perversion of the dialectic while I mentally undressed her. Then it was off to some brick wall folk club where Josh White sang about chain gangs and a man "takin' names" while in the back there was a man from the FBI taking names. Finally, back to her house where she darted pell-mell to get inside and avoid my lunging kiss while my nose got caught in the slammed door.

I struggled always to hold my own, but who was this Steppenwolf? And did I agree with Sidney Hook on what? I never saw her again, and because I had fallen in love with her I came to realize that I had some catching up to do; Stendhal and Dostoevsky would now replace Felix the Cat and Little Lulu. So I read. Some of it I liked, some of it I did not. I was not an omnivore who couldn't get enough literature. Reading was always competing with sports, movies, jazz, card tricks, and just plain not reading because the print looked too dense. I still am taken aback at the cruel spacing of *The Magic Mountain*. Still, I feared I would never measure up socially if I only knew things like who is strangling all the people in *The Spiral Staircase* or the lyrics to "Ragmop." I read the novelists, the poets, the philosophers; I struggled with Faulkner and Kafka and had a worse time with Eliot and of course Joyce, but I loved Hemingway and Camus because they were simple and caused me to feel, but I couldn't get through Henry

James, hard as I tried. I loved Melville, the poetry of Emily Dickinson, and I took the time to learn about Yeats's life so I could enjoy his poems. I was so-so about Fitzgerald but loved Thomas Mann and Turgenev. I loved *The Red and the Black*, especially where the young hero keeps wondering if he should make his move and hit on the married woman. I wrote the Broadway comic's version of that scene in *Play It Again, Sam* and played it with Diane Keaton. I read C. Wright Mills and *The Ginger Man* and learned about polymorphous perversity from Norman O. Brown.

I read indiscriminately and there remained great gaps in my knowledge, but I listened to classical music in addition to jazz, and visited museums more and more and educated myself best as I could, not for a degree or any noble aspiration, but so I wouldn't seem a dodo to the women I liked—although in most ways, I remained a dodo. To this day, the Tin Pan Alley poets are my poets, and nothing in *The Wasteland* or Pound or Auden moves me as much as Cole Porter's "You're not worth the ransom of asparagus out of season."

I know Edith Wharton and Henry James and Fitzgerald all wrote about New York, but the town I recognized best was described by that sentimental Irish librettist on the sports beat, Jimmy Cannon. You would be shocked to know what I don't know and haven't read or seen. After all, I am a director, a writer. I've never seen a live production of *Hamlet*. I've never seen *Our Town*, in any version. I never read *Ulysses, Don Quixote, Lolita, Catch-22, 1984*, no Virginia Woolf, no E. M. Forster, no D. H. Lawrence. Nothing by the Brontës or Dickens. On the other hand, I'm one of the few guys in my peer group who read Joseph Goebbels's novel.

Yes, Goebbels, the gimpy little suppository who flacked for the Fuhrer tried his hand at a novel called *Michael*, and don't you think the main character had all the anxiety of the nervous lover anxious for the girl to like him.

As far as movies go, I never saw Chaplin's *Shoulder Arms* or *The Circus* or *The Navigator* by Buster Keaton. Never saw any version of *A Star Is Born*. For all my Saturdays at the Midwood Theater, I never saw *How Green Was My Valley* or *Wuthering Heights* or *Camille* or *Now, Voyager* or *Ben-Hur* or many others. *They Drive by Night*, *The Uninvited*, *The Bride of Frankenstein*, never saw them. I'm not disparaging these works; this is about my ignorance and why glasses do not make one a particularly literate person, much less an intellectual. And these are just a small sampling of holes in my erudition. To this day I've never seen *Mr. Deeds Goes to Town* or *Mr. Smith Goes to Washington*.

As with books, there are also a certain amount of films I have seen, particularly growing up, and I've seen my share of foreign movies. Still, I think you'd be surprised at my taste. Example: I prefer Chaplin to Keaton. This doesn't sit well with most critics and students of movies but I find him funnier though Keaton was a better director. Chaplin's also funnier than Harold Lloyd, who executed great visual gags brilliantly, but I could never warm up to him. I was never a huge Katharine Hepburn fan. Though she was terrific in *Long Day's Journey into Night* and *Suddenly Last Summer*, her best, I find her often very artificial. Weeping was her go-to emotion, whereas Irene Dunne: Loved her. And Jean Arthur. Spencer Tracy always seemed so real except in *Pat and Mike*.

I was never a great fan of Lenny Bruce's, and my

generation went nuts over him. I didn't for a second think I was a better comic, not by a long shot. I have a very critical opinion of my own stand-up comedy but I'm not talking about that phase of my life yet. I'm just pointing out a few icons that surprisingly didn't mean as much to me as to the general public. Like *Some Like It Hot* or *Bringing Up Baby*—to me, neither was funny. Nor do I like *It's a Wonderful Life*. Frankly, would love to strangle the cutesy guardian angel. Could never buy into *An Affair to Remember*. Adored Hitchcock but can't see *Vertigo* no how. Crazy about Lubitsch but never found *To Be or Not to Be* funny. *Trouble in Paradise*, however, I find a knockout, a Faberge egg.

Love musicals: *Singing in the Rain, Gigi, Meet Me in St. Louis, The Band Wagon, My Fair Lady*. Never liked *An American in Paris*. Never laughed at Eddie Bracken or Laurel and Hardy or, God forbid Red Skelton. Of course, the Marx Brothers and W. C. Fields are the absolute greatest. I also liked Rex Harrison in the movie *Unfaithfully Yours* and Leslie Howard's version of *Pygmalion* with Wendy Hiller. I think *Pygmalion* is the best comedy ever written and much prefer it to any of the Shakespearean comedies or Wilde's or Aristophanes', although sometimes Aristophanes reminds me of Kaufman and Hart, whom I do like. I'm a total sucker for *Born Yesterday*, especially as done by Judy Holliday and Broderick Crawford. On the other hand, I never found *The Great Dictator* or *Monsieur Verdoux* remotely amusing. I certainly do not find when Chaplin kicks that balloon of the globe up and down in the air an example of comic genius by any means. But who cares what I think—it's taste. You may find those willowy lingerie models beautiful and sexy and I may not. Except I do and there's nothing I can do about it. So much for taste.

Meanwhile, high school is droning on. I am slowly realizing that one day in the not-so-distant future, I will have to make some life decisions. College? Where? Must go though, or mother will put her eyes out in the manner of Oedipus. To be what? A second baseman? A card cheat? It's quite obvious I'm no musical talent. Do I have the nerve to get up onstage and be a comic for real? And aren't I most happy in a room by myself? I was not a performer, just a nervous wise guy with failing grades. Meanwhile all around me, nice boys and girls with passing grades who didn't cheat at cards or dice and were rooted in reality, were ready to challenge life and compete. These kids read books because they loved books and loved learning and were not speculating on lunatic professions but aimed to be doctors, lawyers, teachers, businessmen; here a nurse, there a psychologist, an architect. And then there was me, bored, cranky, full of nutsy escapist fantasies, a worm reading only to keep up with the cute little bluestockings with the blunt-cut hair and overbites.

Yes, I was learning little by little, but in an undisciplined random way that prepared me for nothing substantial. Talk about stupid and disconnected from reality. I thought maybe I'd be a cowboy! I really thought I'd go west and herd cattle. Sleep under the stars. Right. On the ground with the tarantulas. Meanwhile, I bought a lariat and using a pail in our basement as a target, practiced learning to throw a rope around a steer. Never mastered it. Probably would have gone into a fugue state if I had come face-to-face with a steer in any other form than adjacent to a baked potato. Christ, I'm afraid of dogs. And I'm talking about all dogs, including

Yorkies. You'll hate me, but I don't like pets. Naturally, I don't like being bitten and I hate being shed on, licked, or barked at. On the evolutionary scale, I always regarded all animals as failed humans. I also don't like being sung to by a canary or when fish in a tank look back at me. Recently, our daughter came home from college with a pet mouse. She then left the mouse with us for a weekend while she went to the Hamptons with friends. The mouse got sick. It was an emergency, and Soon-Yi and I were forced to take the mouse to the animal hospital ER at midnight. People are walking in and out with hurt dogs and cats and I'm sitting there with an asthmatic mouse. Soon-Yi got me through it, but you haven't lived till you tried sitting in an emergency room holding a rodent at 2 a.m. next to a man with a sneezing parrot. Anyhow, so if not a cowboy, then maybe I'd join the FBI. Of course you had to be a lawyer or an accountant, so pass on that. But I took being a G-man very seriously before coming to my senses. I bought the necessary equipment and learned how to fingerprint and how to read prints from the delta to the whorl.

From there, it was a very short psychotic jump to private eye. I saw *Murder My Sweet, The Maltese Falcon*. I read Mickey Spillane. Private eyes had a pretty exciting life. Solve crimes. Hot dames. Fifty an hour plus expenses. I called a few gumshoes out of the yellow pages to see if one would let me hang around and intern. No takers. But, anything to avoid a life of boredom. To not have to punch a time clock or sit all day at a desk balancing books or telling patients to open wide or telling customers, "You'll get a lot of good wear out of this shoe."

Time was passing; my skills were not promising. Maybe a

gambler. I bought some loaded dice and practiced with real dice so I could throw them both against a wall and box in the lower one with the upper one so I controlled at least one I needed to make my point. There were a few games and I won a few bucks from the suckers, but the women I dreamed of swooned over artists, poets; cultivated babes who valued Rilke over Sugar Ray Robinson. I noodled around with writing, and interestingly my first efforts were not only not comic, they were lurid and morbid. Although in class, anytime we had to write something I wrote comedy, and not only did it make the other kids laugh when it was inevitably chosen to be read aloud but was sometimes passed from teacher to teacher. Let me digress for a moment.

Years earlier, as you now know, my family started out in Brooklyn. We moved from Avenue J to Avenue L. Big move. Two letters. Then, in 1944 we went to Long Beach for the summer, renting a bungalow. It was cheap, as Long Beach was totally primitive, not built up. It was in the summer streets of Long Beach where my uncle Abe taught me to catch a ball, and as the years passed I got good at it. The summer was blissful. I swam in the ocean or only a few blocks away, in the calmer bay. I fished with my father, with friends. I'm telling you, I had a nice childhood. I should not have turned out to be the way I am. So the summer ended and the war was on and my father earned so little that Mom and Dad decided to stay in the bungalow for the winter. The bungalow was not heated but my father bought plug-in heaters, making sure to get the kind that go wrong, set the house on fire, and burn the family to death in their sleep.

I attended public school in Long Beach, and it wasn't too bad because the classes were much easier. After school my friends and I could walk the two blocks to the ocean and have the entire beach to ourselves. Some days we'd go to the bay and set up crab traps and fish. The local movie house opened only at night or if it was a rainy day. In the spring, my friends and I went barefoot. Even to school. Imagine that—me, who saw himself on Fifth Avenue adding just the right touch of vermouth to the gin and then pulling one of those long silk cords by the drapes that ring for Alan Mowbray, was living like Huck Finn or the barefoot boy with cheek of tan rather than Noël Coward.

We lived in Long Beach for a few seasons, and now I come to the point I digressed for. In school, I was ten years old and I wrote a composition in which I referenced Freud, the id, and the libido, not knowing what I was talking about but having some odd instinct for knowing how to parlay a jot of knowledge, in this case just the words, into a comic bit that works and makes the reader or audience think I know much more than I do. The teachers were greatly amused by what I wrote. They passed my writing around, whispering to each other and pointing at me. This odd flair has stayed with me my whole life, and knowing how to use references has grown into a useful tool. End of digression, and if I haven't lost you totally I'll get back to the main theme of the book: man's search for god in a pointless, violent universe.

And so, I was closing in on the final term in Midwood High getting bad grades and not helped by the romantic notion that a life of crime might be the most fun of all my options. Then one fateful afternoon, after a particularly good volley of gags directed at the screen during a movie, someone said, "You should write some of your gags down. They're funny." A casual remark, but through the noise of the Flatbush streets, I heard it. I had the stolen typewriter Dad had fenced, and so I went home and sat down at it. I made up a few jokes and banged them out on the Underwood. On a roll, luck always being my portion, my mother, a serious woman with a heart of liquid nitrogen, paused in her daily ritual of slapping my face on spec and said surprisingly, "Why don't you show your wise cracks to Phil Wasserman [not the other Phil Wasserman—the original, the press agent] and get his opinion? He runs always with those Broadway wags."

I followed her advice. Phil was impressed and said, "You should mail them in to some of the newspaper columnists— Walter Winchell, Earl Wilson, Hy Gardner of the *Herald Tribune*. They're good gags." Here I have to warn the reader the one-liners were not the equal of Voltaire or La Rochefoucauld. They were mother-in-law jokes, parking space jokes, income tax jokes, maybe an occasional topical one. Example (and don't shoot me, I was sixteen): "There was the gambler's kid who went to school in Vegas. He wouldn't take his test marks back—he let 'em ride on the next test." So I mail a few of these Akoya pearls in to various Broadway columnists and I hear nothing. Life goes on and under pressure, with bamboo splints pushed under my fingernails by my parents, I toy with the notion of pharmacy. My date with Janet S., a to-die-for girl in my class with the face of a Raphael Madonna and hair and wardrobe by Jules Feiffer, ends in disaster as I take her to a jazz concert and it turns out she hates jazz. Not to mention she's got a crush on Sheldon Lipman, who wanted to be an anthropologist, which she finds so "breathtakingly fascinating." Much as I try and sell her on the glamour of sharing life with a mortar-and-pestle jockey, she can't see her future with me, and I'm heartbroken yet again. I come home from school, practice my horn, sitting in with Johnny Dodds on my twelve-dollar Victrola.

I go hit baseballs and moon over Ellen H., who is also so beautiful that I lapse into Urdu every time she talks to me but she's going steady with Myron Sefransky, budding journalist and all-'round mensch. She can't stop raving about having been taken to the Village to see Theodore, who was a flamboyant storyteller on stage, of tales by Bierce and Lovecraft, and the new idol of the black-clothes, silver-earring set. Brother Theodore, as he billed himself, had dramatic flair and held audiences spellbound. Years later I cast him in my first hapless play *Don't Drink the Water*, but David Merrick had to fire him because he had no craft and could not hold a performance from one night to the next. I played chess with him during rehearsals, and he kept me in thrall with horror stories, too. These stories were not H. P. Lovecraft or Ambrose Bierce, like in his one-man show, but about the Nazis in Europe bursting into his house and simply throwing his relatives out the windows to their deaths.

So I'm home, daydreaming of Ellen and her perfect round, no lipstick face and her leather shoulder bag holding a red paperback by Par Lagerkvist of *The Dwarf* and cursing a nonexistent god for the fact that when I asked her to go out with me, she lamped me like I was Quasimodo and gave me the full Fuller. That same night, crushed with rejection and before I sacked out, I got a call from a friend who said, "Hey, you're in Nick Kenny's column."

Nick Kenny was a sweet columnist for the *Daily Mirror*, a sparse rag that would have gone out of business were it not for the fact it housed Walter Winchell's column. Unlike Walter Winchell (you all saw *Sweet Smell of Success*), Kenny was a benign softie who'd write little poems in his column; one ended, "and dog spelled backwards is God." So you get the idea. Kenny printed some gags each day, and bolting from my bed to race to Avenue J and pick up the *Daily Mirror* I saw my name in print for the first time. Allan Konigsberg says—and then some stupid gag that I mercifully can't remember. My heart beat like Krupa's "Drum Boogie." You'd have thought I won the Nobel Prize for Literature. I was already fantasizing my flight to Hollywood to write for my favorite comedian, Bob Hope. The down payment on the Fifth Avenue penthouse would come later, after a few years on the road with Bob entertaining the troops. Home in Beverly Hills, naturally. Tennis court. Porsche. And how 'bout that Mulholland Drive—the view up there is really something, innit? Especially if you're looking into the back seats of the parked cars—no, but I wanna say...Finally, I could show my parents who are convinced I'm destined to wind up eating out of dumpsters or on the Ten Most Wanted list, that my life may not be limited to dispensing Vitalis and Preparation H. Next morning, a shower, and off to school where if I continue to fail, so what? My future's mapped out for me.

As I sat in class, smugly listening to the teacher drone on about alternate angles on the same side of the transversal, it occurred to me that some of my classmates might see my name in print. How embarrassing. But why embarrassing? Why not proud? That is one of those vagaries of the human personality I will never grasp. All I know is I was a shy kid and being a public figure embarrassed me.

One can hear the voice of the shrink saying, "You wanted to be famous so much, the wish embarrassed you." A possible insight, but even if true, how does that knowledge butter any parsnips?

Meanwhile, there were still a few gags that bore my name out there floating around with columnists and I felt I had to change it quickly. Changing my name fit perfectly with my daydreams of going into show business. At that time all the performers and some writers and directors and even producers changed their names, and this gesture would make me more one of them. Over the years many people have speculated as to why I changed it to Woody Allen. Some said it was because of the clarinetist Woody Herman. I liked Woody Herman, but the connection never for a second occurred to me. If you can believe how stupid some people are, one speculation was that I played so much stickball in the streets of Brooklyn and the broomsticks were wooden. The truth is, it was arbitrary. I wanted to keep a germ of my original name, so I kept Allen as a last name. I toyed with J. C. Allen but felt I'd be called Jay. I toyed with Mel, but Mel Allen was the famous Yankee broadcaster. Finally, my ADHD set in and I plucked Woody from thin air. It was short, went with Allen, and had a light, vaguely comic touch, as opposed to, say, Zoltan or Ludvicio. The name has served me well, although now and then, since we both played the same instrument, people have called me Mr. Herman; and once a saleslady at Bloomingdale's, who recognized me from *The Tonight Show* and waited on me nervously, said, "Will that be all, Mr. Woodpecker?"

Only rarely have I regretted changing my name and thought my given name was fine. Konigsberg had a serious

Germanic ring. Kant was from Konigsberg. There's a monument honoring me in Konigsberg these days (unless it was pulled down by irate citizens with a rope like Saddam Hussein's) and there is no reason to honor me in Konigsberg. I'm not from there, I've never been there, and have certainly done nothing to enhance the lives of the people there, but my name is the same and perhaps they are hard up for heroes. I chose the piece from many submissions in a contest. I was surprised at how good and clever they all were, and I finally chose the simplest and most modest, which consisted of a pair of glasses on a rod. It looks better than my description of it. There is also a statue of me in the lovely Spanish city of Oviedo, and that statue is a true likeness. They never solicited my opinion or even informed me they were putting one up. They just erected a statue of me in the town, a real bronze statue of the variety pigeons like to roost on. Again, unless a hate-driven mob has pulled it over, it is there to be seen. From the moment it was put up vandals stole the glasses I wear off the statue. The glasses are bronze and embedded in the sculpture, which is full length, and it takes a blow torch to get them off. No matter how many times they redo it, someone steals my glasses. I'd like to say I did a noble and courageous thing in Oviedo to deserve this honor, but apart from visiting, filming there a bit, walking the streets, and enjoying the great weather (like London, in the hot summer, it's cool and gray and always changing), I did nothing to merit any kind of sculptured likeness short of being hung in effigy. Oviedo is a small paradise, marred only by the unnatural presence of a bronze image of a schlemiel.

*　　*　　*

And so with Nick Kenny begins the Woody Allen era, an era that shall live in infamy. I managed to hit Nick Kenny's column several more times, but the big hit was one school day when my first gag appeared in Earl Wilson's column. While Nick Kenny's column was soppy and square, Earl Wilson was the voice of Broadway. His stories and gossip were about show people, plays, movie stars, showgirls, nightclubs, supper clubs. Midnight Earl was a feature, and when a quip by Woody Allen showed up in his column it was as if I was part of the flashy Broadway nightlife scene. In reality, I was in my bedroom on Avenue K in Brooklyn, but I daydreamed myself cracking wise at Toots Shor's with a couple of Copa girls on each arm. Soon I was mailing in jokes to all the columnists and getting printed everywhere; in Bob Sylvester's column in the *News*, Frank Farrell's in the *New York World-Telegram*, Leonard Lyons in the *Post*, and Hy Gardner in the *Herald Tribune*, and still Earl Wilson and Nick Kenny. I reveled in my private accomplishments, neglecting schoolwork while my marks plummeted. The other kids were visiting colleges. In my eyes I had already made it, and although there was no payment for these quips, I saw myself buying a penthouse or maybe lunching with the Hopes in Toluca Lake.

In those days there was a Madison Avenue publicity firm, David O. Alber Associates, whose job it was to get their roster of famous clients as much publicity as possible by securing stories about them, TV and press interviews, magazine covers, and whatever gimmicks they could think of to keep their names in the public eye. One source of publicity was to constantly have your name appear in the newspaper columns, and to be quoted you needed to say something witty. Someone's column might read, "Overheard at the Copa..."—and then some funny remark about traffic or mother-in-laws or the president or whatever attributed to the client. Of course, the client never made the joke and probably couldn't have if his life depended on it. He probably wasn't even at the Copa, although both the client and the nightclub were paying for the print exposure. It was the press agent who mailed the gag in to the columnists who foisted the myth of a scintillating nightlife on Broadway around celebrities doing one-liners in the manner of Groucho Marx or Oscar Levant. So it was that Gene Shefrin, the dynamic motor power of the David O. Alber publicity firm, couldn't help but notice that this unknown character, Woody Allen, was appearing in Broadway columns all over the papers week after week. Shefrin calls Earl Wilson and says who's this guy?

Earl Wilson says he's some kid in Brooklyn who comes home after high school, sits at a typewriter, and mails us a few gags every few days. Next thing I get a message from Earl Wilson's office to call the Alber office. I do and I'm invited for a job interview. Would I be interested in coming in each day after school, sitting at one of their unstolen typewriters, and knocking out gags for them so the likes of Guy Lombardo, Arthur Murray, Jane Morgan, Sammy Kaye, and others not famous for their wit could fasten their names to my inspirations and claim them as their own? For this, they would pay me forty dollars a week. At that time I delivered meat for a butcher shop, and dry-cleaning for a tailor, for thirty-five cents an hour plus tips.

The work was part-time and if I worked hard and was lucky I might make three or four dollars for the week. My big allowance had dried up, as Dad's liquidity was rather anemic due to some faulty speculation regarding the outcome of certain basketball games. My mother worked five eight-hour days for forty dollars a week, and here all I had to do was take the subway from Brooklyn after school, school hours being eight to one, knock out some lively sallies, and ride home. For this I was going to get forty dollars a week. I decided not to play it coy, pretending I needed time to think it over. I said yes before he could finish his sentence. And so, I went to work five days a week and knocked out about fifty gags a day. It sounds like a feat but if you can do it, it's no big deal. The subway ride was about thirty-five minutes during which I wrote about twenty gags. The rest in the office. There was much teasing from the other office workers because I was so young, and it didn't help my image when after a few weeks of work I got the mumps and needed time off. But I worked there for a few years, their clients turning up in columns all over, spouting what we all took to be funny gags but now, in retrospect, were clearly pretty dreadful. I graduated high school with a seventy-two average and continued working, getting a raise or two with time. I didn't want to go to college, confident of a show business career, but in the interests of keeping my mother from setting fire to herself like a Buddhist monk, I gave NYU a try.

For whatever reason, they accepted me despite my dreadful average. Seeking to work as little as humanly possible in college, I took a limited program, three subjects. I was a motion picture major for no other reason than watching movies seemed nice and cushy. I had to take Spanish, and took English. As usual my first English composition caused trouble and the teacher failed the paper, writing in the margin, "Son, you need a lesson in rudimentary manners. You are a callow adolescent and are not a diamond in the rough." In those days, my style was broadly comic, much influenced by Max Shulman, and clearly I was not the writer Shulman was. I also failed my major, movies. Partially because of my old habit of hooky. I'd ride the train from Avenue J to Eighth Street, where NYU was, the doors would open, I'd wonder—should I go to class or play hooky? I'd prolong my mental debate till the doors closed and off I'd ride feeling exhilarated. As in days of yore I'd emerge at Times Square and kill the morning around Broadway, the Paramount, the Roxy, Lindy's, the Circle Magic Shop, the Automat with its delicious food. At one I'd show up at Madison Avenue for my joke-writing gig. When I did go to class, I was learning to play the drums at the time in keeping with my jazz obsession and I'd sit in class practicing my foot pedal work—left right, right left right left, left right, trying to keep paradiddle rhythm steady, I was never paying attention to the conjugation of tenses or to *Piers Plowman*. It was in this way that I managed to fail all my courses. They decided to throw me out. I asked for one last chance to save my mother from self-immolation. They said if I went to summer school and did well they'd reconsider. Biting the bullet, I agreed.

At work, David Alber was in some way connected with or knew Jimmy Saphier, Bob Hope's manager. As a nice gesture he had me write some sample material for Hope and sent it. A note came back saying, "Your boy writes pretty good stuff. (None of that callow adolescent crap.) Might be able to use him for Hope in the fall."

It's hard to exaggerate what Bob Hope meant to me. I had adored him since early childhood and to this day never tire of watching his movies. Not all his movies, not the later ones, and not even so much the very early ones. But *Monsieur Beaucaire, Casanova's Big Night, The Great Lover*, for example. Yes, the movies are silly and the humor is not Shavian, but Hope himself is such a very great comic persona and his delivery is out of this world. Often, when I grabbed strangers by the lapels in the manner of the Ancient Mariner and waxed euphoric about Hope, they would say, "You mean that cornball Republican reading from cue cards and making Miss Universe jokes for G.I.s?" While I saw their point, that was not the Hope I'm talking about.

I meant the comedian in *Road to Utopia* or *Fancy Pants*. Again, I know, the movies are silly. Hope may be carried off by a gorilla—but that's not what to focus on. It's his acting, his character, his commitment, his timing, the great one-liners. Like Jerry Lewis, a huge talent but with silly films, although Hope's were much better than Jerry Lewis's. Anyhow, I was walking on air when I heard Hope's camp liked my jokes enough to consider hiring me. I was, after all, a college freshman, and as summer school limped on I was submerged in Keats and Shelley and did not agree truth was beauty, beauty truth. Nor did I relish hearing my professor discuss the work of Pudovkin or the structure of *Greed* while I kept wanting to make *Road to Bali*.

I toyed very briefly again with being a comedian, and one of my office workers on Madison Avenue, Mike Merrick, who had been a comic and whose black-rimmed glasses I thought were great looking, lent me his old loose-leaf book of stand-up routines. I went on once again at a local social club and killed them and getting laughs from an audience gave one a great high. But Mike Merrick explained to me, "It's a tough life. You've got to want it more than anything else." And I didn't. I was drawn more to writing. I liked the anonymity, and many of the girls I dated went ape over Updike and Mailer and not Buddy Hackett or Fat Jack E. Leonard. My goal subtly shifted. I would do some gag writing for a while, perhaps, for Hope, perhaps for Berle or Jack Benny if I could make them aware of me. But perhaps I should write deeper things than mere one-liners. It was somewhere at that time that my relatives suggested I have a talk with a very distant relative by marriage, Abe Burrows. Burrows was a famous comic writer and director and had coauthored the book of *Guys and Dolls* among other things. Perhaps an aunt who married into the family was circuitously related to him. I could never figure out the lineage. I asked the aunt, who said she couldn't help me except to say he lived at the Beresford, the stylish West Side co-op. "How can I contact him?" I asked shyly. My mother, more aggressive than General Patton, said, "You don't have to contact him. You know where he lives. Just go over to his house."

Against my better judgment I dressed for a royal wedding and set out for the Beresford. I told the doorman I was there to see Abe Burrows. Tell him it's Nettie's son.

Just as I waited while he called up, out strolls Abe in a dark suit with a Homburg hat. The doorman points to me and says he's here to see you. I tell him who I'm related to, a tenuous connection, like maybe ten degrees of separation.

Burrows, who is heading out to an appointment, re-
verses himself, takes me by my shoulder upstairs, tosses his
Homburg away and proceeds to chat with me for an hour,
feeding me and showing great interest in seeing my jokes.
The guy was so nice, so decent, so wonderful. I went back to
that apartment a number of times. He liked what he read of
my jokes. He criticized the ones he thought I missed on. He
wrote a letter on my behalf to Nat Hiken, the fine comedy
writer of *The Phil Silvers Show*. Nothing came of it, but he
tried. During one of our chats when I told him my ambition
to be a TV writer, he said, "You don't want to be a TV
writer all your life." I said, Movies? He said no, theater. But
don't all the playwrights want to write movies? No, all the
screenwriters want to write plays.

I turned my focus onto the theater when I had seen only
part of one play in my life. I say "part," but it's not that I
left after an act. I saw some half of the whole play. It came
about years before when I longed for a beautiful blonde in
school named Roxanne. Realizing a creature so heavenly,
who could charm a Cary Grant or Tyrone Power, would
never give a tumble to a lad closer in essence to Edward
Everett Horton. I daydreamed sadly until one day a light
bulb went off. I had heard that Roxanne was dying to see
The Fourposter, a two character play with Hume Cronyn
and Jessica Tandy, two wonderful performers. Slyboots that
I was, I got up the nerve to call her and said if she was free
Saturday night, I just happened to have two tickets to *The
Fourposter*, and would she be interested in seeing it?

One could sense the silence on the other end while she
was forced to choose between wanting desperately to see
the show and having to do it with a zook. In the end, she

opted to accept. Now, having no experience with Broadway I didn't know that there were shows that were sold out and you couldn't get tickets for them. I learned this from the man at the box office who said he could accommodate me several months from now. Gripped with panic, I called one of my friends who advised me to try a ticket broker. I did and learned I could score a pair of seats in a box for twenty dollars. I did not have twenty dollars and couldn't think of how to get that without holding up a filling station. Finally I asked my father for it. It was a huge sum of money, especially for two theater tickets, and I couldn't bear to tell him the embarrassing truth of why I needed twenty rutabagas fast, no questions, but as always, he came through for me and got the double sawbuck. Come Saturday night, I pick up the girl. Charmingly, she feigns interest in my spate of self-aggrandizing anecdotes in which I come off like Rhett Butler. We go to the show. We are ushered into the box, which overhangs the stage from the second floor on the extreme right. The type of thing Lincoln was murdered in only not as well placed as his so half the stage is not visible to us.

My first Broadway show and I see only actors on stage right. When the broker said box seats, I thought of Yankee Stadium or Ebbets Field, where box seats are great. We watch the show and Roxanne is a good sport. She doesn't complain but when we leave she passes on drinks and is suddenly stricken with a mysterious illness. I can't remember; I think she said she was coming down with the flesh-eating virus. Nearing her apartment house, she has already phoned her brother saying she'd be home in six minutes. He is waiting at the open door to let her in, precluding any chance of me making a pass at her. I think how funny it would be if I simply kissed him good night. Anyhow, years later when Abe Burrows asked if I liked theater, since I'd seen only half a show, I fumfered. But I took to heart his saying I shouldn't settle for being a TV writer nor a screenwriter my whole life, and with my new obsession I read every single play and saw every opening on Broadway for years. But I'm getting ahead of myself.

I was still knocking out one-liners with David O. Alber to furnish gags for the tabloids. If I could be a writer for Bob Hope, that would do it. But living in the future I would be a playwright and oddly not like George S. Kaufman, my idol from days past, but like Eugene O'Neill or Tennessee Williams. Of course right now I was failing out of summer school and I was called before a panel of deans. A panel of deans is not like an exaltation of larks. It's more like a bevy of ghouls. It's a humorless quartet who are there to tell you you're out. I listened politely as they indicted me on several counts from being a no-show to failing everything. They asked me my goal in life. I said, to forge in the smithy of my soul the uncreated conscience of my race and see if it could be mass-produced in plastic. They looked at one another and suggested I see a psychiatrist. I said I worked professionally and got along well with everyone and why would I need a psychiatrist? They explained that I was in the world of show business where everybody's crazy. I didn't think a shrink was the worst idea, since despite all my creative interests and promising start as a comedy writer along with all of the love I was shown growing up, I still experienced some moderate feelings of anxiety—like when you're buried alive. I was not happy; I was gloomy, fearful, angry, and don't ask me why. Maybe it was in my blood-stream or maybe it was a mental state that set in where I realized the Fred Astaire movies were not documentaries.

I started seeing a highly recommended psychiatrist named Peter Blos once a week shortly after my expulsion, and although he was a terrific guy, it didn't do me much good. He eventually suggested I see a psychoanalyst four times a week, where I lay on a couch and was encouraged to say everything that came to mind, including describing my dreams. I did that for eight years and cleverly managed to avoid any progress. I finally outlasted him and he came in one day waving a white flag. I saw three more shrinks in my life. First was a very fine man named Lou Linn, whom I saw twice a week in a face-to-face situation. He was quite brilliant, but I easily outfoxed him and remained safely uncured. Then I saw a very bright lady for maybe fifteen years. That was more therapeutic and helped me over some of life's tribulations, but no real changes for the better in my personality occurred. Finally a highly recommended doctor who has tried face-to-face therapy with me, couch psycho-analysis for a period, and back to face-to-face therapy, and I'm still able to fend off any meaningful progress.

So I've had many years of treatment and my conclusion is, yes, it has helped me, but not as much as I'd hoped and not in the way I'd imagined. I made zero progress on the deep issues; fears and conflicts and weaknesses I had at seventeen and twenty, I still have. The few areas where the problems are not so embedded, where one needs a little help, a push, maybe I got some relief. (I can go to a Turkish bath without having to buy out the room.) For me the value was having a person to be around to share my suffering with; hitting with the pro in tennis. Also for me a big plus was the delusion I was helping myself. In the blackest times it's nice to feel you're not just lying dormant, a passive slug being pelted by the irrational lunacy of the universe, or even by tsuris of your own making. It's important to believe you're doing something about it. The world and the people in it may have their boots on your throat, stomping the very life out of you, but you're going to change all of that, you're taking heroic action. You're free-associating. You're remembering those dreams. Maybe writing them down. At least once a week you're going to discuss this with a trained expert, and together you will understand the awful emotions causing you to be sad, frightened, raging, despairing, and suicidal.

The fact that solving these problems is illusory and you will always remain the same tormented wretch, unable to ask the baker for schnecken because the word embarrasses you, doesn't matter. The illusion you're doing something to help yourself helps you. You somehow feel a little better, a little less despondent. You pin your hopes on a Godot who never comes, but the thought he might show up with answers helps you get through the enveloping nightmare. Like religion, where the illusion gets one through. And being in the arts, I envy those people who derive solace from the belief that the work they created will live on and be much discussed and somehow, like the Catholic with his afterlife, so the artist's "legacy" will make him immortal. The catch here is that all the people discussing the legacy and how great the artist's work is are alive and are ordering pastrami, and the artist is somewhere in an urn or underground in Queens. All the people standing over Shakespeare's grave and singing his praises means a big goose egg to the Bard, and a day will come—a far-off day, but be sure it definitely is coming—when all Shakespeare's plays, for all their brilliant plots and hoity-toity iambic pentameter, and every dot of Seurat's will be gone along with each atom in the universe. In fact, the universe will be gone and there will be no place to have your hat blocked. After all, we are an accident of physics. And an awkward accident at that. Not the product of intelligent design but, if anything, the work of a crass bungler.

Anyhow they bounced me from NYU summer school, but I was by then a working comedy writer. Not only was I doing it for David O. Alber Associates, but Abe Burrows had recommended me to Peter Lind Hayes, who had a radio show, and I got hired to write for him. Arthur Godfrey hired me to write for his radio show as well for a while. Meanwhile I was hitting the theatrical agencies, and a nice agent at William Morris named Sol Leon introduced me to a wonderful comedian named Herb Shriner, who did what was called a simulcast—he was on radio and TV at the same time. He was a very fine comedian in the rural Will Rogers style but better. He told great jokes and he liked mine and hired me. A writer named Roy Kammerman was his head writer, and he was a nice man and a fine comedy writer. I was such a rookie that when I wrote my first show for him—or really contributed some gags—I took a date to the TV studio where the show aired so I could play the big shot with the hopes it would grease the skids to the boudoir. Anyhow I went to the show and got in line behind hundreds of people waiting to get in to see it. Suddenly Herb Shriner's manager sees me there and says, "What the hell are you standing in line for?"

I said, "I write on the show."

He said, "Yes, but you don't have to get in line to get in, you come in backstage."

"I do?"

"Come on." And he took me and my date in the stage entrance and we watched from the VIP room and I played the big shot. I took my date to Lindy's after. Another line to get in. I had been told to tip the doorman, so I greased him with two federal diplomas and I got taken care of toot sweet. A big night till that moment at her front door when, key in hand, she gives me what basketball players call an up-fake. She snaps upward, I fall for it and leave my feet as if to block her jump shot, and she goes right past me inside.

I'm eighteen, making triple what my parents earn put together. I have a chance to help out at home, particularly my father who keeps betting and losing and owing the bookies. The next step in my relentless drive to succeed comes when a guy in the neighborhood named Harvey Meltzer, who lives in an apartment house nearby, has heard about me, the neighborhood wunderkind, and comes over to talk to me about being my manager. My understanding of the business end of show business is slightly worse than my grasp of the Hodge conjecture. He says his uncle is a big wheel at William Morris in Hollywood and he has the inside track on something called the Writer Development Program, a program NBC is forming to develop and train promising writers. Apparently some suit up there has read, In the beginning was the word. Their well-meaning idea was to find potential writers for drama and more so for comedy, to put them on a steady salary, a hundred seventy-five a week, and to have them write, to apprentice on shows under veteran writers, to blossom, with NBC cashing in on the fruit. I am all for this, as my salary at Alber is meager in comparison and the radio shows I write for wax and wane with the host's popularity. A hundred seventy-five steady every week sounds good plus getting placed on some big-time show. I forgot to mention one small fact: Herb Shriner, my biggest credit, and his lovely wife, died in a car accident. Two nicer people you couldn't meet, and with so many more I could think of who would have instantly made the world a better place if they showed up somewhere DOA, these two lovely, undeserving people buy it.

So I agree to let Harvey, who resembles a less robust Tommy Dorsey except with a kaleidoscopic smorgasbord of facial tics, be my manager and sure enough, he nails the NBC writer development deal. I reward him by signing the seven-year contract he presents me with. One of his many mistakes—a much-too-piggish agreement I never should've signed. First, seven years was too long. He was taking advantage of my naivety. Not only that, instead of the usual 10 percent an agent gets, he says he is a manager, which is different, and so earns more. Thirty percent, he says. Fine. Hey, look, I'm a teenager. What the hell do I know? Not only that, there's a thing called a sliding scale which normally slides in the direction of lessening the agent's percentage the more the artist earns. The higher the salary the artist makes, the less the agent needs to clean up. In the deal I signed, the sliding scale slid in the wrong direction. So, the more I earned, the higher Harvey's cut was. Over seven years, a lot happened and I was wised up. But I never tried to break the contract; I served the whole seven years honorably. Let me illustrate what a hayseed I was at that age. I had never seen anyone with a hairpiece in my life. One day I met with a comic who wore one. He wanted to pay me a hundred bucks for a routine. As we spoke, I noticed a thin rim of cheesecloth bordering his hairline. I couldn't believe what I was seeing, thought it was growing, and felt he should be in the circus, rather than doing stand-up.

Now about the Writer Development Program. There were about eight of us, after much vetting of our audition material and personalities, deemed worthy of NBC's investment. For all their scrutiny, though, they did not choose wisely, and there came a time when they would realize only a feeble return on their money. Most of the group wound up in occupations that have no resemblance to what NBC had in mind. The creepiest of the group wound up writing "warmth lines" for Richard Nixon's speeches. Aside from him, they were all nice people but for one reason or another didn't become dramatists or TV comedy writers. Heading the program or shepherding the flock, as the press used to say, was Les Colodny, an ex–William Morris agent who was amusing but who had no lesson plan and didn't know where to begin to transmogrify this group of maladroit dreamers into professional comedy writers. I took the money and used the subsidy to learn how to write, to practice writing sketches and jokes, to self-teach by hard work. I was hired and left to flounder like the others but, riddled with ambition from years of maternal hectoring, was sensible enough to make use of the time and money. We might meet up at NBC, sit in a room while young comics would show up and show us their stuff, and we'd pick ones to write for, thus presumably developing writers and comedians. Mostly, we saw stiffs. But a young Don Adams, a young Jonathan Winters, a young Kaye

Ballard came in. Of course they needed little or no help from us. The real talent created their own acts and never used us. I wrote one single joke for Don Adams. Jonathan Winters needed nothing from anyone; he was simply a genius.

At that time, I met Harlene, the girl I would soon marry. It was yet another social club. I was the emcee at one of their functions. I did jokes out of Mike Merrick's loose-leaf book of routines, and I had decided to delight the audience by playing my soprano saxophone for their delectation (years later, a music critic would describe my playing at a concert as "excruciating"). New Orleans addict that I was, I chose "Jada" and "At the Darktown Strutter's Ball." Someone told me about a senior at James Madison High School who played piano. Somehow a meeting was set up. She was pretty, she was bright, she came from a good family who had a lovely house and a boat, and she played classical music and took acting lessons. In short, she was much too good for me and would prove to be so after we married.

We practiced our two tunes together and started dating. I must say, for a college-age kid, I took her to very romantic, sophisticated places. Off-Broadway shows, Birdland to see Miles Davis and John Coltrane. Candlelight restaurants in Manhattan. I held my own as a charmer and lover with the exception of when her family took me out for a day on their boat. I was being a good sport and wanted to appear impressive but once out to sea, just when I was chug-a-lugging a beer and intoning a chorus of "Heave ho, blow the man down," I turned chartreuse and dropped to the deck, groaning and begging to be euthanized. As I lay there describing a Mobius loop, my seasickness soon to go into the Guinness Book of World Records, I vowed never to step on a boat again and didn't until over a decade later. I was trying to impress, or should I say, not seem like a nincompoop (I am a nincompoop and often go to great lengths to disguise it) and so I went out on a sailboat at the urging of the very beautiful Janet Margolin while we were filming *Take the Money and Run*. The results were the same. After boasting of my exploits at sea and calling the crew "me hearties" I was soon lying on the deck ready to trade Janet for a Compazine. As we were only in San Francisco Bay, a short distance from the shore, my pleading for a helicopter to airlift me to a hospital went unheeded. Sailing back and staggering from the vessel, pale and shaken, I made some lame excuse blaming my unraveling on a recent middle ear infection, picked up in the Sudan where I was teaching the Nuba to perform "Floogle Street" and "Who's on First."

Harlene and I each lived with our parents, and I called for her every night. We did everything a dating couple does. By the way, by then I had a car. I had purchased a 1951 Plymouth convertible for six hundred bucks. I had entertained great fantasies about how a car would change my life. It would liberate me; I could drive over the bridge to Manhattan anytime I chose, spin out to Long Beach to visit nostalgic old haunts, go to Connecticut on a spring morning to commune with nature. I don't know what the hell I was thinking; I hated nature, and more than nature I hated being a car owner. Like all mechanical objects, we were instantly archenemies. I'm not a gadget lover. I own no watches, carry no umbrellas, own no cameras or tape recorders, and to this day I need my wife to adjust the TV set. I own no computer, never have gone near a word processor, have never changed a fuse, emailed anyone, or washed a dish. I'm one of those

and wanted to exit the Plymouth and leave it forever in the midst of a jammed street. I drove around endlessly unable to find parking spaces and then couldn't squirm in. I bashed in many a headlight and taillight of parked vehicles trying to fit between them and then pulled out and sped off in panic, leaving the scene of the crime. I got lost continually. I had no sense of direction. Once, driving on the Sunrise Highway, Harlene said her parents were away and we could go to her house and use the bedroom. Inflamed by the idea, I made a quick U-turn and knocked over a telephone pole. I got flat tires on the West Side Highway at 3 a.m. Only the kindness of strangers bailed me out. If the total stranger who was nice enough to stop in the black night and instruct me in how to change a tire hadn't been so patient and had been say, the Zodiac Killer, I wouldn't be here.

Yes, it was, as all girls' mothers feared, a hotel room on wheels, but every time I began smooching, a flashlight appeared at the window and some cop moved me on. Many drivers screamed at me, and when I accidentally hit another car broadside on Atlantic Avenue, a raging monster who was bodyguard and driver for a mob boss charged to my window as I suddenly had visions of myself as the subject of a candlelight vigil. Quickly, I rolled the window up and got his hand caught in it. Erupting like Vesuvius, he bent it back like it was a sardine can. Had not a crowd intervened I would have ended up in thirty-seven separate mason jars. And yet I did drive because everyone I knew seemed to be able to manage a car and why shouldn't I? But I never could, and gave up on it shortly after. I tried driving once or twice years later with the same results and finally packed it in for life.

The moment I sold the Plymouth was like having a tumor removed.

So Harlene and I did everything and we looked up one day and decided we would marry. We were kids; there was nothing else to do. We had seen all the movies and shows, hit the museums, played miniature golf, sat over cappuccino at Orsini's, and spent a day at Fire Island. What was left? So we got engaged. Between my steady salary with the NBC Writer Development Program and the money I was making selling special material to nightclub comics, I could afford to be a married man. Special material is a branch of comedy writing that goes unsung, and the public doesn't get to really appreciate. There are millions of comedians around or certainly there were when I started. They play nightclubs, or on TV, or at private functions, and they all need material: jokes, bits, routines, something to say. Most of them were not very good as evidenced by the fact that they needed other people to put words in their mouth, funny words. If left on their own, they couldn't coax a chuckle from a manic fat man on laughing gas. Naturally, truly gifted ones like Mike Nichols and Elaine May or Mort Sahl or Jonathan Winters needed no one. They didn't have to buy jokes; they created material themselves because they were indeed funny.

The icons of an earlier era like Bob Hope and Jack Benny had also created their own strong comic personas, and by the time they were superstars, they could hire writers to feed the character they had themselves earlier established. So I, like assorted colleagues who kept their stoves warm by the servicing of various mediocre wannabes, and depositing the worm of funny into their anxious open beaks, wrote special material. I was forever sitting at some nightclub hearing the sad whining of an uninspired tummler who couldn't figure out why he was stalled at the bottom rung, "I need an attitude. I don't have an attitude. Alan King's got an attitude. I have to get an attitude." What he needed no writer could give him. All we could do was sell comedians some jokes or a routine, which they would memorize and perform with varying degrees of skill, but nothing ever stuck. The audience never went home with anything—no human being, certainly no funny human. Just an extrovert who bought some one-liners is out there getting laughs and applause and then wondering why he's not "making it."

"What I need are truisms," one poor soul said to me, coining a lubberly neologism as he medicated his chemical imbalance. "The audience identifies with truisms." I presumed he meant insights where the joke resonated with the house in recognizable experiences. Still, the field of special material provided many of us upcoming writers with our daily tuck, although it could get hairy. It sometimes went like this: Comic and writer meet. Comic needs new routine. Writer throws out ideas. Comic likes one. Comic gives down payment to writer. Writer writes comedy bit. Comic tries it. Bit doesn't work. Comic blames writer's writing. Writer blames comic's delivery. Much anger. Comic loses deposit, winds up with nothing. Out a few hundred bucks. Invective ensues and threats of a lawsuit or two broken legs depending on the comic's capacity for remorse.

It was at this time that I got the news from NBC that they were flying their developing writers to Los Angeles because one of the big shows, the *Colgate Comedy Hour*, was failing and maybe we could help save it and in the process learn something. I had never been away from home, never had any interruption with my relationship with Harlene, and most of all had never flown. In those days the planes had propellers and couldn't make the trip nonstop and, worst of all, traveled through the sky. On the other hand, going to the city I knew only from listening to Bob Hope monologues seemed exciting. Hollywood and Vine, Mulholland Drive, the La Brea Tar Pits, all of us who loved Hope on radio or later TV knew of these places only from his jokes, just as radio had taken us every Sunday night to the home of Jack Benny in Beverly Hills. I might even get to meet Hope or Benny. Excited, I assumed Mom would sew name tags in my clothes and off I'd go. But as the day of departure drew close I began feeling a little panicky, and at the airport, when I saw the other writers purchase flight insurance at a vending machine (you inserted your coins and out came a policy so if your plane crashed, a designated beneficiary would collect), I grew pale. My fear was not so much dying in a crash but crashing in the wilderness of some mountain, lost for weeks, no food, and the other writers elect to eat me as I was the youngest and hence most tender.

As luck would have it we didn't crash, I made it to LA without winding up anybody's main course, and the policy buyers lost all their quarters. After pausing at the airport for an English muffin and a fresh cup of smog, I got into a waiting limo and was soon checking into a hotel on Hollywood Boulevard. A horror worse than an aviation disaster was the news that I would be sharing a room with a man named Milt Rosen, an older, portly comedy writer who'd been out there struggling to save the *Colgate Comedy Hour* with a half dozen other veteran scribes. Not only would I be sharing a bathroom—oh God, could this be happening to me?—but the bed was a double bed. Stricken, I staggered around, thinking I'll pay for my own room. But could I? Or should I feign a family crisis and go back to New York? But I'm a comedy writer with a real opportunity. I'm in Hollywood. This is where it all happens—the movies, the homes with swimming pools, Bogart and Bacall, *Gone with the Wind* only blocks away, Bob Hope lives here, Sunset Boulevard. This is where you strove to make it. I stayed. I shared a bathroom and a bed. (Bruno Bettelheim writes about how in the concentration camps, one accommodated quickly to hideous conditions, which without the threat of torture or death would have required long years of analysis with dubious results. Of course, he wasn't thinking of sharing a bed with Milt Rosen.)

As it turned out Milt was a nice man and a smart man and a funny man and I liked him and, fifty years later, having not heard a word from him in all that time, I found out he was ailing and in need and I sent some dough and he was surprised I remembered him. Still, I found it pretty disgusting to bunk with a chubby stranger who had XY chromosomes. We had a few days off to get settled before my assignment, and as I walked around Hollywood, loving the palm trees and the sunsets, I was warmed by the knowledge I was being given a chance to be a part of history I'd grown up mesmerized by. I drank the local orange juice, ate the sweet rolls (Danish, we call them) and one day marched into a room with a couple of writers and got introduced to the head writer, who had been brought into town to turn the moribund hi-jinks around and hopefully get some mileage out of us. His name was Danny Simon and I knew of him from his credits as a TV writer. He and his brother, Doc, had been a sensational comedy writing team that all of us in the business knew of by their great reputation. We'd seen their shows, for example, *The Red Buttons Show*, and they were deservedly hot stuff. The brothers had just broken up the team as Doc Simon, whose given name was Neil, wanted to begin a career as a playwright.

Danny surveyed us schlumps and asked to see examples of material we'd written. We handed over pages of stuff, which he said he'd take home and read and discuss with us. I was the youngest one there by far, and he was polite but slightly skeptical when he accepted my binder of material. I went home not discouraged or encouraged but hoped I could factor in and contribute. There were other veteran writers out there working. I say veteran—they were more veteran than me, already established, but not old guys. Norman Lear and his partner, Ed Simmons, were a team. So were Coleman Jacoby and Arnie Rosen. Ira Wallach was out there trying to help out and there was an assortment of comics trying to bolster the show, from a newly emerging Jonathan Winters to an old vaudevillian, Joe Frisco. I dined alone and went to sleep, keeping one eye open all night lest Milt Rosen roll over onto my side of the bed. I was prepared to let out a piercing shriek. The next day, when Danny Simon called me into his office, my life changed forever.

He proceeded to tell me how terrific my jokes were and said if I never learned to write sketches or plays or anything else, my jokes were so good I could make a great living with them alone. Needless to say, this was encouraging. He wanted to work with me and since the departure of his younger brother, he was constantly searching for a working partner and maybe I was it. We began to collaborate on writing comedy sketches. Let me give you the picture. Danny was a very compulsive, demanding guy who fought with every partner he worked with after Doc. Writers on Danny's level had no patience with his scrupulous demands, his constant rewriting, working all day on a single page to get every straight line and punch line perfect without stopping the narrative flow and then he'd reread the page, destroy it, pop yet another Miltown, the fashionable tranquilizer of the day, and begin again. Collaborators rebelled and he was merciless with them, and how many could follow in the footsteps of a comedy writer like Neil Simon?

I, on the other hand, was a soft-spoken kid who knew nothing, idolized Danny and Doc Simon, could never imagine disagreeing with Danny because what the hell did I know, and so he found himself an ideal collaborator. He loved my jokes and thought me personally very funny. I suppose he enjoyed being so looked up to, and he taught me some key things. For example: Great straight lines make great punch lines. Never have the character say something that wasn't perfectly natural just to get to a great punch line I had waiting. He taught me to throw out even my finest jokes if they in any way halted or slowed the narrative; to always begin at the beginning and go right to the end of the sketch, never to write a scene out of sequence, never to write when you're not feeling well because the material will reflect the lack of energy and health. Never to be competitive. Always root for the success of your contemporaries, as there's room for everybody. And most important, he taught me to trust my own judgment. No matter who tried to tell me what's funny, or what isn't, or what I should be doing, I was to go with my own judgment. Unless of course the person was him, because he fancied himself a gifted teacher on a subject that many tried to explain and analyze from Freud to Henri Bergson to Max Eastman and have come up empty. And he was a great teacher. He imbued in me a confident quality when it came to comedy, and this firm point of view has helped me enormously.

At summer theater, which I'll come to, my first week I wrote a sketch to go before a live audience on a Saturday night show. After a few days' rehearsal there was a run-through, and all the contributors naturally came to the run-through to see their material mounted and tweak it. I didn't bother to come, so confident was I. When a girl asked me, "Where were you?" I said I didn't need to go. I wanted my sketch to play as was and it didn't need tweaking. And she said, "Of all the pieces in the review at the run-through, yours died." And I said calmly, not trying to be aloof but undoubtedly oozing unearned hubris, "I'm not worried." When the show went on and some numbers faltered and failed, mine played to big laughs. I had held my ground as Danny had taught me, and my sketch was one of the hits of the show.

So I was learning how to be a writer, and that meant being at the typewriter at nine and hard, even agonizing work and reworking until six. Other great comedy writers I later wrote with did not work that way, but it was my foundation and I'm glad I went to a tough school. I made friends with some of the older writers, and they liked me because while I had some talent, I showed great respect (which I felt), and none of them were ever competitive, only helpful and encouraging. While out there I was taken with the romance of Hollywood. By now we had been moved to the Hollywood Hawaiian Hotel, into a charming suite with a kitchen and bedroom where I lived alone. The hotel had a courtyard with a swimming pool that all the writers and comics hung out around, and there were the sunsets and the balmy nights, not to mention per diems.

I wanted to share it with Harlene, so I suggested she fly out and marry me. She had just graduated high school and was seventeen. I was twenty. She talked it over with her parents who said she could if she wanted to. Her parents were lovely people, a gigantic cut over my parents, who by comparison lived ten decibels higher. The Rosens lived well, they were not always arguing, they were cultivated, traveled, had a fine home. Next to them my parents were cave dwellers who raised me as a Cro-Magnon, and Harlene's parents never should have let their daughter marry me. True, I was showing promise in my field, but I was not showing much as a person. I was still stupid (it's like driving—you never lose that), uncivilized, neurotic, totally unprepared for marriage, an emotional mess who was coasting ever since sixteen on what Noël Coward called "a talent to amuse."

When Harlene did fly out and we married, the words "I do" sounded to me like they were spoken in a cavernous echo chamber like Orson Welles's lips saying "Rosebud." It took place, however, in some rabbi's living room (a nod to her parents), and I could imagine a vault door closing on my life. A crypt door. Yes, I loved Harlene, but I had no idea what love meant, what to expect, what not to expect, what was required. What followed was a nightmare for both of us, but it was my fault. Inexperienced as she was, she was up for it and was a larger person, had better personal resources. I failed at it so miserably and made her life miserable in the process. I'll paint the picture for you, and it's a sad picture. We both survived it, but let me take you back to those years of early marital agony. Two very young people, she's on the verge of starting college, I'm earning enough to support us, the Writer Development Program starts to fray, its ranks thinning as the duds get weeded out. We return to New York as the *Colgate Comedy Hour* quietly succumbs.

We take an apartment. Park Avenue and Sixty-First Street. Naturally I gravitate instantly to the Upper East Side; all those penthouse movies. Except we don't live in a penthouse. It is a very small one-room apartment, and I mean one room. This tiny rectangle costs me a hundred and twenty-five bucks per month and since neither of us was experienced it didn't occur to us that being the first apartment in a multiple-dwelling brownstone, and contiguous to the building's front door which had all the doorbells on a panel, that every time someone enters and rings, the ring back, a loud electric buzz, reverberates throughout our apartment like an Evinrude. In our one small room we have a sofa bed, a kitchen table with four chairs, a bookcase, a television set, a piano, a comfy chair facing the sofa bed, a few lamps, and a stand with a large tape recorder. My typewriter is on the kitchen table because it's where I work.

I'd love to say we were cramped in a Fibber McGee's closet, poor but happy, and didn't we have fun in those days. We did not. On the plus side, I was putting Harlene through college. She went to Hunter, just six blocks away, and I walked her to school every morning before digging into work. I was so glad when she was gone because there was not a single thing we could agree on, not a single compromise either of us was capable of making, and we battled like hit men in the Castellammarese War. I was moody, unhappy, nasty to her very nice parents for no reason other than I was an obnoxious swine. I couldn't stand my wife's friends. I got on her nerves with my constant, sullen unhappiness. I began getting nauseated often, usually in the dead of night. I attributed it either to a fatal disease or her cooking, but my yearly physical had me in good health and the middle-of-the-night nausea set in even if we ate out. When I think back how precarious it was. Three a.m. I rise with unbearable queasiness. We call an emergency service, which sends one of those anonymous freelance doctors on duty all night. A stranger comes. He injects me. The nausea abates. I sleep. This routine happens often. It was not until I entered psychoanalysis as a last resort to my unending misery that the nausea was diagnosed as psychological, and in no time after entering analysis, I became completely cured of the attacks. If couch psychoanalysis did nothing for me but that (and it didn't), it would have been worth it.

Somewhere in this time frame, a letter arrived in the mail. I sensed it might be that offer from Bob Hope which had never materialized. A letter from an unknown source is an exciting thing, and I couldn't wait to open it. As it turned out, it was a draft notice. Well, you can imagine my surprise and how thrilled I was. Finally a chance to live in a men's barracks, to shower with two dozen strange males, to share a bathroom with guys called Alabama and Texas, and I'd be Brooklyn. To snap awake at five thirty, drill all day, take orders from a buzz-cut Neanderthal with a Planck-length brain. And the food! Free at last from a diet of New York sirloin, lobster, the burgers at Twenty-One, and my Reuben's Special. It would no longer be General Tso's chicken but

General McArthur's chicken. Or what is that they serve in the army on a shingle? Naturally I longed to see action. To sit cramped and seasick as my landing barge rocked ashore and I hit the beach against a volley of enemy machine guns. The wounds, the hospital, Harold Russell. Here was my chance to be a hero, a Medal of Honor winner, proud to serve.

I quickly contacted every physician I knew and begged for notes, claiming I was physically handicapped. On the day of my examination, I showed up with a wheelbarrow of alibis, declaring me a crippled specimen, and prescribing bed rest. Flat feet, asthma, poor eyesight, gall bladder, allergies, curvature of the spine, hiatal hernia, torn rotator cuff, frozen shoulder, vertigo, Alice in Wonderland syndrome. All stamped by the examining doctors, "No Evidence." Down to my final interview with the psychiatrist, where I brought notes certifying my psychopathology from my shrink to the last cabdriver I had. The situation looked like I was a sure 1A. The examining doctor told me to hold out my hand. I did, and it was steady and not trembling. Then he asked, "Do you always bite your nails?" I was not a severe nail biter, but I confessed it was a habit of mine. He perused my fingertips and abruptly stamped me 4F. Rejected by the army because I was a nail biter. Was it a first? And so lucky for the other soldiers who would have been in my barracks. Now they wouldn't have to bunk next to a guy who sobs himself to sleep clutching a small cloth bear. I have since, at my wife's insistence, given up nail biting, replacing that disgusting habit with the more socially acceptable coprolalia.

The grim days of unhappy wedlock drifted on. Winter passed and with the exception of a deafening crash that woke us up in the middle of the night, nothing eventful happened. The horrible noise came from a man in 525 Park, a large apartment house next door, who had jumped to his death and landed in the small alley between his building and ours. Hopefully you'll never hear a suicide hit the pavement, but take it from me, it's much louder than you think.

Summer came and now I will take a moment to talk about Tamiment. This was a summer resort in Pennsylvania which had a theater and a theatrical company who put on highly professional revues every week. Costumes, dancers, singers, sketches, production numbers. The original *Once Upon a Mattress* was done up there by the summer theater people. Max Liebman, Danny and Doc Simon, Sid Caesar, Mel Brooks, Joe Layton, Danny Kaye. They were all veterans. It was a cornucopia of incipient talent, comedy writers, songwriters, directors, costume and set designers, all began there and went on to big careers. There was a full orchestra with fantastic musicians and crackerjack arrangers. Danny Simon urged me to spend a few summers there as he and Doc had. He felt the constant pressure to turn out a sketch or two every week that would immediately go into rehearsal and play for better or worse Saturday and Sunday nights was the learning experience of a lifetime. Seeing material done live, seeing how audiences responded; a life-and-death situation every week for ten weeks. And the cherry on the cake was that as the summer passes, I would accumulate playable sketches that then could be done in a Broadway revue.

Ever since I moved to New York, someone or other was always trying to get a revue produced on Broadway. *New Faces* had been a big hit, and everyone in town with a song or a skit in his trunk wanted to have a revue. Eager and talented young people would meet with a gung-ho producer in one or another Upper West Side apartment and pound out satirical songs on the piano and love songs and the comedy writers would read their sketches to the hilarity of the others and blood oaths were sworn to get a revue on. By God, this time we will! I know a backer from Texas, from Florida, an Argentine who's crazy about American theater. Almost none ever saw the light of day. The few that did usually died the death of a dog. I supplied three sketches for an ill-fated infliction called *From A to Z* starring Hermione Gingold. All three sketches had crippled the audiences at Tamiment. The first was a sketch about two guys who go to a party and all the girls are replicas of Groucho Marx. The sketch did not amuse the commercial Broadway critics, though Ken Tynan, writing for the *New Yorker*, found it hilarious. The second was a thing called "Psychological Warfare," in which soldiers clashing on a battlefield fought psychologically. "You're too short—you're too short and your mother never loved you." You get the idea. It played quite well. The third involved a general at Cape Canaveral phoning the mayor of New York to prepare him for the fact that a nuclear missile they were testing had misfired and was headed toward his city. "So here's why I'm calling, Mr. Mayor, and try not to be a baby about it—"

The Groucho sketch and "Psychological Warfare" made it from out of town into the opening. The missile-toward-NY sketch, which convulsed them at Tamiment, couldn't wrench a smile from a single seat holder. Don't know why. The only thing I could think of was that the show was previewing in Connecticut and Philadelphia, and perhaps the audience didn't find the predicament comic because New York wasn't their town. You never know why they don't laugh at stuff you think they should love. It's not an exact science.

So Harlene and I spent the summer at Tamiment, where I wrote sketches that played well. The other sketch writer was David Panich, an odd and brilliant character whom I owe much to. He was ten years older than me, dazzlingly brilliant, immense erudition, could draw with the precision of Dürer or Dali. He wrote poetry, he read everything, and he played boogie woogie on the piano. He hated modern jazz but had lived among all the great modern jazz giants, Monk, Miles, and had a romance with Charlie Parker's wife. He was a gifted sculptor who carved the famous carving on Charlie Mingus's bass. His apartment on Roosevelt Island was like entering a spaceship: ultramodern, his own paintings on the walls, always morbid subject matter, like his poetry. He earned his money as a schoolteacher in Harlem and was quite racist about blacks and yet all his students loved him and he took them to museums and restaurants, always on his own dime, and to his house. He imitated them offensively. He had been in a mental institution, in a straitjacket, and he fascinated me with tales of how terrible it was when they'd come to knock him out with electricity for his shock treatments, which was the crude way they did it then. He had spent time walking over the George Washington Bridge and contemplating jumping. He had gone to the roof of his apartment house to spit down on people. His only distant relatives in New York had him committed. At first he agreed, then panicked as the attendants marched him down a long corridor. He got violent. The straitjacket, the shock treatments. And all because of a woman, an affair with one he thought was perfect and who dumped him for another woman after some time together.

In an era before marijuana became a middle-class cliché, he was high a lot. His connection was a black woman named Hazel in Harlem. He risked much in those days, jail and his teacher's license. He was a user, not a dealer, but being high made him laugh easily, and he was a great audience for me. He opened my eyes to just how great S. J. Perelman was, superior to all other funny minds, an axiom I hold to this day. He made me improve my vocabulary. Often we discussed women. He worshipped them but did not like them. I was an unhappily married young man trying to make it work. "Call it quits," he counseled me, sucking deeply on his reefer while we sat together by the lake of Camp Tamiment, schmoozing on those late afternoons. "And dump that excuse for a manager who's an embarrassment to you. He's a fish peddler. Not to mention he's robbing you blind." Harvey had no office, just an answering service. He would go up to all the agents' offices and say, "Any work?" Any rags, any bones, any bottles today? Then, he would use their phones. Still, I owed Harvey my first job, and so I would complete the contract.

"And your wife?" David would ask me. "You married too young. Break it up, cut your losses. You're not doing her any favor struggling to make it work." "I don't know," I said. I didn't know. It certainly served a function; it got us both out of our parents' houses and thrust us into the world. I was a working New Yorker. She was a philosophy major at Hunter. She taught me philosophy and I developed a crush on it. We read together and hired a student from Columbia to come in once a week and discuss a different great work. But the arguments we had over free will and monads, while heated, were never as combatative as the ones we had over our marriage. I knew I was in trouble when, in one philosophical discussion, Harlene proved I didn't exist.

I had a great success at Tamiment that first year and they wanted me back the second year. I discussed it with Steven Vinover, a gifted lyricist who died prematurely, and he felt I should not return unless they let me direct my own sketches. I met another great lyricist my first year at Tamiment. He was not working there but visited to see the show on a Saturday night. He was just six years older than me, and great things were predicted for him. It was Stephen Sondheim, and after that first meeting I did not meet him again till dinner at his house many years later with Mia Farrow, who was a great friend of his.

My second year at Tamiment I directed my sketches and had another successful year there. I hung out that summer with yet another lyricist who worked on our weekly shows, Fred Ebb. We had lots of laughs together at Tamiment and shared much heartache in the darkened balcony of rehearsals of the ill-fated *From A to Z*, where we commiserated with one another over the problems of struggling with a failing show. Fred would go on with his partner, John Kander, to write *New York, New York*; *Cabaret*; and *Chicago*. A few years later, and I don't want to get too far ahead of myself, but Larry Gelbart called me from Boston or Philly while he was struggling with *The Conquering Hero*, and it was then he told me the now immortal gag he had quipped to producer Robert Whitehead: "Don't hang Eichmann, send him out of town with a musical."

I had some great times at Tamiment and returned for a

third season. I'm glad I did because the third year one of the comics was Milt Kamen, a hilarious and funny man but a difficult one. He played the French horn, he had a temper, and in the winters he was the stand-in, the lighting double for Sid Caesar. Caesar had the great comedy show of those years. Caesar and *The Honeymooners*—two very different great comedians, Sid and Jackie Gleason. Sid had a cerebral band of writers, Mel Brooks, Larry Gelbart, Mel Tolkin, Lucille Kallen, Mike Stuart, Shelly Keller, Neil Simon, not to mention contributors like Carl Reiner, Howie Morris, and Sid himself. Sid's brilliant weekly show was the cynosure of all who dealt in or appreciated smart comedy. To get on his staff alongside those names was a true prize. Sid was a genius, a flamboyant one, and his material was brilliantly written and brilliantly executed. I had another strong year at Tamiment, Milt Kamen returned to work as Caesar's stand-in and raved to Sid about me. Sid had already heard my name from Danny Simon. He agreed to meet with me. I went up to his office and he sat at a desk along with Larry Gelbart. Gelbart was ten years older than me, around thirty. We all spoke for a while about politics, sports, life, and it seemed like nothing much was happening. As the clock hit around six and both men planned to go home, Sid turned to me in that grandiose way he had and said, "And you, you're hired." I rode down with Gelbart and I said, "I'm hired?" and he said, "If you'll work for the minimum." "I'll pay the minimum to be in a room with you two guys," I said.

Larry Gelbart by the age of thirty was already a veteran and a legend. His father was a barber who pushed his son's gags on a captive audience of stars whose hair he cut. Larry had written radio, *Duffy's Tavern*, for Danny

Kaye, for Berle, for Bob Hope, and now for Caesar. When he died, I was asked for a comment and I said, "He was one of the only people in my life who lived up to the hype." He was a fabulous guy and a truly great comedy writer; a Jewish writer the way Mailer was a Jewish writer, that is they were both Jews but you never saw it in their work. Together Larry and I clicked, and the show we wrote won a Peabody Award. We satirized Ingmar Bergman and Tennessee Williams and we also won some kind of Writers Guild thing and there was a lunch to honor the winners at Toots Shor's and I walked up to the door but couldn't enter, a phobia I wrestle with to this day—entering phobia. I once sat outside Sidney Lumet's lovely town house on Lexington Avenue while all the dinner guests arrived and I was to be among them and I couldn't enter, and I sat and tried to get up the courage and I saw ones I knew and liked and who liked me. Bob Fosse, Milos Forman, Paddy Chayefsky—but I couldn't bring myself to enter.

When I had to go to an event I made sure I was the first one there so maybe then I could enter. I was invited by President Johnson to the White House once. I left my apartment, flew to DC, changed in the airport bathroom into a tux, raced to the White House to be the first one, and not have to miss this opportunity. I entered but I was beaten by Richard Rodgers, whom I had never met, but he threw his arms around me and said, "If our grandparents could see us." He had his little quirks, too, and I wondered if entering phobia was among them.

Incidentally, years later I did attend a crowded party at Sidney Lumet's and somehow entered, and I was sitting on the sofa which backed against a wall of windows. The social ramble, as Satchel Paige called it, was getting too much for me and when a famous lady singer was urged to perform, I got ultra-antsy. As someone sat down at the piano and began to play a song she was associated with, I longed for nothing more in the world but to be out of there. Why? Who knows? I only know hot flashes crippled me with discomfort. The hitch was I was quite far from the front door and couldn't gracefully push my way through the people and split as the guest had started her number. I did not want to be accused of boorishness. Then it hit me—the window right behind me was half open. Lumet lived in a town house, so I was on the ground floor. Everyone's attention was focused on the piano. I was behind the ecstatic revelers and with a bit of choreography, I could slip out the window and on to Ninety-First Street, and who would be the wiser? I quickly slid the window up a bit more so I could ease through. The one thing I did not want is for anyone to turn and catch me in midescape. Quietly, I began my exit. The singer sang, I eased—one leg at a time to be precise. Suddenly it occurred to me that if I was spotted by pedestrians on the street climbing out the window, I could look like a burglar. What if, God forbid, a rookie cop sees me and takes a shot at me? Panic set in, and I manipulated my way back in and onto the sofa. I sat through the singing, leaving when everyone else did. But you can see how much my psychoanalysis was helping me. Although I had had only about twenty-three years of it when I did this.

So I finished Tamiment, got hired by Sid Caesar, and then again by Sid for a special, and this time with Mel Brooks, who I'd heard was an energetic terror and would eat me alive, but he was also a terrific guy and he liked me, and we'd walk home together every night. He regaled me with his romantic adventures, and I marveled at how such a small Jew could mesmerize one magnificent woman after another. Mel was bright, well-read, and musically talented. Writing for Sid amounted to a group of guys meeting in a room about ten o'clock each morning, lots of chat about movies, current events, general small talk, eventually getting down to actually trying to write something. Everyone would pitch ideas and when one was agreed upon, we'd all go at it, throwing lines, laughing at each other's lines, or shooting down the ones we didn't like. Writing with only one other person, like Larry Gelbart or Danny Simon, was really the same procedure except two guys went through the opening small talk before settling in to work.

Later, when I collaborated with Mickey Rose or Marshall Brickman or Doug McGrath, it was also pretty much the same with the added element that we were personal friends and we would take walks and have dinner together while we continued to develop the screenplay. Lunch with Sid was always fun, since the writers were funny. If we went out rather than ordering in, Sid would never let anyone grab a check. I ate alone with him once and snatched the check and insisted, and he only let me take it after examining it closely and making sure it wasn't a big number. I saw him allow Larry Gelbart to pick up a check once and I could see that it killed him, and I heard him say, when he reluctantly permitted it, "I've finally grown up." Whenever Danny Simon or Gelbart needed a collaborator, I got the call. Two different personalities. Danny, so secretive, would call and say, "Can't talk about it on the phone, meet me at Hansen's." I'd say, "Is it a writing job, or do I have to pass microfilm?"

He got me on *The Paul Winchell Show*. Winchell was a great ventriloquist and so I was writing for a piece of wood. Larry Gelbart would call: "Will you collaborate with me in a special for Art Carney?" "Sure." "Come up to my farm. You and your wife can sleep over. We start today." Once when I was writing for Sid, he, I, and Larry were at Sid's house in Great Neck. Sid decided we'd do all our writing in the steam room. Even though I was new on the job and loved them both, I wouldn't get naked and sit in a steam room with two guys. They both spent the next hour in there while I sat outside on the lawn. Sid always found me a little weird but liked me. Over the years I had lots of good times with Larry. Dinners, walks, shopping in London, exchanging jokes in Paris, listening to jazz in Manhattan clubs. He treated me as an equal whereas to Danny, I was always that kid he discovered in California.

The contract with Harvey Meltzer ran out. I did not re-up. I had heard of a manager who everyone wanted to be handled by but who was very picky. He had discovered and made Harry Belafonte. When Belafonte was an unknown, he said he was destined one day to be a limitless star, clubs, cabarets, and on film. Skeptics scoffed at the notion of a black calypso singer going so far. But Jack Rollins had a vision. They scoffed also at two kids from Chicago doing intellectual improvisations, but Jack said they were going to be big stars, and Nichols and May exploded on the scene. He handled only a few people, feeling he couldn't do a good job for his clients unless he kept their number down. His commission was 15 percent and that was it. A mutual friend introduced me to him. He had never handled a writer before, but when he read my material, he liked it. When I told Jack and his partner, Charlie Joffe, that ever since I saw Mort Sahl I harbored a gnawing urge to be a comedian, Jack asked, "Doing what kind of stuff?" I said, "Well I've been toying with this notion: that the *New York Times* is the only paper with no comic strip and what if they had one and it was like Superman but when he changed his clothes he changed into a Wall Street broker."

From that moment on Jack would not let me get out of becoming a comic no matter how hard I tried. I agreed to 15 percent, a fortune less than what I was paying Harvey, and got a brilliant manager in the bargain. We shook hands, never signing any papers, and remained together till he died at a hundred. He was one of the few people, maybe the only person, I knew who had actual wisdom. He wasn't just smart and a visionary when it came to talent. Wisdom is different, and try as I did to combat his wisdom with my rationalization, fears, prejudices, and cockeyed notions, he prevailed enough to make a gigantic contribution to my career. But at first I fought him. I thought I knew it all when it came to comedy. I had been practically a child prodigy and a success, much appreciated by the finest comedy writers in the business.

At twenty-two I was made head writer of the Pat Boone TV show. I lost that job because I wasn't the right fit, but Pat was yet another very nice man to work for. I was giving him sketches you needed Sid Caesar to pull off. I wound up a writer on *The Garry Moore Show* and lost that job playing hooky. I had a good reputation as a writer, especially with the other good writers in town who asked for me on shows, and I kept working. But I had whetted Jack Rollins's appetite to discover a new comedian, and it became clear he had faith in me pursuing that job even though I did not. Days I worked on TV making lots of money. In my spare time, I was putting together an act just to see if it looked like anything.

And now I pause to tell you what made me think of leaving the isolation of the writers' room and taking a shot at going on stage to be a stand-up comedian. Some few years back, when I was still in the NBC Writer Development Program, Les Colodny, who headed that program, suggested I hop over to the Blue Angel and catch this upcoming comic, Mort Sahl. The Blue Angel was a chic, expensive joint, and NBC would pick up the tab. I grabbed my fiancée, Harlene, put on a tie, and went over there with her. To say that I was blown away by Mort Sahl—it would be like when I first tasted spare ribs. Now when it comes to Mort I could go on and make this book longer than *War and Peace*. I can't do justice to his work as a comedian. I can only say what a sports writer said to me as he extolled Babe Ruth, "You had to be there." In a short time Mort would electrify America, get booked at every college campus in the country, draw huge audiences, conquer every smart nightclub, get put on the cover of *Time* magazine, get profiled in the *New Yorker*, and those of us who were around when it was happening know we shared a comic experience like no other.

It's hard to go into what made him great because the answer is everything and no amount of prose can nail it. Suffice it to say, he ruined my life in the way that Charlie Parker ruined every saxophone player who came after him for years. As one critic who liked me a lot wrote, "If Woody Allen can lose those Mort Sahl mannerisms, he could be a very funny comedian." I wanted to do what he did, I wanted to be like him, I wanted to be him. And that's the problem. You have to be him to get that effect. It wasn't the brilliant jokes, which were the best I ever heard, it was the man. It took me a long time to understand that and to grasp that no matter how hard I tried or how clever I could make my act, I wasn't him. (It's the same problem 99 percent of the actors had after Brando hit the scene. They walked like him, paused like him, posed like him, postured and pivoted like him, but in the end, they were them.) In the end, I was always me. As Marshall Brickman so incisively put it in a discussion about art and artists—"You're fucked by who you are." I did extremely well as a stand-up comedian, but what I did when compared to Mort was second-rate.

I had worked up a routine and did it for Jack Rollins, Charlie Joffe, and Jack's wife, Jane. They found me funny. Everyone (except me) thought I was a natural comedian. Jack wanted me to test the waters at the Blue Angel. The Blue Angel was the hottest little club in America. As I said, it was very chichi, very sophisticated. Example: one of their acts was John Carradine reading Shakespeare. Mort and Mike and Elaine and Jonathan Winters had played there. The club had a policy on Sunday nights, after the show, of spotlighting a new act. It could be a singer or a comic. I had terminal stage fright, but Jack would not take no for an answer when I tried to back out. After Shelley Berman, the star and a very successful comedian, did his show to a packed house one Sunday night, he asked the audience to stay and gave me the nicest, most helpful introduction a star could give a beginner. I mounted the stage, a mass of terrors, and began, and the laughter came back so strong that Jack Rollins told me I went right into my shell. I had a half hour, and when it was over I was backstage being criticized by Jack, a ritual that would be repeated many times over the next few years.

Despite my retreating onstage, becoming shy in the face of loud laughter and applause, I must have done well because the next day offers came in. Club owners who had seen me wanted me. So did TV producers who were present that night. Jack turned them all down and said I was nowhere near ready. Now the real work would begin. He wanted me to perform over and over, month after month, until being on stage was "baked into" me. The writer in me suggested I could just go out and read my material. The jokes are strong. What's the difference? Jack explained patiently, "If they like the man. That's it. If they connect with you, they will like your jokes. If they don't, the best gags in the world won't get you there." I disagreed. I disagreed with the unquestioning confidence of the truly ignorant. I balked at every sensible and correct thing he said, but he was patient and insistent and said if I just shut up and did what he told me and then looked up in two years, we could reassess and see who was right. You can be a very successful comedian, he told me, but I couldn't see it. Still, I liked him so much that I agreed to shut up and let him run things.

So that's how I wound up leaving a television writing career that paid me thousands a week to accept a no-salary job at a place called Upstairs at the Duplex for a lovely lady named Jan Wallman. Every night I cabbed to Sheridan Square along with Jack Rollins, or Charlie Joffe, usually both, and the two men along with Jan Wallman would pull and push me out onstage where I might work to forty people or ten people depending on the weather. Another comic on the bill was a funny guy named Garry Marshall, who went on to produce *Happy Days*, a huge TV hit, and also to direct movies like *Pretty Woman*. I can tell you, he was a funny stand-up comic, too. I usually did well but some nights were clinkers. People dropped down to see me and encourage me. David Panich marveled at my "delightful invaginations." Mel Brooks came, so did Phil Foster, the very funny Broadway comedian. Jack and Charlie never missed a show. The night Charlie got married he and his wife hurried down to this little dive I was doing my routines at, his bride fresh from the vows in her wedding dress.

Each night after the show, off to the Stage Delicatessen to talk about it with Jack, to hear why some of my references were too obscure, too inside, "too high-pitched so only dogs can hear them," Jack would say. Comics would come by the table, sit down, chat. Jack E. Leonard, Buddy Hackett, Henny Youngman, Gene Baylos. They were all funny and they liked me and rooted for me because I was polite and respectful and was not a new comic disdainful of the older Borscht Circuit comics. Quite the opposite, I loved their acts and let them know it.

They were paternal in a way. I once wasn't sure whether to tip a coat-check girl for lending me a tie. In those days, a big tip was a buck and it wasn't the money, I just wasn't sure of the protocol. I asked Phil Foster, "Do I tip her?" He said, "You got ten dollars?" I said yeah. "Gimme it," he said. I did. He tipped her the tensky. "My God," I said. "Ten dollars? I never tipped any coat-check girl ten dollars." "You'll always remember this moment," he said, "and you'll always remember to tip. If she lends you a tie, a jacket, you tip. Now you'll remember." Incidentally, it was not that

I was a cheapskate when it came to tipping. I just didn't grasp the finer points and once tipped a process server who knocked on my door and handed me a summons.

In those days, the Stage Delicatessen on Seventh Avenue was a late-night ritual. Next to the stage was the Dawn Patrol Barber Shop, open twenty-four hours, and you could get a haircut or a shave at three o'clock in the morning. Also open all night was the Colony Record Shop, where one could browse and pick up girls during the wee hours. Then there was the Larry Matthews Beauty Salon, where guys would also pick up girls. And what girls. All the beautiful showgirls and chorus girls went there when the nightclubs closed to be made even more beautiful. I never was good at picking up chorus girls and proved much more adept at getting haircuts.

OK, I'm married, last stages. Harlene and I have grown apart. She has become understandably impatient with my moods, my gloominess, my annoying personality. I am developing as a comic and she is in the final year of college. Because of her, I have become familiar with some Kant, Kierkegaard, Schopenhauer, and Hegel, and while I can't really say I knew my en soi from my pour soi, I was able to grasp that "being in a bad marriage" and "Being in a bad marriage" was not too dissimilar no matter what Heidegger would say. By now, we were living right off Fifth Avenue in a brownstone two-and-a-half-room apartment. It was relatively uneventful except for one morning we woke up and a note was pushed under our door from the middle-aged lady who lived in the other apartment on our floor. It read, "I have gone out the window, call the police." What was it about our neighbors and their compulsion to jump? Oh, and once I came home and found our apartment robbed. Some crook broke in, took nothing, but left us a portable TV set. I assume he stole it from another apartment, was in the midst of robbing us, panicked, and ran out leaving it there. It was serendipitous, as we needed a second set.

One night, we went out on a double date with another couple. The girl, as it turned out, was not happy in the relationship with the other guy, though I didn't guess it then. I was not thinking of other women, preoccupied as I was with becoming a comedian. I wrote routines, practiced, tried to quell my nerves, went to my psychoanalysis dutifully every day hoping for that Perry Mason moment. Eureka! I remember now, I accidentally came upon my parents having sex, and the trauma that I've long repressed has caused my inordinate fear of being nailed shut in a cello case.

The girl on the double date (good title for a thriller) lived near us. We were on Seventy-Eighth Street off Fifth, she lived with her parents on Seventy-Third and Fifth, and there was nothing special about the evening and I can't remember if the girl and the guy broke up or he moved out of town or what but since she was a neighbor, my wife and I invited her over for dinner. She came, the three of us spent the evening talking, watching TV maybe. She was quite pretty and very charming and I didn't realize how much she impressed me until I awoke in the middle of the night with a burning desire to marry her and live on the moon. She said she wanted to sing in clubs and was going to appear downtown for a few nights and invited us. I said we'd love to see her but we were going to Washington, DC, on a trip for a week. We wished her luck and she left, though her smile remained like the Cheshire Cat's and, riddled with guilt, I quickly tried to put it under a sofa cushion.

Soon after Harlene and I went to Washington, a vacation that presumably would save our marriage. A week away from the tensions and familiar routines of Manhattan would reverse years of Hun-like aggression. So off we went by train to see the National Gallery, the Freer, the FBI building, the Mint; dine at Duke Zeibert's and the Occidental and there, in the nation's capital, among the unspeakable beauty of the cherry blossom trees, we fought. We argued, and the inspiring monuments to liberty and amazing veal francese at Anna Maria's were not the magic bullets we'd hoped for. Home, hunched over my typewriter while my wife was at school, I took a break and called "the girl on a double date" to see how she had done in her cabaret debut. It was about three on an April afternoon. She was home and told me it seemed to go okay and how was my trip? I babbled a bit about the Liberty Bell, forgetting it was in Philadelphia, and then with that sudden rush of impulsivity that Dostoevsky imputes to his gambler, "I'm going to buy a jazz record. Feel like taking a walk?"

"Sure," she said, and with that one word my life made a seismic shift, though I didn't realize it. Moments later I was in front of her building on Fifth Avenue and the door-man, eyeing me like a spore culture, would not let me past him but called up and said she would be right down. And there she was, she was twenty and startling in her impact as she bounced out of her building to greet this mere peasant deemed unfit to enter her lobby. She smiled and said hello, and as I stared at her, smitten, I never dreamed that one day she would be my wife and eventually we'd part but remain friends for life, and now I'm eighty-four and she's eighty-one and if Chekhov were alive, he'd know what I'm groping for. She was Louise Lasser; the Ls in her name were formed with the tongue, which was immediately sexual. The Ss didn't hurt, either. She had just dropped out in her final year from Brandeis. She was a blond, beautiful creature, and while years of terrible illness and suffering have taken a great toll on her, you must believe me when I say she was a knockout.

OK, don't believe me, hear these two testimonials. First the milder one. I was in a cab with her, and when we came to our destination, she exited first, leaving me with the cabbie as I paid. "Who is that girl?" he said in astonishment. "She's amazing. So beautiful and so alive and charming." OK, so that's one impartial voice. The voice of the common man. When she was going to Brandeis, the journalist Max Lerner and Jack Kennedy both hit on her. Not such common men. The second piece of evidence: her father took us to see *Fiddler on the Roof*, second- or third-row seats. We see the show and I noticed among the pit musicians were a few I knew from the Tamiment orchestra. After the show was over, I walked the few feet to say hello.

"Who is that girl you're with?" the drummer said to me.

"Her name's Louise. She's my girlfriend."

"All the guys in the orchestra couldn't stop buzzing about her. We thought it was Brigitte Bardot."

Okay, no one was as devastating as Bardot, but at twenty and with that ponytail, Louise somehow gave off a reminiscent vibe. She also resembled the very young, remarkably beautiful Mia Farrow and would get sent newspaper photos of Mia with notes from friends and acquaintances saying,

I thought this was you. Many years later I once showed a photo of young Louise to Mia's son, Fletcher, and asked him who it was. "It's Mom, isn't it?" he said.

The long-winded point I'm making here is she was beautiful. But that was only one small part of her greatness. She was charming, smart as a whip, quick, very funny, and witty; she was educated, raised in a Fifth Avenue duplex like the ones I'd seen on screen at the Midwood. She shopped with charge accounts at Tiffany's and Bergdorf; her father was a highly successful CPA whose red-and-blue tax book appeared in every bookstore in town. Her mother was an interior decorator. Her family took her to the best restaurants where all the maître d's had known her since she was little. While I was growing up on linoleum eating Del Monte string beans out of a can, she was knocking off escargot on Fifth Avenue, where a liveried doorman would get a cab for her so she could speed off to the theater and after to Giambelli's restaurant. She had a chesty voice, and carnal promise oozed out of every pore. She was also a little nuts, because God has a variety of dirty tricks up the heavenly sleeve of his white robe.

But the bedlam was yet to come. Now it was April and we walked through Central Park, then to the Jazz Record Center, a grubby walkup shop that specialized in jazz records. One mounted a staircase that had a sign reading EVERYTHING FROM BUNK TO MONK, and entered a large room brimming over with jazz vinyl. As a kid I could spend hours up there browsing, picking out a single record because one was as far as my nest egg stretched. The owner was an obese man named Joe who sat somnambulistically as one rummaged through the bins and could barely mumble answers to my questions. I was reminded of an essay by one of those great essayists, Hazlitt or Lamb, bemoaning the fact that as a boy growing up with only a few cents, he spent so much time selecting a book to buy and how pleasurable it was. Now that he was older and could afford many books, the thrill was gone. But for me there was a new thrill as I scanned the racks with Louise. I found the Johnny Dodds or George Lewis I wanted and bought her a Billie Holiday album, *Lady Day*. After all, she was a singer so she had to worship Billie Holiday, which of course she did.

We strolled home and when I came to her building, I thanked her for the walk and said I had some free afternoons if she'd like to spend some more time walking or seeing a movie. She said she had the following Tuesday free. We made a date to meet at the fountain of the Plaza Hotel Tuesday at noon. Very Scott Fitzgerald. Who knew she would be Zelda? I walked home in a daze. Her head was swimming, too. I don't know why. I had nothing magical to offer. I think it was that I was good company, hip enough and amusing. I can't think of what else would have sent her into cloud nine. I was married, a runt, ill-clothed, a wannabe comic. Of course I couldn't imagine she liked me. I only knew this person was the fulfillment of all my dreams and fantasies, and come Tuesday at noon I could spend the whole afternoon with her till evening. I guess I was extra nice to my wife that night, although she was already bringing up the logistics of a looming split. Spellbound, I planned my afternoon with Louise, certain a call cancelling was imminent. I trekked to the Duplex and told my jokes. Jack Rollins and I ate, discussed comedy, but my mind was only half on my Max's special. Here was the plan and see what you think of this: I wanted to have a fun, exciting afternoon with Louise. I didn't want to sit silently in a movie, the relationship not moving forward. What activity could I do with her where I could get a sense of how she felt with me, first off as a married guy, and second as a swain, a lothario, a candidate for her heart?

It was then I hit upon the perfect date. The racetrack. We could go out to Belmont, we could pick horses together, win some, lose some, laugh, commiserate. It was something different, most important, something active and alive. After, if all went well maybe a quick dinner at the Cave of Henri the Fourth, a walk-down, candle-lit French joint that reeked of romantic atmosphere where I would order wine and strike brooding poses like Montgomery Clift.

Cut to Tuesday morning. I rise, shave, shower, and dust my recluse's body with so much talcum powder I look like the wolf who tries to fool the seven little goats by coating himself with flour. I say good-bye to my wife, who will be gone at school all day. The fly in my sartorial ointment was my shoes. I had lousy shoes, and so I ducked into a shoe store en route to our rendezvous and bought a pair of handsome, if too small, shoes. Funny, they fit in the store. At noon I sat on the lip of the fountain at the Plaza, and moments later she appeared, looking smashing with her beautiful long blond hair, saucer eyes, chesty erotic voice, and me with my imbecilic smile.

On the train to the track. Conversation seems to be going well. Then Belmont. Placing bets, having laughs, handicapping by the names, losing mostly but one win. Then, on the train home, an icy depression sets in and I start to sense things have not worked out. I'm so exhausted from being charming, it's like I ran the marathon. Now, a waxing panic steals over me and as the silences between comments grow longer I am drowning in the conviction I've blown it. Flop sweat. My life is passing before my eyes like a movie and I am being played by Franklin Pangborn. It's six thirty and I suggest dinner, expecting to be dusted. Ink in the blow-off. But wait. What's this? She's up for it. Suddenly, we're over candlelight and I'm ordering a bottle of Bordeaux. I know as much about wine as I know about horses or bipolar women. The trick is to position your eyes so it looks like you're checking the year on the menu but really checking the prices. Stay with the most expensive you can afford. So we drink and chat, and after two glasses fuel my courage, I take her hand and she's okay with it and I can feel the ground beneath me shaking. There is some talk of my marital status, but I assure her quite truthfully that we married too young and while my wife is lovely and brilliant, we both are on the verge of ending it. I leave out the part that Harlene is a nice, normal young woman perfectly capable of having a fine and healthy marriage but not with an immature, maladjusted wreck like me.

I get the check, we rise, and in the shadows of the cave I kiss her. She meets me halfway and I'm standing there, my lips suctioned to hers thinking, I am now kissing Louise. You wanted to know what it would feel like, says the little man who lives in my head and hates me, well, this is it. Now it's ten minutes later and she is pulling cash from her bag. I'm tapped out between slow horses, new shoes, and a bottle of Gruaud Larose. She is plunking it down in the palm of a carriage driver's hand. It is the first of three payments she shells out for as we do Central Park over and over, kissing relentlessly in the privacy of the buggy. When I get home, my eyes are rolled heavenward like the praying saints on the walls of the Vatican. "Why's your tongue so black?" asks my wife.

"Must be something I ate," I flute back in a guilty falsetto, "some berries."

"You hate fruit," the ball and chain says.

"I gave them a try," I say, my nose growing with every word I speak.

"I want to talk to you. I want to discuss how we'd do it if we broke up," she announces.

I am ready for this dismantling, having fortuitously stumbled upon the neurotic's philosopher's stone, the overlapping relationship. And so we did break up, and Louise and I began a love affair. And I remember exactly where we were when I first realized what love was and what it felt like and finally I got what they mean, the poets, the lyricists. We had been dating for a few weeks. I had moved out and taken a very romantic apartment with a fireplace in the bathroom, not that I ever used it. I used the bathroom, not the fireplace. But we used the fireplace in the living room and spent all our waking and sleeping moments together. And one afternoon we were at the Museum of Modern Art having coffee in their restaurant, and for whatever reason I was looking at Louise and felt, ohmigod, I love this woman. I never felt like this about anyone before. Now I see what they're talking about. And somewhere in heaven, that same character that toyed sadistically with Job had come across my picture in the files and was rubbing his hands together with anticipatory glee.

*   *   *

It turned out Louise's mother had some serious mental problems, and when I say serious I mean she was in and out of institutions and needed shock treatment for bouts of at least depression. This in-and-out had wreaked havoc on Louise, an only child, as it would have on anyone. I chose to overlook certain red flags from the start because I really wanted this to turn out right. For one thing, when I asked Louise why she had dropped out of Brandeis in her final year it turned out, upon persistent questioning, to have been some psychological problems, not just to pursue acting and singing, as she had said. Then there was the manic energy, which was so invigorating, especially coming from a bright, funny sex dream. It seemed a shade too manic, too frantic, but what the hell did I know about manic behavior? In my family there would have been no suspicion of mental problems, as nothing short of running naked down the street brandishing a meat cleaver was recognized as odd behavior.

Probably the most obvious sign something was amiss was her room. Picture a beautifully decorated Fifth Avenue duplex apartment housing father, mother, daughter. The furniture, some of which was designed by the mother, is sleek with every lamp, ashtray, chair, and table, understated and tasteful, arranged with a gentle simplicity. The colors are muted pastels, soft blues and grays, there is much cherrywood. Everything is in place and looks perfect to the eye. One gets the impression the objects have a number on them that corresponds with their number on the table.

The effect is meticulous and lovely. One ascends the staircase and comes to Louise's room. One opens the door to it and sees Hiroshima. The bed unmade, drawers wide open, clothes strewn about, creams, lotions everywhere, jars and squeezed tubes uncapped, the tops God knows where. The bathroom cabinets are wide-open and many items normally used and put back after are on the sink, on the edge of the tub. There is a box on the night table with a half-eaten slice of cold pizza from what day one can't estimate, along with a wax half cup of coffee with the drowned butt in it. Open books and lots of sheet music lie scattered about on top of and under laundry. The room is the dramatic opposite of the meticulously calculated beauty of the rest of the apartment; a statement. But saying what? Inside I am out of control? Or, this is how my mind is furnished? Or mom, this is how I react to your compulsive neatness. To your scrupulously arranged interior decorating. To any simpleton that room would have told the whole story; foretold the whole future. But I wasn't any simpleton. I was a simpleton extraordinaire, in love with the apotheosis of my dreams and wading through the debris, I chose to rationalize it. "I guess the maid's been sick," I piped. "She was here yesterday," was the answer and then I was making love to a goddess, and if fastidiousness was not her thing, I'll accept the trade.

Louise and I would go together for eight years before we married. During that time we lived together on and off, mostly on. In that eight-year ride on the Wild Mouse, she would be unfaithful, on diets, in and out of hospitals, on grass, on drugs, recreational and medicinal, manic, very self-deprecating (see *After the Fall* by Arthur Miller), followed abruptly by a category 5 hurricane of euphoria, trying to act, trying to sing, trying to stay alive, trying to be my girlfriend, incredibly exciting to be with on the good days (which got fewer and fewer), deceitful, charming, helpful and encouraging to my career, maddening, adorable, sad, full of sharp insights, always funny.

In all my future writing over the years she remained my blond lady of the sonnets. When I did a scene acting with Anjelica Huston and duplicated Louise's bedroom, that terrific actress looked at me incredulously and said, "Who did you ever know who had a room like this?"—and I'm thinking, Oh, just some girl I married.

So now I'm playing the Duplex, and in addition to Jack Rollins and Charlie, Louise is there coaching me, criticizing me, helping me, throwing her insights in with Jack's. They hit it off, and he tried managing her abortive singing career but she proved to be unmanageable and too erratic to make it work. *I Can Get It for You Wholesale* opens on Broadway and she understudies Barbra Streisand. Still, she comes faithfully to my shows after her final curtain on Broadway. She was always helpful as I moved out of the Duplex and over to a coffeehouse on Bleecker Street called the Bitter End, where under the further encouragement of its great owner, Fred Weintraub, I emerged as the new hot thing. The Bitter End sold coffee, no liquor, and it had the signature brick wall to back the acts. They were mostly folk acts. Lucy and Carly Simon; José Feliciano; Peter, Paul and Mary; and the Tarriers, a folk group that included Marshall Brickman, its bass player and a hugely funny talent I later collaborated with on a number of films, including *Annie Hall* and *Manhattan*. Marshall was authentically funny and that was a gift hard to come by.

Hilda Pollack worked the register and paid me off in cash with a rubber band around it. Adam Perelman worked there, the son of S. J. Perelman. I had many chats with Adam, who eventually committed suicide. I met Bill Cosby when he was just starting out. Dick Cavett tried his hand at stand-up there, and as with everything Cavett attempted, he did it well. My friend Mickey Rose tried being a comic there but gave it up. But I was a big hit. Arthur Gelb, a journalist from the *New York Times*, came down and did a flattering piece on me, and on the six o'clock news David Brinkley quoted Gelb's piece and said if you go to the Bitter End you can see a comedian who doesn't mention JFK. At that time the Kennedys were the nation's most sensational family, and every comic did political jokes. This was the bad part of the Mort Sahl legacy. Mort was a genius who did a lot of political humor which really had not been done as well before, and a million lesser talents figured they could do political humor, too. While a few could, most failed.

One difference was between a comic choosing the political route and Mort being a genuinely informed, articulate political person. But finally it was that Mort had a dazzling personality and the others did not. He was gifted hugely as a performer. So much so that other comedians didn't give him credit for performing but said denigratingly, "He just comes out and talks. Anyone can do that." So while others might do political jokes, even some very good ones, the audience was locking in to Mort's personality. Don't get me started on this again. Topical jokes had the advantage of being news on everyone's mind every day, and the comic starts out ahead by using well-known subjects that almost elicit a laugh the minute you bring up the issue. I always felt

Mort was even greater and funnier when he wasn't doing political material. I never ever did topical jokes; not for any reason, it was just that the subject matter didn't interest me to talk about. To listen to news, yes, but not to talk about in my act. But right after the *Times* piece the lines started to form at the Bitter End. The shows were packed, requests for interviews came in, TV shows like a show called *P.M. East* asked me on, and I did it many times. It was hosted by Mike Wallace, and they paired me for one show with their other favorite upcoming guest, Barbra Streisand.

I got an offer to do a record album, and soon I was back headlining at the Blue Angel. In those days, small, smart clubs that catered to sharper patrons had caught on and the new comics played them all. I played the Hungry I in San Francisco along with Barbra Streisand. I also played Mister Kelly's in Chicago where I met Judy Henske, during a period Louise and I were on a hiatus from one another. I dated Henske and found her to be bright, funny, and charming. She was from Chippewa Falls, Wisconsin, which I later made Annie Hall's hometown. Judy towered over me and we made a silly-looking couple but it was a treat to spend time with her. The problem was that at that time, no woman I dated had a chance to develop anything serious with me because I loved the mishugana whom I couldn't seem to straighten out, nor could I grasp the seriousness of her illness. What the hell did I know from manic depressives? My uncle Paul saved tinfoil. He peeled it from cigarette packs and rolled it into a larger and larger ball. That was as crazy as I knew.

At Mister Kelly's in Chicago I also met John and Jean Doumanian, and we became great friends. I will tell the story of me and Jean as I go along, and it is a strange one. I played the Crystal Palace in St. Louis where an emerging artist, Ernie Trova, showed me his sculptures, which eventually scored big in the pop art world.

At the Blue Angel I appeared with Nina Simone and working there I met Paddy Chayefsky, Frank Loesser, Billy Rose, Harpo Marx. Of course they all came in to see Bobby Short in the lounge. But I was a big hit there and that is where I met Dick Cavett, who was sent to scout me by the TV show he worked on. He became a fan straightaway, and we became good friends, hanging out together and pounding the pavement on both coasts, sharing our love of magic, Groucho, S. J. Perelman, W. C. Fields, and the duck wonton soup at Sam Wo's. Cavett is the kind of guy whose life is one adventure after the other. He can go to the corner to buy a newspaper and wind up at a party with Greta Garbo, J. D. Salinger, and Howard Hughes. OK, I'm exaggerating, but not by much. He is so witty, well-read, and interesting that since he came to New York from Nebraska he has been a magnet for the great and near-great who relish his company. Just as his fabulous TV talk show stands as a record of culture with a guest list that includes the Lunts, Katharine Hepburn, Noël Coward, Fellini, Kissinger, Muhammad Ali, Olivier, Judy Garland, Bette Davis, Fred Astaire, Alfred Hitchcock, Gloria Swanson, Ingmar Bergman.

His private life has always been an unending series of lunches, dinners, weekends, and conversations with a huge spectrum of luminaries from hosting Tennessee Williams to riding on police calls with Walter Winchell to trading magic effects with some of history's greatest conjurers. I think back with a pleasant nostalgia when we both had more free time and we could call one another any morning, go for breakfast, take a walk, then maybe go over to Charles Hamilton's to look at rare autographs, and then he would be off to lunch with some star; Orson Welles or Gore Vidal. When he took me with him to lunch with Groucho I remember it was thrilling to meet the great comedian whose voice made everything he said sound funny, but I also felt sad thinking Groucho was exactly like any number of Jewish uncles or relatives I had who cracked jokes or teased at a family wedding or bar mitzvah. The difference was, in Groucho's case, that urge to comment with funny remarks took a quantum leap into comedy genius.

Once Cavett and I found ourselves together in Los Angeles. He was a writer on *The Jerry Lewis Show* while I was appearing at the Crescendo. We went to see all the movie star homes like starstruck fans and stood speechless before Jack Benny's house and W.C. Fields's home. During my shows at the Crescendo, Jack Kennedy was murdered. Here is a telling anecdote that demonstrates either my discipline and ambition or my lack of connection with reality. Nights I did my act for the club on Sunset Boulevard. Mornings I spent at my portable typewriter writing my first film script, a commissioned job that turned out to be *What's New Pussycat*, a dreadful film—but that's coming up.

So I'm writing and the chambermaid says, President Kennedy's just been shot. They think he's dead. I turn on the TV and every channel is frantic with the tragedy. I watch for two minutes, digest the information, turn off the set, and go right back to work on my screenplay. Nothing distracted me. That night my show was cancelled and Cavett, Mort Sahl, and I sat around bemoaning the news.

Years later Cavett was stricken with depression. He was home, gripped in the clutches of it, and his TV producer called me and said maybe I could go over and cheer him up. He always lived near me and I rushed over. He was despondent, filled with irrational fears of going broke or never working anymore. I couldn't do more than keep him company. Neither could Marshall Brickman, who came over and tried to help, but the sickness was much beyond us. It took years of doctors, therapy, medicine, shock treatments, and Dick's sheer intellect before he could overcome it and allow himself to lead a fulfilling and productive life. Even at the height of his mental misery, Cavett retained his social poise and cosmopolitan charm. Jean Doumanian and I went up to visit him at Mount Sinai Hospital when he was receiving shock therapy. We wanted to cheer him up and keep him company before we scooted up to Elaine's for dinner. We hoped Dick wouldn't be too down, too wrecked by irrational demons and the prospect of electrical voltage. So we go up there, he's in front of a mirror dressing in a tux. "I only have a few minutes," he tells us, "I'm meeting Jack Nicholson and we're going to a dinner party." With that, we exchange a few words and he exits like Fred Astaire for an exciting evening and we're left standing in a mental ward. The next day they'd be putting the electrodes on his head, but God forbid he should miss a dinner party with a great star.

It seemed like I was surrounded by great and wonderful people unstable as uranium. Louise would be a delight one moment and the next complaining: Her skin hurts, her hands are becoming stiff. She can't breathe. She's dying. This episode might be at three in the morning, waking me

up. Now she's off the bed on the floor hyperventilating, terrified. Suddenly, she's gasping for air. What am I supposed
to do? In my family, the only distress at 3 a.m. could be
cured by a few Tums. It looks like she's having some kind of
exotic fit, so I call an ambulance, which drives us to Lenox
Hill. She's examined, shot up with some needle, and we're
turned out. A cab at four in the morning, not easy to find.
Back to the house. I don't have my jacket and the key is in it.
I thought you had the key. I thought you had it. A cab to the
Americana Hotel. By now her sedative has kicked in and she
can't keep awake. I'm navigating her inert body through the
lobby while the bellhop shows us to a room. The following
day the locksmith lets us back into the house.

The next week this pretty girl convinces herself irrationally she's too fat. I prove to her with geometric logic that
she is not too fat, in fact, not fat in the slightest. But it's
to no avail. Crash diets ensue, clearly unhealthy radical
nonsense. Fasting. Only protein for several days. Then only
salad. Carbs, then no carbs. Only liquids. More fasting.
Again the middle of the night, she awakens. I'm starved,
she tells me. No wonder. She goes to the kitchen and opens
a half-dozen cans of tuna fish, and by a half dozen, I mean
six cans. She pops the contents into a huge bowl and puts
in plenty of mayonnaise. She mixes it all up. Here we go
again, it's 3 a.m. and we're both back in our bed sitting
up. I'm exhausted and forlorn; she's gorging herself on tuna
salad. The next day we sleep in and she's consumed with
guilt over breaking her diet, convinced she's gained five or
six pounds overnight. Louise couldn't cook. She could only
make spaghetti and her recipe was for eight people, which
she could not pro-rate. Hence, the two of us would always

be eating spaghetti with six portions leftover. Soon, she's back on speed again for the latest crash diet. I'm wondering if the few good days per month, which have dwindled down from five to two, are worth it. Then, a few days later the madness subsides and she's the best female pound for pound in the world. She's sweet, brilliant, very funny, very charming, very sexy.

And by sexy I will give only one example because it's embarrassing. The tip of the iceberg. We're sitting at a restaurant, having placed our orders. I am looking forward to my succulent Nova Scotia appetizer. She is suddenly overcome with lust. I have done nothing to provoke this except to be my usual loving, amusing, buoyant self. "Come on," she says, rising. "Where?" says I, salivating over the imminent delivery of a plate of lox. "I feel like making love," she says. "But I ordered my appetizer," I complain. "Let's go," she says, wanting what she wants when she wants it.

"Where?" I squeal, being pulled up and dragged to the door. "We'll be right back," she tells the waiter. "But where are we going?" I ask. "I saw a little alley around the corner," she says. "But we're in midtown New York," I say, "we're on Fifty-Fourth between Broadway and Seventh. The whole city is out there." "It's a tiny, dark spot," she says, "down some steps, it's pitch-black, no one will see us."

Now, being hustled through an ensemble of garbage cans, I am pushed into what is a dark, secluded outdoor spot in midtown Manhattan. All around us, traffic and pedestrians barely out of sight. Finally, lust trumps lox and I succumb. We make love and not too long after I am sitting over my portion, a beatific smile on my face, her cheeks rubicund with fulfillment. Women like that do not grow on trees. Incidentally, going to restaurants with Louise was always a special trauma because she'd order, then change her order, then go back to the original order, and I was always the breaker of news to the waiter that the order needed to be switched yet again.

"I shouldn't have had the waiter debone my fish," she once said at Lutèce. Horrified, I asked, "You don't want the bones put back?" I braced myself. Would I have to make that request? But anything for that woman because I did love her.

And all during this time I was working as a comedian, developing technically, and my reputation growing.

Sometimes Louise would go on the road with me, and sometimes she'd stay home and yank some other guy out of his seat and hop into bed with him. She was supersonically promiscuous, and yet she loved me, and if I ever threatened to break up with her, she got panicky and depressed. She'd make a real effort to be the perfect girlfriend, but she never met a mattress she didn't like and had a cottontail's libido. She was a good influence on me in many ways, and getting me out of my reclusiveness was one of them. She made friends easily. People liked her: her energy and intelligence, her charm and humor. She came with me to Chicago where I played Mister Kelly's; she was the one open to the warmth of John and Jean Doumanian, and were it not for Louise I would never have followed up on their overtures of friendship. Their image of Louise is at the Astor Towers Hotel high above Lake Shore Drive, John and Jean waiting in the suite to take us to dinner, me ready, Louise late as usual, standing, her head tilted so her long blond hair could hang down on the ironing board as she ironed it over and over to make sure it was straight.

Jean and John eventually divorced but remained close friends their entire lives, and both moved to New York. I became close with Jean, and it's not an exaggeration to say that for decades she was the closest person in my life. Jean and I were true friends. We saw one another through good times and bad, held each other's hand through rocky relationships with the other sex. We ate dinner together every night, either the two of us, or with other friends, or with whoever each or either of us was dating. She was the last person I spoke to before turning out the lights to go to sleep when I lived alone, and the first I called upon awakening. We walked the streets together, watched a million movies together, traveled in Europe together. For the many years she was with her boyfriend, the man she met while I was in Paris filming in the 1970s and whom she has stayed with since; the three of us were inseparable. She fixed me up with dates at times, I helped her get work in TV when she moved to the city. We had no secrets, we were closer than family. This extreme and pleasurable closeness continued decade after decade until I sued her.

And believe me, I still don't get it. I guess it began when Jean and her wealthy boyfriend decided one day to be producers and started by backing a number of my movies. The films were mostly profitable and I let my share of the profits stay with them, feeling more secure than if I had put it in a bank. They said I should take my cut as we went along but I said, "I'm not in this for the money, I just like making movies." It was true that I almost never did anything, and certainly nothing I cared about, for the money.

As Jack Rollins always said, don't choose projects for the money, choose artistically, concentrate on doing good work, and the money will come. It was something I didn't need him to tell me, but hearing it from him confirmed my own feelings. And so I gradually accumulated a sizable amount of money from films I did that went into profit. I always took a very meager salary to keep budgets low. I was probably the lowest paid filmmaker of my generation. And I'm getting way ahead of my life's story here, but it's the clearest way to explain what I still can't explain.

I'm married to Soon-Yi, we have a child. I just bought a house because our apartment was too small for a growing family. My business manager, Steve Tenenbaum, says, "I'd like you to dip into the pot of your profits a little as there are some large expenses coming up." Utterly, inexplicably, from these two lovely people, Jean and her boyfriend, he gets a small stall. Mindful of a close friendship, he goes about it gingerly over and over but always gets a little runaround. A year passes with no action. Now if Jean and her boyfriend had come to me and said, We're short, we have to use the money, bear with us, I would have said, Of course, you're my best friends. Pay me when you can afford it. But this was not the case. Her boyfriend, a Safra, was a billionaire, and what I was asking for and which was my hard-earned profit, was chump change to any billionaire. If I was unaware of some financial catastrophe that required the expropriating of my money, all they had to do would be to tell me and I would have sympathized and been fine helping out. But there was no financial catastrophe, and more time passed amid tactful requests, stalling, and evasion.

I would have thought that, given my closeness with Jean,

she would have said to her boyfriend, I'm dealing with my closest friend. The last thing I want is for an issue of money, which destroys so many relationships, to have the slightest impact on this one. Let's resolve this instantly in the most friendly way.

That didn't happen, and despite my pleading to resolve matters, we were finally forced to audit. The audit showed I was owed considerably more than we were asking for. I suggested they give me the smaller sum and we quickly put this behind us and move on. No response. Still more time passes, and it starts to become apparent they have no intention of giving me anything. It is unfathomable to me as both are hugely generous, supportive friends. Jean explains that her boyfriend, through whatever tortuous train of thought, does not agree he owes me money. I point out the audit to no avail. I suggest we go no further down a path that can harm a lifelong friendship and we should simply dump it into the hands of an arbitrator, walk away, and whatever he says, we do. They are willing to arbitrate, but it cannot be binding arbitration and I am told point-blank if it works out where they have to pay me, they will not be bound to do it.

The absurdity of everything is now beginning to become irritating and I want to preserve the friendship, but I can't figure out where to go with this. I can't afford to just forget the money as we are talking about millions of fairly earned dollars over a number of years of work and while I would gladly take a fraction of it just to keep peace, no fraction is on the table. Meanwhile we all have dinners together like there's no elephant in the room. And for me, there wasn't. I enjoyed their company and never gave a thought to the issue at hand. We didn't discuss it and had many a great time and lots of laughs. Now, more time goes by and Jean calls the last minute before our next film together and says they are backing out from sponsoring it. I accept this news and mention that the others already hired might not be so amenable to a sudden, last-minute rug being pulled out and could sue. Uncharacteristically, Jean says, Let them sue, it'll cost them and take them forever. This is not her. She is a wonderful, lovely person. What kind of lovely, wonderful person talks like that? As the lawyers say, did there come a time when you decided to sue?

Well, yes. I couldn't get to first base on any aspect of the money owed me. When Jacqui Safra said he didn't like arbitrators nor trust them, then I suggested we turn to God. I said, Find someone you trust, a rabbi maybe. Let him study the matter and come to a decision. Unacceptable, he replied. We owe you nothing. So, yes, there came a time when we threatened to sue. Still they remained unwilling even to settle for a lesser sum. And all the while, Jean and I and Soon-Yi are having dinner together every night. Others join us, we talk, gossip, laugh. If the subject of our conflict comes up, which it hardly ever does, it gets deflected. Jean's boyfriend is not present at these dinners as he was often in Europe. He was by law permitted only four months a year in America, and even a day longer would have meant he would have to pay income tax, and he had a worldwide network set up to efficiently deal with the minor irritant of his fair share.

Finally, at Cipriani one evening, Jean and my wife and I sat and ordered and laughed and I said, Please, this is the eleventh hour. Tomorrow my lawyer is going to file a suit against your company. Isn't that the dopiest thing you've ever heard? Let's settle this dumb conflict and get on with our lives. Charm from Jean but no response to my plea. Soon-Yi and I go home. It's midnight. I call Jean on the phone and we talk and I beg. Please, get a friend we both respect to arbitrate, get a rabbi, get someone. Don't let my lawyers serve papers. What good does a lawsuit do? We all lose that way. More charm, wit, but no engagement on the gathering clouds of a showdown in court.

So next morning we serve papers and I, like a schmuck, raised on Hollywood movies, have fantasies of the two of us in an adversarial lawsuit by day but best friends over dinner at night. *Adam's Rib*. You'd think it was a little late in life for me to learn that real life was not an MGM production. The tabloid headlines branded Jean and her boyfriend crooks, and neither ever spoke to me again. I wrote Jean a nice note saying, Let's leave this as a matter for our lawyers to work out but we won't clash, we'll remain aloof from conflict throughout. It will be like a Tracy-Hepburn movie that will be a unique experience and provide us both with screwball-comedy laughs. After all, it's not that we dislike each other; we just have a disagreement over a single issue, and sober men in dark suits will navigate through the shoals while we do the town each night popping champagne corks and trading sharp banter. There was no answer to my letter. Not only that, I had referred to the *New York Post*, one of the tabloids, as a rag and she turned my letter over to them.

And did there come a time when you went to court? Yes. And my case was so overwhelming that they folded midstream and settled. One juror told me the jury was prepared on the basis of everything they heard to give me everything I was going for. Looking back on the sheer stupidity of it all, I am still completely bewildered. Everything could have been avoided. My legal fees, her company's legal fees, which were considerable, the public embarrassment of friends winding up in court, her testimony, which was demolished by my lawyers and the press. Her boyfriend's perpetual exposure publicly to sensitive business mechanics. It cost them much more than the meager settlement offer we had made them originally. So how could this happen between close friends?

I have only two theories, neither brilliant. The first is that while Jean was a lovely person, her boyfriend was not as kosher as I thought. He came from a very successful banking family that had been involved with a number of questionable encounters. Various others had either sued or wanted to sue him but couldn't afford it. And so much of his energy went into setting up ways to beat the income tax. Conclusion: He was trying to bilk me out of my hard-earned cash. I don't put a lot of faith in that idea because from spending years with him, I found him compassionate, generous, and a very nice man.

My other theory is that Jean and he were making a moral choice and sincerely believed that I was not doing the right thing as a friend by asking for the money, since not every movie of mine made a profit and the profit from those that had should cover the loss from those that hadn't. They had been generous friends backing my films, so I could continue to work with absolute freedom and here I was, unappreciative, with the nerve to ask for money. Only a moral choice made sense to me for them to stand their ground so irrationally and squander such a deep friendship. Ironically, if you added up what the films cost and what they earned, there was a profit. It was all so bewildering, a lose-lose for everybody.

OK, now back to life with Louise, or The Agony and the Ecstasy. Let's just say we had ups and downs, breaking up, coming back together, breaking up. Meanwhile I'm getting better as a comic. I did well at my first shot on *The Jack Paar Show*, but Paar did not like me and thought I was dirty, which I wasn't. He was vile to me until I made it, and then he claimed credit for discovering me and suddenly was my biggest fan. Ed Sullivan also accused me of being dirty. At a run-through of his show, his staff said, don't do your actual routine since we're only rehearsing. You can do anything you want and save your real material for tonight when the show goes on the air. So I did some other stuff not right for his show, but I was never a dirty comic. (By today's standards, Lenny Bruce would be tame.) If you've ever heard any of my albums you know I'm right about that.

Anyhow, after I get off, Sullivan gets me in my dressing room and starts to berate me mercilessly. He tells me I'm the reason kids burn their draft cards and rages on with apoplectic fury. I'm sitting in a chair, shocked, thinking, Should I tell this guy to fuck off and leave? Why not? Do I care about Ed Sullivan and his show? Not in the big picture. After all, the sun will be burning out in five billion years and no one will ever remember. For whatever reason, I hold my tongue. And I swear to you, it was not fear, it was a calculated decision on how to best play the moment, and simple silence seemed the move.

Sullivan finishes and exits with steam coming out of his ears. I do the show with the originally intended material, which was totally uncontroversial, got my laughs, and went home. Well, from that day and for the rest of his life, Sullivan was my greatest fan, supporter, and even friend.

He never stopped praising me in his column, he plugged my albums, my Broadway show. He had me back on his show a number of times. Once we found ourselves at a small dinner table at Groucho's house and he just could not have been nicer and more complimentary. To this day I can't figure out what happened to the man. Head trauma? Mini stroke? Was he anguished by guilt? Who was he confusing me with?

I did Johnny Carson eventually. Loved him. I did Merv Griffin, also a lovely guy. Another religious conversion. I'm on Merv Griffin with Henry Morgan, that nasty, cantankerous curmudgeon. He steps on my opening punch line. He goes after me. I try to go to a routine about my childhood. He says, "Don't gimme that. I had two parents, too." I said, "Really? What were they?"

The audience goes crazy laughing, seeing this monster get nailed by a young comic he'd been persecuting. Morgan shuts up. No good-byes. A short time later, when I'm struggling out of town with my first, poorly written show, *Don't Drink the Water*, Henry Morgan comes to see it in Philadelphia. Suddenly he's my best friend. He comes backstage, offers help. He dines with me, sees the show several times, walks the streets with me, tries to help me diagnose which spots are weak, does his best to make meaningful suggestions. Go figure.

I'll tell you about the out-of-town nightmare of my first play, a play I wrote mostly in Europe, but first: What was I doing in Europe? you ask.

I was a hot comic, doing all the TV shows, even hosted *The*

Tonight Show on a few occasions, replacing Johnny Carson for two weeks. I was all over the press, really making it, yet interestingly never drawing. I'd kill them on Ed Sullivan and on Johnny Carson, I'd be the talk of the town in every paper, and club owners would book me eagerly. The only problem was, not a lot of people came to see me. In Vegas I didn't feel in all conscience I could take the enormous salary they were giving me and tried mightily to give it back, but the bosses at Caesars would not hear of it. Every contemporary of mine cut record albums; Bob Newhart, Shelley Berman, Bill Cosby, Mike and Elaine, Lenny Bruce, Mort Sahl, Vaughn Meader, who did a JFK imitation that was astonishing. They all sold like they were being given away. I recorded an album—three, in fact. All sold weakly. Down through the decades one company after another couldn't believe the prior company couldn't sell a million copies. They blamed it on poor packaging, poor marketing, phases of the moon. Some new company would buy the album and reissue it with superb new artwork. I would plug the albums on TV, on radio, in press interviews. Still, very modest sales.

One fresh new company taking over from the last disillusioned company, full of marketing ideas and jazzy liner notes, only to sink with it in a sea of red ink. The albums were always very well reviewed, to be admired but not purchased. Meanwhile, I'm making a bundle from these albums, which are not topical and, therefore, timeless. As I write this in 2019 they are coming out yet again with new packaging. So not an album seller, no huge crowds in the clubs I played, or a concert draw. Then why don't you quit? I can't, I'm a star. I was white-hot. You can imagine the look on the nightclub owner's face when he books me, expecting lines around the block, and by the second night they're moving around the potted plants to make the room look smaller. Third night, they need more potted plants to make the place look less empty. By the third week, there's no people. Just plants. I'm doing my jokes to foliage.

Okay, so how did I get to Europe? I'm working New York and Warren Beatty catches my act. I don't know him but unbeknownst to me he talks me up to his sister, Shirley MacLaine. One night at the Blue Angel, she and the legendary agent turned producer Charlie Feldman come in to catch me along with the still photographer Sam Shaw. Sam took the famous photo of Marilyn Monroe with her dress blowing up for the *Seven Year Itch* movie. I didn't know they were there, but a day later Sam comes up to Jack Rollins's office and says, "Does your boy want to write and maybe be in a movie?"

Now Sam, if you didn't know him, is a rumpled Norfolk jacket guy with cameras slung over his neck, a mustache, bushy hair, and a distracted look. He was described to me as the kind of guy who says, Here, can you hold this, handing you a camera or a briefcase, and then four years later shows up and says, Do you have that briefcase I gave you?

A true original, but when he came up to the office un-announced and inquired about me doing a movie, Jack and Charlie figured they had a head case on their hands. He then explained that Charles Feldman wanted to do a comedy starring Warren Beatty, and they both wanted me to write it and I could write myself a part in it. For this, I would receive the princely sum of forty thousand dollars. Jack and Charlie played hard to get for about fifteen seconds before they said, "When does he start?" The money was never an issue, and Jack would have said yes to that offer for forty dollars. I finally met Warren, who couldn't have been nicer, more supportive, encouraging. He came to see my act on numerous occasions, we walked the streets and talked, we had dinner, and got along well. I met Charlie Feldman, a large power in the business, an ex-agent and now producer who knew every legendary writer, star, and director in Hollywood. He had been a big deal throughout its Golden Era, and he loved my humor. He was astonished how fast and effectively I could turn it out and considered me (his words) "a beatnik."

I was a T-shirt-and-sneaker guy but no beatnik, in fact an Upper East Sider. Anyhow, the Beatty-Feldman axis wanted me to write a comedy with many beautiful women in it set in Paris so we could all go and have a great time. This is not a bad proposition to be presented with by a major movie star and a big-time producer. I set about doing it even as I kept working as a comedian, and I told you how I did not even let myself get sidetracked when Oswald shot the president. After a short time I had a finished scenario. It was not called *What's New Pussycat*, as that title didn't emerge till Charlie Feldman heard Warren say it to a lady friend over the phone and thought it would make a good title. And so, screenplay under my arm, typed on Corrasable Bond, I came before Warren and Feldman at Feldman's hotel suite. I can't remember if I read it to them or if they had read it— it's probably the latter. Feldman thought it was funny but winced at everything fresh in it and responded best to its few clichés. Warren felt that the lead role that was written for him was not as funny as the small role I had written for myself. He was probably right in the sense the leading man needed to be romantic, believable, adept with women, whereas a minor character like mine could be much broader, sillier, and so more comic.

Hearing their verdict on my script and having graduated from the Danny Simon school of comedy writing, I of course felt utterly confident in my own judgment but was not in a position to argue. I agreed to have another go at it and felt I would do my best to see if I could improve Warren's part without stepping on his charm, but there was no way I could bring myself to satisfy Feldman by turning the script into a formula Hollywood commercial story. Nevertheless, it was back to my Olympia portable and the rewrite drill. I can't give you the accurate details of what happened over the next months except that I wrote and played clubs, did TV, and loved, lost, loved, lost, loved Louise. Here's all I remember. Somewhere down the line Warren dropped out. As I got the story, it was nothing rancorous, but for certain reasons he had decided not to do the film.

By then I had finished at least one more rewrite and I was informed the script was being submitted to Peter O'Toole, a huge star hot off *Lawrence of Arabia*. I knew him to be a fine actor but had no idea if he could play comedy. At that point in his life, in my opinion, he could not, although when he got older he demonstrated he could, so maybe it was just that material. Maybe it was just my Marx Brothers–bred dialogue he couldn't execute well. But he loved the script, found it hilarious, and committed immediately. Shortly after, the second big role was gobbled up by Peter Sellers. Sellers was a genius at playing comedy, truly a hilarious man, also white-hot coming off *The Pink Panther*. The only problem with Sellers was that he was one of those comedians one hears of that is so terrific he is allowed to wield unlimited power. Artistic power in a movie has to reside with the director, not the star. Not any star. The director here was a lovely man named Clive Donner, who did not have a great flair for comedy to begin with but was decent and civil and open for discussion and flexible and I really liked him. The rub was he was no match for Feldman or the two Peters, who were full of ideas. Sellers's were funny, but wrong for this script. Feldman, a hands-on producer, was a weird combination of risk taking and also a hack. He'd take chances on who he might hire, but then get in their way. Or at least in my way.

He hired Dick Williams, the brilliant animator, to do the titles, his first movie. He had Vicky Tiel and Mia Fonssagrives as the designers, fresh from school, their first movie. He had Burt Bacharach, who wrote the very effective title song, a big hit by Tom Jones. He had me, a total novice to movies.

The cast swelled as Feldman signed Ursula Andress, another big name, fresh from the first James Bond movie. Romy Schneider was hired, a European star. Finally in response to my begging, he hired the wonderful Paula Prentiss, a fabulous and beautiful comedienne. I should say he interviewed her at my begging and the second she entered the room with that face and figure, he handed her the role. My picture was written for Paris. I was flown there, put up in grand style, given a handsome per diem, and kept fidgeting with the script. I flew to London first, my first time abroad. I loved London but was thrown for a loop when I ordered bacon and eggs and it came with only one egg. Obviously the trauma has stayed with me because I still wake up in the middle of the night screaming, "One egg! Only one egg!" In those days, it was not easy to get a good meal in London. Today the town's full of delicious food.

The movie office was in London for whatever reason and after a week, in Jolly Olde, we flew to the South of France and I'm sitting with all these movie people, friends of Charlie Feldman's, like Daryl Zanuck, John Huston, William Holden, and I'm at the Du Cap Hotel and gambling at the casino at night. Me, the schlemiel who was dragged up the stairs at P.S. 99 by Miss Reid, the bulldog assistant principal, for trying to exit the building two hours early. Then it was off to Paris and it was love at first sight. I loved everything about that city and still do. When the movie was finished, the two young costume designers, Vicki and Mia, decided to stay on and live and work there. For a fleeting moment it crossed my mind to do the same, but it would have been tough since I was an American-speaking comedian not established in movies, a born New Yorker, and I couldn't bring myself to. Often I have regrets, but my list of regrets in life is so long I'm not sure if I have any more room for another one.

Meanwhile, a week later we are suddenly told we are disembarking for Rome. The picture will be made not in France but Italy. Rome lives up to the hype. Fabulous, beautiful, the food, the culture—the movie culture. Yet my script had a Gallic flavor and Rome was the wrong place. Even Feldman would soon see that. But all this uncertainty was beyond me. It had to do with business, with women, with gambling, gambling debts, deals. We were in Rome a month and with my free hotel and generous per diem I'm living high off the prosciutto.

Of course my phone bills to Louise more than wiped out every cent I had. I call, we talk, then maybe a brief silence on her end, the silence creates a sense of insecurity in me which leads to some fumbling, the need for reaffirmation. Call ends. Must call back fifteen minutes later—maybe it ended a little too coolly for my taste. Just want to call and be reassured she still loves me. Second call. Reassurance does not come. Tone of call degenerates. Too much dead air. Hang up. Half hour later, just one more call but don't want to be a noodge, needy and clinging, an insect. I'll make up a pretext for calling. Hello, hey, I just had to tell you—I finally saw the Sistine Chapel. "Oh, that's nice," she says. Perfectly reasonable but insufficient enthusiasm. Pause. Silence. Now I'm pressing and lapse into Bob Hope. "And how 'bout that ceiling. He had to use very long paintbrushes. No, but I wanna say—" Nothing. Unfulfilling ending. When the next call is five in the morning New York time and she's not home, my anxiety level sets off the sprinkler system in the hotel. I know the truth but sweep it under the rug. Over the next years, the rug will be fully packed, and I will need an industrial size carpet to cover the compromises.

Finally, the decision is now made by Charles Kenneth Feldman to go back to Paris and do the movie. I'm thrilled. We go back and locations are chosen by the director and his minions. The art director was Dick Sylbert, extremely talented and extremely charming, but I never liked him. He was too much Feldman's man. Plus a relentless name dropper. But you couldn't deny his talent and he had a fun personality.

Shooting began, bringing with it instant chaos. For one thing, every crazy line or notion Peter Sellers came up with was considered gold whether it fit in or not. Personally, I wasn't crazy about him either; years later Paul Mazursky, who directed him, agreed with my take. But no question, he was a truly brilliant, authentically funny comic talent. Meanwhile, my script was being mangled. I knew I was dead when I wrote a scene where the lead character stops an elevator between floors so he can make love to Romy Schneider while irate pedestrians keep ringing for it. It was meant to be in a busy office building, but since the film was basically a Hollywood project, the elevator they found was so overproduced, so beautiful, so period with lovely curtains and black wrought iron and glass windows. There was nothing funny about making love in it, as it was more beautiful than most bridal suites. I protested, but authors in Hollywood were one step beneath the caterer.

Peter O'Toole was a nice man who bought me a first-day-of-shooting gift, an Irish sweater that I still have. He explained that the knit design in those type sweaters were all different so that if the wearer drowned at sea, his bloated, disfigured body could be recognized by the family knit pattern. From that moment on, I was confident that if I ever fell into the Seine and they fished out my corpse, my mother would be able to identify me and cancel my magazine subscriptions. Still, I couldn't bear the liberties they were taking with my screenplay. Peter O'Toole runs into a cameo crossover by Richard Burton, who visited the set as they'd just done *Becket* together, and they circle one another and say, "Hey don't I know you?"—It was supposed to be gut-splittingly hilarious, but I reached for my airsick bag. I was so embarrassed by what I was seeing but could only grouse impotently.

When I viewed the film put together for the first time, I quoted Willie Sutton when he learned Frederick "the Angel" Tenuto had killed Arnold Schuster, for turning Willie in. "This sinks me," Willie said, and *Pussycat* sank me. And I didn't spare myself. I could see I was pretty nothing. My first film, I didn't know exactly how to command the frame and be funny. I'm up there dressed in a terminally cute hat at a sidewalk café, wondering if what I'm doing is scoring. It was no fun. But I did live at the George V for months. I met and dined with icons like Jack Lemmon, Orson Welles, the Burtons. Interesting about the Burtons. They were in Paris making *The Sandpiper*, and I had lunch with them at the studio cafeteria, and these two giant movie stars kept pushing to be funny to impress me with their banter and comedy insults. She'd call him a pockmarked Jew, he'd make some crack about her weight, and they're doing this all for the benefit of me, a total nonentity. I wanted to say, Hey, you can relax and eat your truffles, I'm truly not worth the effort. But I guess the natural insecurity that dogs all actors and actresses no matter how big and accomplished never abates. Another red flag went up from Louise while I was in Paris (like I still didn't get she had some issues).

Remember we'd been lovers for a while, lived together, on and off, mostly on. So I call her one day and we're chatting and in the middle of the conversation she says, "The leaves are starting to turn. You'd love them. You love fall colors. And what else—oh, my mother committed suicide." "Pardon me?" "She took sleeping pills." "When?" "Oh—last week." "You didn't call me?" "What for?" Now I feel awkward because what am I going to say? "I could have..." "Could've what?" "Gee," I fumfered, "I would assume you would call the person closest to you." "Why? You're in Europe." Yes, I definitely was in Europe. She had me there. Still, it seemed so odd, it happened six days ago. Her mother had saved up her prescription pills and overdosed. "Well," I said, "I could have consoled you." But she didn't need consoling. She didn't seem upset; in fact, she seemed relieved that this poor, mentally suffering, lonely woman had ended her misery. All I can say is, the whole deal resembles no known social interaction I recognize from Avenue J in Brooklyn to lands appearing in the work of Margaret Mead.

At the time, Lyndon Johnson was running for president against Barry Goldwater. I was part of a group called Americans Abroad for Johnson. Now, I've never been political in my work. I did not consider *Bananas* political in the slightest, and I was surprised that when I went to Europe to promote it, all the foreign press wanted to talk about in relation to that silly, just-for-laughs movie was the politics they read into it. Now, I'm certainly into politics as a citizen. I stood on street corners handing out flyers to vote for Adlai Stevenson in the Democratic primary against Jack Kennedy. I campaigned and did shows for George McGovern, for Eugene McCarthy. Watch who I campaign for and bet the other horse. I have voted Republican only once in my life, for John Lindsay for mayor of New York. But I was never interested in making a political film. Anyhow, here I was, campaigning for Lyndon Johnson by doing my stand-up act in Paris. I think I can safely say I'm the only American stand-up comic who played the Eiffel Tower.

When *Pussycat* was completed I made ready to go home.

I bought my mother an alligator bag at Hermes for an ungodly sum, and she never used it but kept it in the vault at the Dime Savings Bank in Brooklyn. Then the news came that instead of going straight home, I would be flown privately to Washington, DC, to be part of a big inaugural stage show for Lyndon Johnson. It was January 1965. Rudolf Nureyev and Margot Fonteyn were to perform along with Barbra Streisand, Nichols and May, Alfred Hitchcock, Harry Belafonte, Joan Baez, Carol Burnett, Johnny Carson, and me. I flew back on a big plane and the only three passengers were Nureyev, Margot Fonteyn, and me. I never spoke to them nor they to me during the entire trip. We landed at Dulles, were treated like royalty, and we did the show, which was great. Note that among all these crème de la crème performers, three acts had been discovered by Jack Rollins: Belafonte, Nichols and May, and me. I did my moose routine and exited, as *Variety* used to say, "to hefty mitt."

It was the only time I met Alfred Hitchcock. We gabbed backstage, and he was charming and funny. He walked out onstage in front of the black tie multitude and the Lyndon Johnson family, including the president's wife and daughters, and said in that fabulous voice, "I warned you *The Birds* is coming."

I flew back the next day to Manhattan thinking that after all those months away I would be hailed the conquering hero. I had just finished my first movie, hobnobbed with my betters in London and Rome, lived five months in Paris on the arm, private plane to the nation's capital, show for the president with illustrious colleagues. I get off the shuttle, and as I walk through the airport to get a cab I see the newsstand and I see my photo and Johnny Carson's side by side and a banner line the size of the attack on Pearl Harbor. It reads: COMICS IN BAD TASTE AT INAUGURAL. Apparently, Dorothy Kilgallen, the columnist, was present at the show, and whatever Johnny Carson did offended her taste and so did my moose routine. Of course my moose routine wasn't in bad taste, but I guess her Hearst mentality thought it would sell papers.

Johnny Carson and I had two different reactions, mine the nerd's and his the mature man. He called me and asked if I'd like to go on his show and respond, as he certainly intended to. I thanked him for the opportunity but passed. I was too busy saving that copy of the *Journal American*, as I was convinced that as long as I lived and no matter how active I would be over the years, I would never again in my lifetime be on the front page of any newspapers. I got that one wrong.

The truth is I was not at all affected by the criticism. But I'm lucky that way. For better or worse, I sort of live in a bubble. I gave up reading about myself decades ago and have no interest in other people's appraisal or analysis of my work. This sounds arrogant, but it's not. I do not consider myself superior or aloof, nor do I have a particularly high opinion of my own product. I was taught by Danny Simon to rely on my own judgment, and I don't like to waste precious time on what can easily become a distraction. Friends have often encouraged me to at least treat myself to the enjoyment of once in a while reading some respectable person's high praise and maybe even in extreme cases consider responding when attacked, but I have no desire to do either. I guess Johnny Carson had the more understandable attitude—challenge your assailant, which he did strongly and decisively that night. Was it really worth it to me to engage some dopey yellow journalist and defend not the Constitution of the United States but my moose routine? I felt if you believed everything you read in the tabloids you deserved your life.

So I'm back living on Seventy-Ninth Street. On again, off again with Louise. What did we fight about? Everything. The subject matter was just a medium for her to hang her rage on. Like we're on the street and I can't flag down a cab. What could I do, there were no cabs to be had. I couldn't pull a cab out of the air. Then, when my head's turned in the complete other direction, a free taxi whizzes by. She yells, I turn rapidly, but it's too late. So suddenly, she's screaming at me like I'm a private on Parris Island. I'm incompetent, a rookie. I'm surprised she doesn't order me to give her fifty push-ups. Naturally, I start getting a little perturbed. Suddenly she decides the evening's ruined and she's storming back inside the house. Soon she'll calm down and she'll be making me laugh, running her fingers through my hair, and saying my name in that voice that causes the windowpanes in the room to steam up. Another time we're having dinner with an acquaintance who recites a hard-luck story. "We'll lend you the twenty thousand," she says as an air raid siren goes off in my head. We don't have twenty thousand to lend or even twenty thousand to fondle in private. Then I have to get us out of it. So we argue and I'm left to break the pledge.

Or there was the time the electricity went off on Christmas morning. After much searching she gets an electrician willing to come over. He leaves his family in Queens to take the gig. Moments before he shows up, the electricity goes back on. Now he's at the door and she's saying, forget it, we don't need you. He's saying but I should be paid for a service call. She's saying, Paid for what? You didn't do anything. He's saying he traveled over to the house. Yes, she says with consummate illogic, but you didn't fix anything. I try and intervene and explain to her it's not his fault that it's a false alarm but he should get a service call fee. The guy, a nice man, is getting understandably annoyed and threatens to go down to the basement and turn off our electricity unless we pay him. I can take it no longer and can see this will ruin the day, but the man's right. I pay him, he leaves. I'm the object of much derision. The next few hours are spent in contemptuous ignoring of me and I wait it out, knowing it will pass, and then heaven's prurient little seraph will cool down with her long blond hair and pout and we'll make love over our fat Christmas goose and plum pudding and God bless Tiny Tim and her Parnate. Regarding my relationship to Louise, I refer you to Shakespeare's Fifty-Seventh Sonnet. He doesn't actually name me in the poem, so I can't sue.

About that time I met another great character and his name was Mechel Salpeter, but he had long ago changed it to Max Gordon. Max was a producer during the Golden Age of Broadway. He was friendly with George M. Cohan and lent Eugene O'Neill the money to get married. He had produced wonderful plays like *Born Yesterday*, *Dodsworth*, *My Sister Eileen*, and *The Bandwagon*, to name a few, not to mention some by my boyhood theater idol, George S. Kaufman. I was taken by Kaufman at a very young age. When forced to pick a book to read in the library of P.S. 99, I randomly chose *Six Plays by Kaufman and Hart*. I turned by sheer chance to *You Can't Take It with You*. The stage direction read, "The home of Martin Vanderhof—just around the corner from Columbia University, but don't go looking for it." That to me was an amusing stage direction and very unlike the dry books prescribed for schoolkids that turned us all off reading for life. I read the play, and, like so many people, the characters and chaos reminded me of my own family. Like the Sycamores, we always seemed to live with aunts, uncles, grandparents, cousins—never just my parents, sister, and me, or if so, for negligibly short times.

I saw Kaufman on TV, where he was a regular on a weekly show, and he was witty in a refreshingly sarcastic way. When he said on a show in December, "Let's make this one show where nobody sings 'Silent Night,'" and was instantly off the air forever, he was a hero to me and my group. When the idea was floated years later that I devote myself to playwriting rather than TV or screenplays, the figure of George S. Kaufman loomed large, and while I aspired to do serious plays, I knew that to get started comedy was my most direct road. Kaufman and the great Moss Hart had written some wonderful comedy shows, and I identified with the more silly-looking partner of the two. I, like GSK, made many sardonic cracks, was pessimistic, and had a low tolerance for publicly exploited sentimentality. When I found out Kaufman's mother's name was Nettie, same as my mother's, it erased all my scientific skepticism, and I felt there was some karma we shared.

Now, through a concatenation of random events I met Max Gordon. Max had retired from the theater but was on the lookout for that great play that would fuel his come-back. Many tried to please him, but he was demanding. He had been used to the best and would not settle for less. I told him my idea for a play, an idea that could easily have come to either Kaufman or Hart and they would have written it to perfection, light-years ahead of the clumsy way I messed it up. But it was my first play, and when I told Max Gordon that a bickering family vacationing in Europe in an iron curtain country is mistaken for troublemakers and has to run and seek shelter in the American embassy, he cocked an ear. I spun the tale out of how they couldn't venture out without being arrested and so got on everyone's nerves with their complaints and idiosyncrasies. Max loved it. And he loved me. More important, he loved my nightclub act and thought I wrote the funniest material. We latched on to each other, and I promised to write the play and give it to him. At that same time, Charlie Feldman was setting up the movie *Casino Royale* in London and offered me a small role. My guess was he wanted me handy to hit on me for funny lines if he got into trouble—and he got into trouble, deep trouble, but he did not hit on me. Probably because he was so removed from the business of creativity he didn't know he was in trouble.

Before leaving for London, Louise and I got married. We had been up and back for eight years and always returned to one another despite the breakups. She and her shrink had discussed it, and the notion arose that maybe the act of marrying, the commitment, would put a totally different and more solid cast on the relationship. We were both willing to give it a try. If any of you out there are thinking of this, I don't recommend it. For us it was a disaster from Jump Street. I was appearing at the Americana Hotel. We bought a cheap ring at a novelty shop around the corner on

Broadway, went upstairs to the suite all the performers were given during their stay, and a judge her father knew married us. The judge said in his little speech that he married a number of couples and not one had ever gotten divorced. Records, of course, are made to be broken.

We got off to a bad start because weeks after we married I had to go to London to appear in what turned out to be one of the worst, dumbest wastes of celluloid in film history, *Casino Royale*. Louise did not want to come. I would be gone for months. We'd just tied the knot. She might visit, but essentially this was a golden opportunity for her to run amuck with other men. When I got wind of what was going on I must say I didn't resist the many delectable temptations in swinging London. Some marriage. Here I was, a young man being paid a handsome salary, put up at a nice apartment, given a healthy per diem, and all on a movie that was so ineptly produced that by the time they got to shooting the scenes I was in, I was already on overtime. At that time between the cast in *Casino Royale*, celebrities passing through London, producers, directors, writers, and the cast of *The Dirty Dozen*, which was filming there and included Charles Bronson, Telly Savalas, John Cassavetes, Lee Marvin, there was heavy gambling. This was right up my alley, big poker games every night. We'd play in a private room at a joint called the Pair of Shoes. They didn't cut the game, but having all those celebrities around the place was worth it to the boss. We started every night around nine or nine thirty after a fish dinner at Wheelers and played till dawn. The stakes were substantial without being really high. You could win ten or fifteen thousand dollars, which made me feel like a big-deal card player until the following year when I met

Joe Cohen in Vegas, a poker player who'd bet $350,000 on a hand.

I was a consistent winner because everyone was playing to have a good time but I was a dedicated shark, in the game for profit, not laughs or social niceties. I sat quietly, folding bad hands and playing good ones and winning every night while the others drank, laughed, and actually enjoyed themselves. At the casinos I'd watch Cassavetes and Telly and Charlie Feldman enter, buy twenty grand's worth of chips, lose it in ten minutes, and request a refill. The actors were hanging paper all over town, and if I'm not mistaken, by picking up the gambling debts of ones like John Huston, Feldman was able to get him to do a section of *Casino Royale*, which I'm sure he wouldn't have otherwise gone near.

The Beatles were always around and Saturday mornings one could stroll on the Kings Road and pick up the most adorable birds in their miniskirts. Louise and I talked by phone, but she had no burning desire to be with her new husband and when the movie wrapped I told Charlie Joffe that I'd be just as happy remaining in London, which was a delight, and never returning.

This was not a realistic possibility, as I had finished writing a play for Broadway. I called it *Don't Drink the Water*, and it was a nice try and you could see the influences, but it was crudely done. When I think back to the various times I spent in London, the time I felt most terribly British was probably when I met the queen. To a bloke like me, I'd say it was a corker. It was at this knees-up gala in a theater. I remember days before some bugger who was all mouth and no trousers from Buckingham Palace came to try and teach me the protocols addressing royalty as if I was some damp squib. I remember standing in line next to assorted nobs. I just had a cut of the joint and a pint of bitters, and I was feelin' quite chuffed. All set for my little brush with the quality. Finally Her Majesty greeting everybody in the line with each bowing meekly, comes up to me, and says, "How do you do?" Well, I panicked and went all collywobbles. Don't know what made me do it, but I knelt and stuck my head forward to be knighted. I think the queen was surprised and she gave a look to her footman, or maybe he was a lord or an earl, and I fancied I heard the old girl mutter, "Flush this vontz."

Okay, so it didn't happen exactly that way, but I did meet the lady and loved my summer on the Thames.

Upon my return, Louise and I took up where we left off before we'd made this life-changing commitment which had clearly changed nothing. Sometimes it was great, more often pretty rocky. *What's New Pussycat* had been a big box office hit—I was told the biggest of any film comedy to its time. The correlation between bad movies and big box office was not yet discovered by physicists. Anyhow, I'm home only a short while when I get a phone call. Some guy had purchased a Japanese movie and asked me if I'd dub it into a comedy. It's not a comedy, but if we put our voices in when the Japanese actors speak, we can make it funny. Sounded interesting. So I got some pals, including my wife, went into a studio, put the film up on a screen and ad-libbed the track of this serious adventure movie, making it into a comedy. When I was unavailable to change a few lines, the producer hired someone else to add them. The project turned out not just uninteresting but dumb. My work on it was not very good, and the added few lines by whoever were embarrassing to me. I sued to get my name off, but when the movie came out with the venal title *What's Up Tiger Lily*, it was a hit.

At that point, wiser heads told me to shut up, withdraw the suit, and go with the flow. I did, but both the *What's New* and the *What's Up* movies humiliated me before my mirror, and I vowed that I would never work in movies again unless I had total control, which I've always had since. On the first few movies I had it because the people who hired me were enlightened men and they respected directors, and soon after it became a must in my contracts. But I once again am going too fast.

Interesting sidebar to show what a confident or maybe pompous ass I was at the time. When *Pussycat* came out, it deservedly got bad reviews but did great at the box office. While Pauline Kael found some good things in it, most of the reviews were not raves. What the hell is this chaos? was the theme of the critical community. I thought the financial success would ensure I would be able to direct my own movie, but the word was the film was only a success because of the stars and I was lucky. I noted at that time, privately and smugly, someday *Pussycat* will be not known for anything except that it marked my debut in movies. Can you believe that obnoxious self-importance? In an ironic pay-off, which does not diminish my revolting contumely at the time, I saw a copy of *What's New Pussycat* in a video store, and on the box was printed as the big selling point, "Woody Allen's first movie."

Did it give me any satisfaction? A supercilious smile played across my lips like Professor Moriarty's, though seconds later I was snapped back into the real world where those little ironies fail to justify nature's shabby indifference.

Another example of my disgusting self-confidence was when I was twenty-one and hired by Max Liebman to write on a TV series starring Buddy Hackett and Carol Burnett. Liebman was a very big deal producer of classy early TV shows like Sid Caesar's *Your Show of Shows*, which in addition to great comedy featured ballet and classical music. Liebman loved me and loved Buddy Hackett but the show was ill-fated. I wrote only one half-hour episode of *Stanley*, as it was called, and one critic wrote that Buddy Hackett could have ad-libbed a funnier show. I cut out the review and saved it with imperious presumption, fully certain it would be ironic in later years.

So now we find me home with a freshly written Broadway play which Max Gordon, a different Max, was champing at the bit to read. And there came a time when I gave it to him. Max was justifiably disappointed. A very solid comedy idea was poorly written. It was packed with funny lines and comic ideas, but the construction and attention to detail was amateurish. Of course I couldn't see this, as it read so amusingly to me, and I thought it indeed followed all the kind of structural odds and ends I'd picked up from reading the plays of Kaufman and Hart. Max, trying to be helpful, arranged to have the play read by Russel Crouse, an accomplished playwright and writing partner of Howard Lindsay, with whom he'd written Broadway's longest-running play to date, *Life with Father*. Crouse was kind and encouraging, and he tried to point out the flaws and how I might consider fixing them. I tried ineptly and deluded myself into thinking

I had improved the script, and perhaps I did a bit but not enough.

Max's old eagle eye spotted the unfixed flaws the minute he read it and began losing interest in the show and me as the next GSK he had hoped to discover. I believed there was something there and, despite any criticism, it was funny. I wasn't perceptive enough to see beyond the laughs and that the characters were not dimensional enough to elicit real engagement and the plot was full of clunky writing. Ignoramus that I was, I sent the play to David Merrick, who instantly found it hilarious and wanted to produce it. I wrote Max off as a producer past the heyday of the blood and threw in my lot with a producer whose presence in the room was always accompanied by the smell of burning sulfur. I insisted to Merrick that we hire Bob Sinclair as the director. He had been Max's suggestion, and since I'd spoken with him about the project, and out of loyalty to what I felt was a commitment, I had Merrick hire him. This was the second of many mistakes.

The first was Merrick's decision to produce the play at all. The play had a large cast and Sinclair, Merrick, and I cast it in the standard way, sitting in an empty theater while actors walked out on a bare stage and read scenes with the stage manager. For the male lead Merrick suggested I go see *Barefoot in the Park* with an actor who had taken over when Robert Redford left. Merrick found Redford's replacement funny and an ideal Broadway romantic comedy leading man. This was how I met Tony Roberts, whom I would work with a number of times and remain friendly with down through the years. He was, as Merrick said, an ideal romantic comedy leading man, attractive in a schnooky way, wonderful with comic lines and easy to work with. He was a ladies' man, and later when we acted together in *Play It Again, Sam*, he once left me onstage sputtering when he failed to enter on cue because he was hitting on one of the actresses in her dressing room. Trouper that I am, I froze and lapsed into Esperanto.

Fortunately, a less panicky actress stepped up, took charge, and brought the play back into focus. Anyhow, Tony was a great find for *Don't Drink the Water*. So was the truly hilarious Dick Libertini, a uniquely gifted comedy actor who played the priest. Decades later he appeared in another one-acter of mine and played a rabbi, and killed the audience both times. Our set designer was Jo Melziner, a Broadway icon who designed, under the misguided guidance of director Sinclair, a huge, cavernous set that was oppressive and the opposite of what you want for a comedy. Mind you, it was great set designing, but he had been pushed in the wrong direction. According to Max Gordon, the director Bob Sinclair had been an assistant to George S. Kaufman, which resonated with me but in actual fact meant nothing. He had retired ages ago, was living in Santa Barbara, hadn't directed in years, and enjoyed an occasional belt of the grape. He was, as his replacement Stanley Prager said, an enemy of humor.

Rehearsals began, and there was much mutual masturbation with everyone laughing uproariously at everyone else's lines and behavior. The lead was played by Lou Jacobi, a genuinely funny man who had been great in Neil Simon's first play, *Come Blow Your Horn*. During rehearsals, Tony Roberts and I were always reduced to helpless laughter by Lou onstage or off. Casting his wife was a Merrick inspiration. I had written it for a wisecracking New York type, actually for the actress Betty Walker, whom I didn't know personally but loved. Instead, with an eye to the box office, Merrick chose Vivian Vance, who played Ethel Mertz on the *I Love Lucy* show. She was a fine comedy actress but dead wrong for the role, and she proved to be a huge pain in the neck. The show came to life when she was replaced by Kay Medford who, like Betty Walker, could make the dialogue sing. But the real trouble was not yet upon us. We were going very strong in rehearsal, and I was told word on the street was very positive. The run-through was effective, the dress rehearsal just fine.

We opened at the Walnut Street Theater in Philadelphia. Ironically, a few blocks away the musical *Breakfast at Tiffany's* was trying out, the director Abe Burrows. Anyhow, we opened and died. The reviews were very bad. Merrick sprung into action immediately and fired Bob Sinclair, whom he correctly never wanted in the first place. He asked me to take over the direction for a few days till he could get someone else. I did, and I stayed up nights rewriting. The cast amazed me. I'd give them new lines two hours before the matinee and they swapped them for the old and put them in right away. The only pill, as I said, was Vivian Vance. Onstage, with all the cast present receiving their changes, she complained loud and long about her not getting more to do, more funny lines, more comic business, which she claimed to be a master at from years on the Lucille Ball show. She was talented and a good comic player but struggled by being miscast. She couldn't get with the idea that the changes in the show were not about her role but about the plot in general, all the characters, all the lines that didn't play, the structure, the narrative. She remained a thorn in the side of the production till Merrick finally bounced her and hired Kay Medford. Amazing what a difference the right casting makes.

Stanley Prager joined us and took over the directing. Interesting thing: Although he was no great comic director, he was a droll little guy, good-natured, brimming with energy and confidence, and he immediately made us all feel better and optimistic. He changed the set around, brought the action downstage near the audience as he whipped the cast into shape. One replacement followed another until *Don't Drink the Water* had the most cast replacements of any nonmusical show to its time.

Playing Philly was grimsville. First, because of our notices we were playing to not even half houses. Depressing. Then, I was pounding out changes long into the night, handing them to the actors the next morning, seeing them scramble to insert them, a miracle of memory and adjustment, but there was one big hitch. The new material often did not match the old material as more changes were required to keep the plot and characters consistent so the actors could be playing some of the old show with its now-obsolete scenes and characters and the new scenes, which required different setups in the earlier scenes. What I'm saying is, we were playing two different plots at once, and the two had not yet been smoothed out. The poor audience, stuck with seats to a turkey to begin with, were guinea pigs to our constant fiddling and experiments. Actors and actresses came and went, scenes shifted, were dropped, new twists with no antecedent exposition showed up. David Merrick said to me one late night as I rewrote and labored in my hotel room, "You're really up to your ass in show business." But he never flinched. He stood by me, kept the show running. The thing about David was that he could be wonderful, witty, charming, and a great producer—unless you got into a quarrel with him.

I spent Sunday afternoons in Philly with him watching football on TV. I liked him. He had been a lawyer who went into the theater to meet girls. His words. I did quarrel with him just once over a line of dialogue which must have been pretty nothing because I can't remember it. Unlike in film or TV, where the writer has the same rights as an Indonesian female, the theater union says not a single word could be changed without the writer's OK. I stood on my rights as author, demanding we insert my new joke. Merrick said, "If that line plays tonight, I fire the director." I glanced over to poor Stanley Prager, who deserved the opposite of being fired—he deserved a bonus—and folded my tent. But I liked Merrick.

And as the show left Philadelphia and opened in Boston it was hugely improved. We weren't doing the business of *Breakfast at Tiffany's* or another show that was reportedly wonderful, but we were coming together. A new scene here, an idea by Stanley Prager there, actors feeling more secure as the changes dwindled. A few hints to me backstage by Elliot Norton, the very nice Boston critic used to seeing shows as works in progress, and the show was jelling a bit. Let me say, it was playing better and better. It was still not much of a show, but between the fabulous comic cast and my never-ending substitution of new jokes till the line worked, it became a laugh machine. When we got to New York and previewed in the Morosco, the house crew of the theater said they never heard so much laughter from an audience. And that was what made us run two years. Not the quality of the play, not the reviews which were at kindest, mixed, but if you were an audience member, not critical of a playwright's stagecraft, you paid your ten bucks and laughed all night.

A pleasant surprise I got was that Harold Clurman, an icon of the Group Theatre who was part of the Actors Studio and reviewed, wrote well of my show. He saw virtues in it apart from just jokes or the cartoon comic characters. I don't think there are any virtues, but his appreciation of it meant a great deal to me because I've always said I was born too late for the Group Theatre but would have fit in with them. I sometimes feel I'm a frustrated thirties playwright, out of time, having missed the boat, too late with my offering, but Elia Kazan liked my movies and that made me feel good. That would have been the crowd I really saw myself with—O'Neill, Clifford Odets on through Arthur Miller, then Tennessee Williams. I didn't have their talent, but if they needed someone to get coffee...

The morning after opening night, amidst the mixed reception with the all-important *Times*, not very good, Merrick called me into his office. Red-flocked wallpaper. He sat there satanically; all that was missing was that his assistants had no pitchforks. He said there was some action at the box office, and we would stay open and see how word of mouth treated us. But more important, he said, "I want to be your producer. I want to produce your hits and your flops." A very nice thing to hear under the duress of weak notices. In time I would give him my next play, a better one though still no great shakes, *Play It Again, Sam*. But that morning in the heart of the theater district I was taken with how supportive he was. We took out a full-page quote ad, utilizing every kind word no matter how obscure the critic. To beef up the page, I used my mother in amongst the many legit quotes, and it was high praise from Nettie Konigsberg indeed. And it came to pass that word of mouth was good and we ran nearly two years, and it was sold to the movies and made into a truly dreadful film (not by me), and huge out-of-town successes like *Breakfast at Tiffany's* flopped very quickly, and such is the irony and unpredictability of the theater. Many years later, someone broke into Bob Sinclair, the original director's, home in Santa Barbara and murdered him, I'm told David Merrick had an airtight alibi and could prove he was with friends that night.

Tony Roberts and I did not get close that first show. That came when we appeared together in *Play It Again, Sam.* I wrote that in a hotel room in Chicago while I was doing an act at Mister Kelly's. As I typed the stage directions and I searched to describe this little film critic's room, I wrote, "On the wall is a large blow up photo of Humphrey Bogart." I only picked Bogart because there was a popular poster of him selling around at that time. It was logical then, having the movie fantasies, that Bogart would be in one, and I conveniently used him over and over as I wrote and he became a major character in the story. I wrote and rewrote in that Chicago hotel room. I ate ribs with my friends John and Jean Doumanian. In those days, Chicago had a joint called the Black Angus that had ribs the taste of which gave life meaning you couldn't get from religion, psychoanalysis, or great art. At that age I ate ribs, could knock off racks of them, then I'd do two shows at Mister Kelly's and then late at night go back and knock off more ribs. Today if I allow myself anything pleasurable, a bell goes off in my cardiologist's office and I'm put under house arrest.

Jean, John, and I hung out sometimes at Hugh Hefner's. Not much but now and then. It was an open house nearly twenty-four hours, hung with Picassos and full of celebrities, sports figures, sexy women. The sexy women were the whole draw. Believe me, it wasn't the Picassos. Anytime I hit Chicago I got a call from the Playboy Mansion inviting me to stay there as a guest. I never did, but we dropped in now and then and socialized. I have a cardinal rule in life: Never be anyone's house guest. And I never hit on any of Hefner's housemates. The thought of any of those stacked miracles wasting a quark of their attention on one more aptly cast as a bumbler, freighted with giving the exposition, rendered me timid. Over the years, I have had brief dalliances with centerfolds but it never came about from going to Hefner's mansion. Usually I was mistaken for someone else. I liked Hefner, and I remember one night he explained to me it had always been his dream as a kid to have a house that was going all the time and you never paid any attention to the clock. You woke when you liked, ate breakfast when you wanted, did what you wanted. No matter when. If you rose at 2 a.m. your day began there and your schedule worked according to your own time. Meant nothing to me, as other guys' dreams never do, but if it made Hefner happy to live life that way, and it did, great. All I know is he was a friendly and generous host, rich, successful, and if he enjoyed rising at eleven at night, having breakfast, and then playing Monopoly with celebrities, who am I to gainsay him?

Things were going quite poorly in my marriage, as Louise

had discovered what is today called weed. Then it was "grass." In the distant past, it was "muggles." Satan also weighed in with uppers, amyl nitrate, Quaaludes, and a cluster of new positions to try out with any male registered to vote in the tristate area. I still adored her and found her philandering typical Louise, but it made for a failing marriage and we began talking about chopping up the trunk, which is show business for "breaking up the act." She had made many contributions to my life, among them urging me to submit a piece I wrote to the *New Yorker* magazine. When it came to prose, I lacked confidence, certain of receiving a rejection slip, but she felt otherwise. She was right, and because of her instinct and faith, I became a regular contributor to a magazine I had idolized my entire life, and I was fortunate enough to have Roger Angell as my editor through the decades. But no question, she was a handful, a handful on assorted pharmaceuticals—help.

What happened next to distract me was an idea that popped into my head to do a comedy film documentary style. This had not been done before, and my original idea was to do it dead real, which I did not do and I'll tell you why, but I did finally achieve it years later with *Zelig*. *Take the Money and Run* was a script I wrote with my old school friend and baseball team pal, Mickey Rose. Our friendship went back to Midwood High, where we both dreamed of being in the big leagues and got out on the baseball field in the summer no matter how sweltering the heat, and hit baseballs and shagged flies and fielded ground balls, stopping only to stroll to the corner candy store every few hours for chocolate malteds. Mickey had no discipline but a lunatic sense of humor, totally original. His idea of a joke would be to go to all these show business meetings up at offices with agents and managers in New York and always secretly leave a can of tuna fish somewhere. He could cause himself hysterical laughter imagining the businessmen getting together for lunch and one saying, "Funny thing happened the other day, I found a can of tuna fish in my desk drawer."

"What a coincidence," says the second man, "I found one on my chair." "Me too!" says a third. By now, Mickey is rolling on the floor, tears coming down his cheeks.

Years later when I hired a chauffeur, Mickey wanted me to have the chauffeur drive me every night at eight fifteen to Park Ave and Eighty-Third Street. He wanted me to get out of the car, kiss the lamppost, get back in, and resume life. Again, he'd become crippled with laughter imagining the newly hired chauffeur telling his wife or friend, "Every night at eight fifteen the guy has me drive him to Eighty-Third and Park, he gets out and kisses the lamppost, and we drive off." In some interplanetary way, Mickey was a genius. Anyhow, we wrote *Take the Money* together, but since I wanted to direct it there were no takers. Then, because my professional life was blessed, a new movie company formed called Palomar Pictures, and being new and having hip guys at the helm like Edgar Scherick and Paul Lazarus III, they were willing to take a chance on a first-time director. Now, I did have a track record as an author of *What's New Pussycat*, junk but a big hit, and also *Don't Drink the Water*, more junk but successful. At least they knew I wasn't a serial killer or someone who'd take their budget, pocket it, and fly off to the Cayman Islands.

Putting a watchdog on the film, Sidney Glazer, they gave me a million dollars and here's, as they say, the beauty part: Though it wasn't in my contract, they trusted me to have total artistic control and never once bothered me for a second. I shot in San Francisco, a town that has been lucky for me down through the ages. The Herb Ross movie of *Play It Again, Sam* was shot there. So was *Take the Money and Run* and later *Blue Jasmine*, all did well, and I did well as a comic at the Hungry I and got started as a jazz player at Earthquake McGoon's. My leading lady was Janet Margolin, a beautiful girl from Central Park West and co-star of *David and Lisa*. Much of the cast were local San Franciscans and they were wonderful. Plus there were some Hollywood character actors. I kept within the million-dollar budget and finished on time. The first day of shooting was to be in San Quentin Prison. All my excitement was over the fact I was going into a prison and there'd be felons and I'd see an iconic big house I'd only read about or saw versions of in old black-and-white movies. I couldn't have cared less that I was debuting as a director. It was the prison I was fascinated by. We were warned by the warden that the population was dangerous and if there was a riot, or any of us were taken hostage, they would do all in their power to get us out short of releasing any convicts. I found it interesting that when the hundreds of inmates congregated in the big open yard, all the white prisoners stayed together on one side and all the black prisoners kept together on the other. Not unlike what you might have found in any American college cafeteria, I later quipped on TV to moonscape silence.

So I entered San Quentin and began my career, staging a riot in a prison yard. Convicts were cooperative and we yelled action and the guys put on a real free-for-all riot.

When I yelled cut and they dispersed I remember picking up a shiv from the yard floor. Now remember, I stepped on the set never having made a film, knowing nothing of cameras, lenses, lighting, or directing. I had never studied acting. One of the executives from Palomar asks me, "How do you feel being given a million dollars to direct a movie?" A million then was a lot bigger number than today. "Nervous?" he queried, trying to put me at ease with the same kind of grin Ming the Merciless wore when he had Flash Gordon submerged in lava.

The truth was I couldn't imagine what he was talking about. Why would I be nervous? The whole deal seemed to me common sense. I wrote the script, I know what it is I want to see. I know when I look through the camera if I'm seeing what I envisioned. If not, I correct things. Maybe I need to move the camera a bit left or right, a bit closer or further. If the character I'm filming walks someplace, we follow him as the camera is on wheels. A stand-in is doing my part, and when the cameraman is finished lighting, we're ready to shoot. I tell the stand-in he can go get a beer and I take his place. I do the scene I have written and say it the way I want to hear it. The camera rolls and I yell, "OK, got it?" If I'm not happy with something, I do it again. This is not rocket science, and the fact that I've never done it before means nothing. As long as you're dealing with comedy, particularly broad comedy, all you want is the scene should be loud, lit, and fast. Speed is the comedy director's best friend. Laughs are what you're going for, and if you have some flair for tickling risibles and you put your wares up on the screen clearly and give an audience a chance to see and hear the punch lines, you're well on your way. Shooting

Take the Money and Run went smoothly, and Mickey and I had a lot of fun improvising gags and bits.

Back in New York I cut it together and hired this young kid, Marvin Hamlisch, to score it. I asked for a few melancholy pieces, influenced as I was by Chaplin's films. Hamlisch obliged and got to work on the score. Meanwhile, we tested the movie. Here, my inexperience took a toll. I put no temporary music in it, so the whole film is coldly silent. When no one talks, and let's say someone is walking a distance without music, the walk takes forever on the screen. Plus as we pick to test-screen it, the USO, grabbing on-leave servicemen off the street, filling half a screening room some afternoon and with no rough cut speech, we naturally die like the Valentine's Day Massacre.

Palomar had the same reaction to the film when we screened for them. Even with the addition of some Marvin Hamlisch music, they saw a million garbanzo beans swirling concentrically down the toilet bowl, having put their faith in a fumbling maladroit. They suggested I bring in Ralph Rosenblum, who had saved a number of movies by recutting them, to help me. On the verge of a disaster, I was looking for help from anywhere I could get it. Enter Rosenblum, a sardonic, highly gifted editor who turned my movie from a failure to success, and here's how. Like Stanley Prager coming in to help *Don't Drink the Water*, Ralph immediately buoyed my spirits. First thing he did was take all the funny stuff I had cut out and put it back in. He explained that with no music and to a group of lonely, homesick GIs who wandered into a half-empty screening room, of course the film will die. He stuck in some Eubie Blake jazz in place of Hamlisch's lovely but sad background music, and the mere switch from slower music or no music to lively jazz transformed it, or should I say transmogrified it because the change was magical. He also put some material before the opening credits, which helped speed up the narrative.

Here's how I'd sum it up. Ralph really only changed about 20 percent of the original cut, which he liked much more than I did. But that 20 percent made the difference between the film working and not working. Without him the project would've sunk. Anyhow, the film opened in a tiny theater on Third Avenue called the 68th Street Playhouse. There was a tree in front of it and its branches obscured the marquee. My father volunteered to come with friends in the middle of the night and cut the tree down. Offer declined. The film was a critical and finally a box office success. And that's how I got into making movies. Hard work, some talent, much luck, major contributions from others.

And in the midst of all that, there came a day Louise and I decided to divorce and her father, a mensch to the end, brokered a split that was fair to both of us and we parted great friends. We have always remained great and loyal friends. Anecdote: We went to Juarez to get our divorce, after sleeping together the night before in San Antonio, and we were so lovey-dovey in the waiting room with others waiting to divorce that a man asked us, Which of you is getting the divorce? We said we both were, from each other. He couldn't believe it; that two people so openly loving were splitting up. He stammered, "Oh—well—it's—it's always much nicer this way." She went on to have a good career, starring in a popular TV show, doing small movie roles, and teaching. At the height of her fame when she was plastered on the cover of many magazines, and had truly triumphed over her problems, I wondered just how huge a star she could have been if she'd never had to fight an uphill battle all the way.

So here I am, single, about to cast *Play It Again, Sam* the play with Tony Roberts as my costar. All we need is to find the right girl to play Linda, the female lead. The director is Joe Hardy, a fine director who knows what he's doing. He and I sat in the back of the theater auditioning one talented actress after another. There's a lot of talent out there and not enough good roles. Sandy Meisnter was a famous, highly respected acting teacher in New York who ran the Neighborhood Playhouse, where so many terrific actors emerged. Somewhere, he collared David Merrick and raved about a girl in his class that he found to be sensational. Her name was Diane Keaton. Real name Diane Hall, but there already was an actress with that name and the union does not permit one to use a name already in use.

So after this buildup, we're all sitting in the theater waiting for Keaton to audition. In walks a lanky young girl. Let me put it this way: If Huckleberry Finn had been a very beautiful woman, that's who was up there onstage. Keaton, who apologizes for waking up in the morning, a rube from Orange County, denizen of swap meets and tuna melts; an emigrant to Manhattan who came here and works as a coat-check girl, who had worked the candy concession in a movie house in Orange County and was fired for eating all the candy herself, tried making the few obligatory hello lines to us all. This was a yokel who spoke of her Grammy Hall, the boarder George who got a free turkey from his union every Christmas, and answered compliments with "Honest injun?" But what can I tell you, she was great. Great in every way. One talks about a personality that lights up a room, she lit up a boulevard. Adorable, funny, totally original in style, real, fresh. When she left we knew we had to go through the other scheduled actresses, but in our minds she had the part.

Rehearsals under Joe Hardy went smoothly. Tony Roberts was like a kid in a candy store, since the show had a half-dozen pretty girls who'd appear in the lead character's fantasies. Tony sprang into action the first day, complicating his already baroque social life. I was getting friendlier and friendlier with Tony, but Keaton and I were each pursuing our own social agendas, chatting politely but sparsely. A guy called for her every day, which I naturally thought was her boyfriend but later found out was her manager. I was dating whoever would say yes to my desperate pleas to let me feed them. One time, a week before going to Washington, DC, for our opening I had a date with a very beautiful brunette. I took her to dinner and we had a nice time, and we made another date two nights down the line.

In the intervening night I was rehearsing with Keaton, and Joe Hardy suggested we run lines to memorize them more fluently. She of course knew hers like Eve Harrington but I, despite having written them, needed more time to get them down pat. We broke for dinner, and she and I hopped across the street to a joint next to McGirr's Billiards, where I sometimes shot pool. At that impromptu dinner she was so charming, so lovely, so pretty, so scintillating, that I sat there thinking, Why the hell am I going out with that other woman tomorrow night? Keaton is magical. Of course she ate like Primo Carnera. I never saw a person outside of a logging camp tuck it away like that.

Anyway, to cut to the chase, by the time *Play It Again, Sam* opened in DC, we were lovers. We remained lovers in Boston and back in New York. I had just purchased a penthouse on Fifth Avenue and she lived in a hovel all the way east, a single room made homey and pretty without spending a nickel on it. She clearly had an artist's eye. You can tell by the way she dresses, which is trendsetting if you happen to think a dead monkey's paw pinned to the lapel of your sweater is chic. Let's just say Keaton always suited up with a certain eccentric imagination, as if her personal shopper was Buñuel. But it was not just a fashion flair. She takes great photos, can act, sings beautifully, dances, writes well. We've remained close friends since we met. When I finished recutting *Take the Money* with Ralph Rosenblum, I screened it for her and she said it was good and funny and not to be so worried, and she's been my North Star, go-to person ever since. Because in addition to tasteful and bright, she's totally inner directed. You can intone Shakespeare's praises all day, but if she finds something of his a bore, she doesn't care how revered his poetry is or what the professors or the public says. She's her own person. I have always shown her my work, and she's one of the only people whose opinion I really care about.

So she liked *Take the Money and Run*, our play opened and it was a hit, and Keaton, Tony, and I hung out together. Soon, she would move in with me, first in my old apartment, then in a hotel while I waited for renovations on my penthouse. I wanted a bar, though I don't drink, and two decanters so I could offer scotch or a brandy to friends who also didn't drink.

At that point in my life, I had a very interesting friend. Her name was Mary Bancroft, and I only mention her because I found her an extraordinary woman. She was much older than me, twenty-five to thirty years older, probably in her seventies when I first met her. It was at a party at Norman Mailer's house in Brooklyn. She lived near me on Fifth Avenue, so I gave her a lift home. She was very brilliant, well read, and knew everything from politics to literature to how Carl Yastrzemski's stance made him such a good hitter. She had decided in her seventies to study computers. I used to take her to basketball games. She was a writer, had been a spy against the Nazis in World War II, worked for Allen Dulles, and had been in psychoanalysis, a patient of Jung's. I can't remember if she had an affair with Jung or Dulles, but she was fun to listen to.

We spent lots of time talking and dining. Dulles had wanted to reward her after the war for her spying service, and she had requested a seat at the Nuremberg trials. She was given a ticket to attend, and it turned out the town of Nuremberg was super crowded during the court proceedings and living space was scarce. She was forced to share quarters with a number of wives whose husbands were on trial for their lives for genocide and atrocities, and she found the wives comically stupid as they went around proudly bragging about their husbands and their wartime accomplishments. Anyway, we had lots of nice times together until she passed away. I thought since she was an exciting character in my life for some years, she was a worthwhile digression in the otherwise colorless Allen saga.

The following year I made *Bananas*. Again a script by me and Mickey Rose, and shot it in Puerto Rico. I didn't use Keaton in the movie, as I had Louise in mind when I wrote the character. On the strength of the success of *Take the Money and Run* and *Play It Again, Sam,* United Artists had offered me a three-picture deal. The first script I showed them was a drama, which they did not want from a comedy filmmaker. I could have made it as I had total say in my contract, but I would never force any studio to be involved or back a movie they did not believe in. David Picker, who was a big advocate for me at UA, was relieved when I said, "If you don't like it, don't give it a moment's thought, I'll write something else." And Mickey Rose and I wrote *Bananas*. There was a book about a revolution in South America, a comic novel, and we asked UA to purchase the rights because we had the idea to do a movie about a revolution in South America and did not want to be sued. UA bought the book for a pittance. Then Mickey and I proceeded to write our own surreal nonsense script using zero of the book. The book had a coherent but uninspired plot. We had almost no plot and lots of insanity. I only learned years later that when Arthur Krim, the head of United Artists, saw *Bananas* and realized it bore no resemblance to the book UA had bought, he wanted to sue me for fraud and was dissuaded by Picker and David Chasman.

As I said, before leaving for Puerto Rico I had bought a penthouse on Fifth Avenue, and Keaton suggested when we return, she move in with me more committedly. I hesitated, but in Puerto Rico we had such a nice time and she was a good sport, considering she wasn't in that movie but my ex-wife Louise was. Keaton was supportive and found

Louise funny. Anyhow, upon getting back to New York I gave Keaton a key to my penthouse and there we were, two jerks, as she used to describe us, living amongst the swells high above Central Park where, if you stood in my living room you could see unobstructed all of the city from the World Trade Center to the George Washington Bridge. The seasonal changes were worth the price I paid for the joint. I was the first to see the apartment when it came on the market. I passed, as it cost too much. Another guy gobbled it up, made his renovating plans and suddenly went bust. By now I regretted I had not bought it and since it once again came up for sale I grabbed it, except the price was now much higher. But what views. What vistas. Every inch of Central Park plus more. *Bananas* was a hit and so were my next couple of films, and Arthur Krim, who wanted to pull me into court, became my biggest fan, my artistic sponsor, my personal friend.

Arthur Krim went on to be one of the three people I have acknowledged made my career. I first met Arthur in passing when I campaigned for Lyndon Johnson. I believe he put that all-star inaugural show together, and I recall being invited to Arthur's town house, where I met Adlai Stevenson and Averell Harriman and assorted high-end Democrats. Apart from his political activism and urging of LBJ to push hard on his amazing civil rights initiatives, Arthur ran United Artists, an enlightened movie company that respected its filmmakers. Once over the initial trauma of seeing *Bananas* and wanting my head on a pike, Arthur tuned in to my work. He always said he was proudest to have made films with Chaplin and me. I did fifteen films with him. He said his most satisfying achievement was that he provided me with a home to thrive as a filmmaker. Along with Jack Rollins and the *Times* critic Vincent Canby, Arthur was the third one without whose support I never would have had the film career I had. Rollins's faith in me when I didn't have any, I have described. But Canby, too, saw me as an important filmmaker when I couldn't see it and treated me as such in print. Between Rollins's encouragement, Canby's support in the press, and Arthur Krim's backing as a studio head, I was given every chance to make something of myself in movies. All I can say is I did the best I could, folks. If the films are not better, it's no one's fault but my own. I had complete freedom to do any project I chose (within a given budget) and total artistic control. Bobby Greenhut, my producer, said, "It's like we're working on a grant."

Good days in the penthouse—wasn't that my point? Yes, Keaton and I would rise, press the button next to our bed, curtains would electronically part revealing Manhattan. Either the sunlight would pour in or the gray or the raindrops or the snowflakes would be falling or the park would be full of hot red and yellow fall leaves, dying but not going quietly. We'd take in the paper from the foyer, breakfast, attack the day, each with our own agendas. We'd return at the end of the day and sometimes eat at home but more frequently go to a Knicks game or show and dinner after at Elaine's, if you call that actual food. The fare there was a scandal but it was the most exciting piece of real estate in the city, brimming with high-profile people every night and all night long. Over the years I got friendly with Elaine and, at one stretch, ate dinner there with friends every night for ten years. Any night there, one might see Fellini, the mayor, a Kennedy, Mailer, Tennessee Williams, Antonioni,

browns, marble cheesecake, and tea. Then, twenty minutes later, walking into the door of the penthouse she'd start toasting waffles and downing what for me would be a day's provisions. Amazed, ignorant about food disorders, I just sat transfixed like a man watching a European circus artist perform an eating act.

But Keaton was tiring of Manhattan and was starting to long for the cancer-producing rays of the west coast sun. She was cast in *The Godfather*, and her career was advancing. We parted company as friends and, as I've said, have remained close down through the years. I still consult her on casting sometimes or any creative problems I might be struggling with. We never fought and would work together many times in the future. In time I dated her beautiful sister, Robin, and we had a brief romance. After that I dated her other beautiful sister, Dory, and we had a little fling. The three Keaton sisters were all beautiful, wonderful women. Good genes in that family. Award-winning protoplasm. Great-looking mother. Mandelbrot's similarity hitting the jackpot.

Everything You Always Wanted to Know About Sex was my first big commercial success and while it had some funny things in it, it was not my finest moment, although it was one of Gene Wilder's. What a talent. In one scene he goes to sleep at night and keeps on his wristwatch. I said, "You always keep your wristwatch on when you go to sleep at night?" He said, "Yeah, doesn't everyone?" He might have been eccentric, but how many guys can act that brilliantly opposite a sheep?

We had a sequence where a mad scientist creates a giant breast that breaks loose and terrorizes the countryside. By sheer coincidence, just when the movie opened, Philip Roth came out with his book *The Breast*, also about a giant breast. Roth was a much deeper, more serious man than me in addition to being very funny. Sometimes we'd show up together in some article on Judaism or Jewish humor, but he approached issues from a thoughtful, engaging point of view. I was only interested as far as they gave me good comedy material. He was a thinker, a genuine intellectual. I was a comic turned moviemaker, and we worked in different mediums. There's a big gap between dying in print and dying onstage. Death in print is a private matter. Death in front of an audience is embarrassing, and the comic experiences the same unpleasantness one might feel at one's crucifixion. And speaking of death, allow me a graceful segue to my next film, *Sleeper*.

Emboldened by the success of *The Godfather* and *Lawrence of Arabia*, movies of epic length, both with intermissions, I daydreamed of a comic epic. Until then, there had been no large-scale comedies, and many of the best were actually very short. Some of the great Marx Brothers movies were not more than an hour and fifteen minutes. There had been *It's a Mad, Mad, Mad, Mad World*, which attempted some size but turned out to be a lead latke wasting the talents of a large number of wonderfully gifted performers. So here was my egomaniacal fantasy: I'd do a two-part comedy with an intermission. The first half would be the adventures (which I would dream up) of a guy in New York played by me and at the end of an hour and a half or so of unbridled hilarity, my character would fall into a vat of cryogenic sauce. Frozen by accident. I would later work out the details of why and how a Manhattanite was skulking around a cryogenic joint and somehow got frosted. I envisioned an audience exhausted from laughing over this development as part one ended, rushing up the aisles to buy popcorn and soda, refreshing themselves in eager anticipation of part two coming up. They would gather in the lobby and quote their favorite lines and sight gags from the first part and then, upon the signal to return to their seats, they would clutch their Reese's Peanut Butter Cups and Raisinets and shuffle dutifully back to await a second hour of raucous mirth and zany mischief.

Since part one was in New York in the 1970s, imagine the audience's surprise and delight when part two comes on and we are hundreds of years in the future and the same city looks appropriately science fiction modern. Monorails and flying autos abound and beautiful women in skintight, revealing fashions appropriate to the year 2500, when I was sure they'd be dressed scantily and with ample cleavage. Somehow into this advanced society I get defrosted and find myself a fish out of water, to say the least. The possibilities for brilliant satire and wacky one-liners were endless. I pitched this prospect to United Artists, who liked it and had bought into the myth that I was a comedy genius who knew what he was doing. They green-lit it on the spot and we all congratulated one another, rushing off to make down payments on villas and Oceanco yachts from the projected grosses. For this masterpiece, I would cast Diane Keaton. Till that point, I had never directed her. We both starred in *Play it Again, Sam*, but Herb Ross directed that film.

A fact that people don't realize is that when Keaton and I began working together in the series of films I wrote for her, we had not been romantically involved for several years.

Many people thought we made *Annie Hall* and *Manhattan* and *Love and Death* while we were living together as lovers, but we were by then just lifelong pals. Keaton was available for the project and excited over the idea. Now all I had to do was get it down on paper.

After a few futile attempts to write part one, that is, my adventures in Manhattan, I realized I couldn't think of any adventures. I called my friend Marshall Brickman to collaborate with me, which he did, but he couldn't think of any adventures, either. As the days passed and our conversations drifted to the relative social value of round-card girls and the joys of Schmulka Bernstein salami, dreams of a major opus began to fade and the only bit that held some promise was me waking up in the future. Another writer-director would have accepted the challenge and somehow made this brilliant concept happen, giving rise to a different, more inspirational show business anecdote. But I don't handle adversity well and it wasn't long before I folded, knocking off work early and settling for a normal-length film consisting of only part two. We called it *Sleeper*, and I don't remember much else except there was something about a guy who loses his nose and me and Keaton try and use it to clone him back whole. I remember Marshall and I gave the script to Isaac Asimov and Ben Bova, two great science fiction guys neither of whom we knew, and asked if they would read it. They were kind enough to, and both loved it and both agreed we got the technical stuff right. Eventually *Sleeper* won a few awards, a Hugo, and a Nebula Award for best science fiction film and for sci-fi writing or something. I forget much of the rest except we filmed in LA and Colorado, and I had to check my body for ticks every night since we were in the Rocky Mountains. To my horror, I did find one in my leg and was certain they'd have to amputate—which at the time would've been fine with me.

After *Sleeper* came *Love and Death*, a broad comedy with a Russian-literature atmosphere. I consider it the funniest of my early funny ones. I asked Keaton to be in it, and we both went to Paris and Budapest to shoot. I remember how impressed Cavett was when we were wolfing down some chili at P.J. Clarke's one night, and I said, "Gee, I better split. Gotta get up early tomorrow. Have to go to Budapest."

Exotic city. Full of Russian soldiers at that time. The country was occupied. I used tons of Red Army soldiers in my movie. They could all march and drill, and all they wanted was relief from the boredom of occupying and cartons of cigarettes. Shooting the Paris sections were paradise, and Keaton and I had rooms for months at the Plaza Athénée. I remember sitting with her in the dining room of our hotel, and we ordered caviar after a hard day's shoot. The waiter spooned out our portions. We gobbled it up. He said, "Would you like some more?" I, moron that I was, marveled at how for the initial price one could have all the caviar one could eat. How did they do it without going broke? Miss Orange County was no cosmopolite, either, and we sat there knocking off several kilos of Beluga. When the check came it read like the tab for a Stealth Bomber. Thank god I've since learned about lumpfish.

Love and Death was a fun picture to shoot except for the weather. Cold in Budapest and cold in Paris. When it ended we were happy to get home, her to the sun, me to the rainy streets of Manhattan where I thrive. The movie came together easily with the exception of the music. I began by using Stravinsky, but the atonality rendered everything unfunny. The minute we switched to Prokofiev, the film came alive. The reviews were good, although it would be the last time I'd ever read a review or anything about myself. United Artists inundated me with a bale of national reviews to cull quotes for an ad. Hundreds of reviews from all over, so different, so often conflicting, and to what end? So I can read I'm a genius or an incompetent idiot? I already know I'm incompetent and was not born a genius. Self-obsession, that treacherous time waster.

The fun of making a movie is making the movie, the creative act. The plaudits mean zilch. Even with the highest praise, you still get arthritis and shingles. And is it so terrible that some people are not thrilled with your work? That someone might not like your movie? The universe is flying apart at the speed of light and you're worried some guy in Sheboygan quibbles with your pacing? Or some lady in Tuscaloosa writes you're a genius and you believe her opinion makes you the equal of Rembrandt or Chopin? Stop hondling with trivia.

My advice to young filmmakers who ask me is always: Lay your proboscis on the grindstone. Don't look up. Work. Enjoy the work. If you don't enjoy the work, change occupations. Don't be outer directed. You know what you think is funny or what goals you are striving for. That's all you need to know. You have a vision, try to execute it. Simple as that. Judge it yourself. You know if you've made the movie you envisioned when you started. If you did, great, enjoy a warm feeling of accomplishment, wink at yourself in the mirror, and move on. If you struck out by your own lights, learn what you can, which is rarely anything in an art form, and try harder next time. The fact that *What's New Pussy-cat* was a big success did not soften my embarrassment over the film. Yet a film like *Stardust Memories*, which was not particularly well received, gave me a great sense of achievement. All I'm saying is the fun is in the actual labor. The rest is drivel or piffle—take your choice. I think I prefer piffle.

After the experience of *Love and Death*, I had taken an acting job in a movie called *The Front*. It was the first decent blacklisting movie and it was written by Walter Bernstein and directed by Marty Ritt, two artists who'd been blacklisted during the McCarthy miasma. Walter was a clever writer who knew all about the ins and outs of not being able to work because they didn't approve of your political beliefs. Marty Ritt was what Walter called a graceful fat man. This tough, burly overweight specimen had been a dancer and almost made it to Broadway in *Pal Joey*, but he was replaced out of town at the last minute by a new discovery, Gene Kelly. Marty had been a protégé of Kazan's, and when he couldn't get employment he supported his family by gambling. Poker and horses kept him in protein. Marty was colorful. He had no time for social niceties. He only wore jumpsuits, and when he invited you to his Beverly Hills home for dinner at six (he ate early) he'd be standing out on his lawn at ten to six waiting for your on-time arrival.

Once there, it was dinner straight away, lots of good conversation. "Kazan thought I was a promising director, but he really liked me because I could handle my fists," was typical Ritt. After dinner, more chat, and when it came time for Marty to go to sleep that's exactly where he headed. You were very politely ushered out, and there was something totally charming about his direct demeanor and gruff, lefty politics. I worked with Zero Mostel on *The Front* and had heard some pretty terrible stories about him being a nightmare to work with but I found him very nice, highly cultivated, and interesting. I even contemplated joining him on a trip to Italy where he was headed to study some paintings, but I came to my senses. Still, I really liked Zero and found him fun to talk to.

When Columbia saw the rough cut they were correctly disappointed. It was clear to Walter and me what was wrong, but Marty was the director. Columbia asked me if I'd reedit the movie. Walter and I said, Not without Marty's approval. A very direct man, unburdened by ego, he gave in. The print was sent to New York, and Walter and I recut it and trimmed it. We did the best we could. It helped, but it was never the movie it should have been. Why? Who knows what goes wrong in these things? My guess is that there were flaws in the script none of us picked up on. Marty directed it well enough, we all act it decently, but to pun on no less a maven than Blaise Pascal, "The art has its reasons, which reason knows nothing of."

My theory, after years of being in the movies, is that the problem is almost always the script. It's much harder to write than direct, and a mediocre director can make a good movie from a fine script but a great director cannot make a lousy script into a good movie. OK, I say "never." What I mean is "practically never." And maybe one or two instances contradict what I'm saying, but if I was putting money into a film, I'd make sure I had a great script. Naturally you don't want a hopeless no-talent to direct it or a klutz to act in it, but a decent workman is all you need for a well-written story movie. *The Front* was well written, and none of us ever saw any serious flaws, and I still don't but I'm sure they must exist. On *The Front*, I met Michael Murphy and we became friends. Murphy was a great pal, and I always kidded him about being a secret agent with the CIA. An ex-marine, raised in Goldwater country, his comings and goings were as mysterious as Lamont Cranston's. Still, he was a fine actor and a bright, tasteful, wonderful guy, even if he did carry around a hidden cyanide capsule.

So now the film is ready for release. Of course there was a corny ad, a big billboard that said WOODY ALLEN IS—THE FRONT. Result: Mediocre reviews, mediocre business. Still the film has lived on, and it is shown all the time on college campuses because the blacklisting material is informative. When it came out I was already well into preproduction on *Annie Hall*.

Here I should pause to say something about my casting process. My first movie was cast in California by Marvin Paige, the second by Marion Dougherty in New York. Marion's assistant was Juliet Taylor, and when Marion gave up her New York practice to join a major studio as their in-house casting head, Juliet took over. Juliet has cast my films for decades, trying to retire on several occasions, but I always managed to talk her back into the workforce. Finally, she gave up show business for a life of travel and leisure, and her previous assistant, Patricia DiCerto, now casts for me. But Juliet has been more than just a great casting person. She's been a confidant who reads my scripts, criticizes them, makes suggestions, watches my first cut, makes more suggestions, and has seen me through many casting crises where an actor needs to be replaced on short notice or there is simply nobody that seems right for a certain part.

Many times, when all seems hopeless, she will somehow come up with just the person we're looking for. She reads my script and makes a list of actors worth considering for each part. I read the list and may eliminate a few, and then we discuss the others. There are always ones I have never heard of and she has to acquaint me with. She introduced me to Mary Beth Hurt and Chazz Palminteri, two fine actors who were letter-perfect for the roles I had written, and I hired them the minute they walked through the door.

I don't like the casting ritual. It goes like this: I am in my casting room, and a nervous actor comes in wanting a job. The poor person has to get looked over, may have to read something, act it out. I am not socially adept, and I do not enjoy meeting people. I can never get the actor out fast enough. I have usually seen film on the person I'm meeting, so I know he or she can act. I have nothing to say to any of them. The truth is, if they don't do anything crazy like come at me with a straight razor, I am prone to hiring them. The only thing that messes it up is that the next actor who comes in is just as good, just as talented, and he doesn't attack me, either. Now the session is over and Juliet has brought in ten actors, all very good; if nine became unavailable any one of the ten could play the role, and so I have to choose. But what do I have to go by? A seat-of-the-pants intuition, a nuance here or there. Finally, I choose because the director has to make a decision or the project doesn't move forward.

Once in a while an actor of reputation comes in to meet or one that has flown in from LA especially for the meeting, and Juliet will say, "You can't just have this person come in and out in thirty seconds. You have to spend a little time with her." What follows is an awkward three minutes where the actor is trying to be charming and hopefully impressive. I, on the other hand, am struggling to make conversation and keep the person from feeling he or she is brushed too quickly. I ask what they're doing, their plans, where they're from originally—stuff I couldn't care less about. I only want to verify that since I saw film on them where they were wonderful, they haven't become too fat or had fatal face work or haven't become a member of a terrorist group. If I had my way I'd never meet anyone and cast only people I've already cast, but that is a foolish and unworkable way to live up to my duties as a movie director.

Love and Death had been a broad comedy. Eisenstein and Tolstoy in cartoon. Now, something inside me said I wanted to do a realistic comedy, where I can speak to the audience and bare my soul. Maybe there'd be fewer laughs, but hopefully the characters will be engaging and their lives will be interesting, even if they're not always speaking in joke. For this I called on Marshall Brickman again to see if he wanted to work with me. Marshall, if you recall, was the bass player in the Tarriers, a folk group I appeared with a number of times at the Bitter End. He is the real article when it comes to comedy and a great collaborator. We had a good time plotting *Annie Hall*. At first it was supposed to be my character's stream of consciousness, but that was yet another of life's great dreams that did not work out. It was on *Annie Hall* I first used Gordon Willis, a fabulous cinematographer, and I learned much from listening to him and watching him work. I learned moviemaking from two masters after floundering around and flying by the seat of my own pants: editing from Ralph Rosenblum, a gifted editor, and everything else from Gordon Willis. Gordon knew it all. I saw him on the phone telling Kodak up in Rochester how much silver nitrate to put in their film. He was rigid, hard on his crew, short-tempered, but I never had a cross word with him, and we worked together for ten years. Like with Danny Simon, I knew Gordy knew much more than me and the best way to learn was to shut up and listen. He had great respect for the script, and we went over every single shot before every movie.

The first scene we ever shot together, on day one of *Annie Hall*, was the lobster scene. Keaton, as usual, was full of sparkle. By then, I had become good friends with Tony Roberts, and the three of us had lots of laughs doing the movie. I finished on time with a great sense of confidence that could only mean I was in for trouble. We finished cutting quickly, and when Marshall saw the movie he had cowritten he found it incoherent. The stream of consciousness hadn't worked, and the only thing that worked was my screen relationship with Keaton. We recut. I reshot. We recut. I reshot. I had a half-dozen different endings, eventually ending up with what you see.

We titled it *Anhedonia*, which is a psychological symptom wherein one cannot experience pleasure. UA, who loved the movie, did not like the title. We argued but folded after a while. We chose the title *Sweethearts*, which we then found we couldn't use because there was already a film with that title. Marshall sardonically suggested *Doctor Shenanigans*. I laughed; UA panicked, afraid he was serious. We toyed with *Alvy and Annie*, but I decided on *Annie Hall*, using Keaton's birth name. The movie opened and soon became everyone's favorite. People were in love with it. This instantly made an old cynic like me suspect of its quality.

It got nominated for a number of Oscars. The night of the ceremony I was playing jazz in New York. I remember playing "Jackass Blues," a tune made famous by King Oliver. I used my gig as an excuse, but I wouldn't have gone if I was free. I don't like the idea of awards for artistic things. They're not created for the purpose of competition; they're made to fulfill an artistic itch and hopefully entertain. I'm not interested in any group's pronunciamento as to which film is the best film of the year, or the best book, or the Most Valuable Player. I don't want to get into this and waste my typewriter ribbon, because then I'll have to get that guy over who changes it and feed him. Suffice it to say, Oscar night, I played the blues best I could, went home, went to sleep, and the next morning on page one of the *Times* noticed down below we had won four Oscars including Best Picture. I reacted like I reacted to the news of JFK's assassination. I thought about it for a minute, then finished my bowl of Cheerios, went to my typewriter, and got to work.

I was in the midst of writing *Interiors*, and that's what held my attention. Not a movie I'd done a year ago. Don't look back, Satchel Paige said, something may be gaining on you. I heed that great man's advice. I try never to look back. I don't like living in the past. I don't save memorabilia, photos from my films, posters, call sheets, nothing. To me, when it's over it's over. Don't dine out on it, move on. I had finished my work on *Annie Hall* in the distant past, and it was the last thing on my mind by the time the Oscars came out.

When I told Arthur Krim I planned to do a drama, he told me I had earned the right to write and direct whatever I wanted. Though I was new and inept at it, I was totally unconcerned with the fact it could easily be a miserable failure. Over the years I have avoided the hit-flop trap. I'm not out to make hits, but the best films I can. Failure comes with the territory. If you're afraid of failure or can't handle it when it happens—and if you're not playing it safe as an artist it will surely happen now and then—you must find another way to make a living.

Many studios have refused to work with me because of my control and requirements, but certain backers see it as a very reasonable gamble. If you had bet on me from *Take the Money and Run* to today, you'd be ahead. Not way ahead but enough to buy that fishing rod you've always wanted. I was happy for Keaton and Marshall Brickman and my producers, Rollins and Joffe, and of course UA made a few extra bucks, although I heard *Annie Hall* was the lowest-earning Best Picture winner to its time. It was fine I got an Oscar for directing, but what did that mean? Was my work improving? Was I taking enough risks? Did it stave off my crown baldness? You see my point? One of the nice bonuses of *Annie Hall* was that while casting it I met Stacey Nelkin.

I needed a young girl to play Alvy's cousin, and she had to be pretty and she had to be sexy for the jokes to work. Juliet Taylor called in a number of lovely young actresses, and amongst them was Stacey, a beautiful, bright, charming young woman who caused Marshall and myself to spin around each other like electrons. Much would be made in the press in later years over the idea that I gravitated toward young girls, but it's really not so. My first wife was three years younger than me. So was my second. Diane Keaton was "age-appropriate" as was Mia Farrow, whom

I dated for thirteen years. Of the many women I have been involved with over the decades, almost none were much younger than I was. One of them, I wasn't even involved with. I merely invited her on a trip I was taking to Paris. She turned me down, and that ended it. But I'll get to that, because she is Mariel Hemingway and the story is funny. One young woman I asked to marry me, and her name is Soon-Yi, and blissfully she said okay, but that story comes later and therein really hangs a tale. (And I hope it's not the reason you bought this book.) Then there was Stacey, the truly wonderful young lady that I hired for a small role in *Annie Hall*, which was cut from the movie because the film ran forever at final edit.

So Marshall and I are impressed by Stacey, who is bright, poised and great-looking, in our brief encounter. And when she leaves, we can only ponder the miracle of the homogametic sex. Now, in all the years of filmmaking I have never mixed business with my social life, and I have never dated or hit on, in any shape, manner, or form, any actress up for a role in any of my movies. The fact is I've almost never dated an actress, stand-in, lighting double, in any of my films. I was either already going with someone, which precluded any outside adventure, or was simply not interested in any of the women I was working with. The truth is my focus was always on my movies, which required every erg of anxiety my hypothalamus could produce. So when Stacey left, that was it, though we agreed she was a good choice for the part. I saw her again for a quick moment some days later when she came back to audition by reading, and a third time when I eventually filmed her short scene on the set. Apart from that I didn't give her another thought, consumed as I was with worry over the problems of *Annie Hall*.

In actuality, I would never have dared to dream that I could be in any way attractive to this charming beauty. After all, she was young and probably loved rock stars, drugs, and late-night discos while I preferred an evening at home with tea and Holland rusk perusing the sonnets of Henry Howard, Earl of Surrey. As it turned out, when she came in to shoot her scene, her mother came with her and was also quite charming. We chatted very briefly between shots, and they knew Marshall and I played jazz at a joint called Michael's Pub and said maybe they'd drop down to hear the band. I said, please do, always delighted when anyone shows any interest, but I figured it was the usual benign insincerity that is the hallmark of show business conversation. Then on a Monday night they showed up. I played my usual excruciating solos, and between sets I joined them at their table. Stacey was sharp and educated, and I recommended a book to her. She claims it was Kafka, and that sounds like the kind of fun guy I was. They drank up, made small talk, said good-bye, left, and I returned to the bandstand to torture the patrons with another set. Again, nothing more than a pleasant twenty minutes with some nice people. Cut to a short while later, I am on the street shooting a scene with Keaton and who walks by en route to her home but Stacey. Her scene had been shot weeks ago, so the assistant director recognized her. He called me over. I sighed, marveled as usual at her contours, and she gave me a warm hello. While the next shot was being set up, we chatted, and she mentioned she was home alone on the coming weekend, both parents having gone to the country. I gave her my phone number and said I'd be in and out the next few days and if she was bored, she could give a call and maybe we'd go to a movie.

I still didn't imagine I'd ever hear from her, my self-esteem always hovering at Zabriskie Point. But sure enough, she called, came over for coffee as we lived quite near each other, and we just talked and had some laughs. A pleasant afternoon. Nothing more. A few days later, she left for the South of France, and I flew to Los Angeles to film more scenes for *Annie Hall*. The summer passed, and I did receive a postcard from Europe from her. In the fall, after we both returned to Manhattan, we called each other and began dating. We dated on and off, saw a few films, listened to music, discussed books, and of course jumped into the percales. We saw each other now and then and enjoyed one another's company. We listened to classical music together, I introduced her to some foreign movies, and we took walks. Then one day, she announced she was moving to California to pursue her acting career more seriously. We said good-bye, she flew west, and soon she married.

We remained friendly and our paths crossed over the decades, talking on the phone or seeing one another through our various boyfriends, girlfriends, husbands, and wives. We always stayed in contact, always checked in to gossip and catch up, meeting each other's spouses and children. I told Marshall Brickman many funny anecdotes about my flirtation with Stacey and the pitfalls and joys of a relationship between an older man and a younger woman, and the experience provided us with some good material. When we wrote *Manhattan* together, we called the character Mariel Hemingway played Tracy instead of Stacey in a burst of creative inspiration. I know the picture did her justice, as we have remained friends still. When I fell in love with Soon-Yi, *Manhattan* was revived and I suddenly got a reputation as someone obsessed with young women. I was obsessed with gangsters, baseball players, jazz musicians, and Bob Hope movies, but young women have been a tiny fraction of the women I dated over the decades. I have used the May-December ploy as a comic and romantic theme a few times, just as I have used psychoanalysis or murder or Jewish jokes, but only as good material for plots and laughs. Still, it's a juicier headline than "Man Dates Age-Appropriate Woman."

But I will get to *Manhattan*. First, my entrance into the world of drama. Unwilling to play to my strength as a merry-andrew, I decided to try my hand at tragedy and while perhaps falling short of Aristotle's requirements of pity and fear, the audience did pity me and the investors learned the meaning of fear. This would not be what passed for drama in American movies. I wanted a genuine drama, a European-style drama, and not a melodrama. Anyway, I failed, but not because I didn't try. My goal was to make a film about a family of girls with a cold mother, and their father remarries this hot-blooded dame, the opposite of the icy elegant interior decorator wife who wouldn't let the poor guy relax in his own home lest he move an ashtray. So the mom eventually walks into the Atlantic and her daughter tries to save her and dies trying but the new mother gives her mouth-to-mouth, the kiss of life as they call it, and the kid's reborn from the new, warmer, more loving woman. Sounds interesting, and in the hands of a more experienced or gifted dramatist it might've been.

My first mistake was doing something I hadn't done before and have never done since, and that is rehearse. I don't have the patience to rehearse, and doing comedies, the more I hear the material the less amusing it becomes. That's why when I finish a script and go over it once and fix the bad parts, I never look at it again till we shoot. If I reread it, it keeps getting flatter and flatter. And I lack real powers of concentration. I'm not a patient person when it comes to rehearsal demands. That's why, over the years, I shoot long masters and don't cover. I can't sit through doing scenes over and over. I like to do it, go home and watch basketball. The actors love long masters because they can sink their teeth into a scene. Of course, they don't have the problem I have later, stuck in the cutting room with scenes that don't work and wishing I had some coverage. So I invite these two fabulous actresses, Maureen Stapleton and Geraldine Page, over to my apartment to rehearse or at least discuss the characters.

God, what a mistake. I never get deeply into those actor discussions of character. If the actor accepts the role, I assume he or she feels he or she can play it. Of course if a question arises, I am happy to answer it. If I've botched something in the writing and lumbered the actor with a line or speech that's awful, I'm happy to change it. I always assure actors they will not have to say anything they don't want to. They can put my dialogue in their own words, they don't have to wear clothes or hairstyles they're not happy with. I don't want them uncomfortable.

So here I am, high above Fifth Avenue, in over my head with two of our country's greatest actresses, my first venture away from comedy, and I make mistake number two. I say, "Would you like something to drink?" You can see where this is going. Cut to two hours later and neither one of them can stand-up. Maureen, one of the nicest and truly funniest women I've ever met, is trying to find the door the way the old movie actor Jack Norton would do it. You'd recognize him from those thirties and forties films. He was mustachioed and specialized in teetering drunks. Geraldine, eccentric when sober, is now testy and she's leaving, having sluiced my bar dry and ricocheting from wall to wall. The following day Maureen was back to her fantastic self. She really had a great personality and could top me no matter how mercilessly I teased her. Geraldine, I called in for a talk and she was sweet and a little apologetic, and I learned my lesson about mixing social drinking and work.

During the shooting of *Interiors*, Gordon Willis and I spent a lot of time together in the Hamptons, where some of the movie was shot. We dined together every night and over dinner decided we would shoot my next movie, a New York love story, in black-and-white and wide-screen. We had always seen wide-screen used for war films and by outdoor westerns, where the size could be exploited visually. Our idea was to use it to convey the intimacy of love affairs. Like Geraldine and Maureen, Gordon liked his little taste of John Barleycorn, and as it got dark early those winter days in the Hamptons and there was nothing to do, he would sample a wee dram of Courvoisier at five. Just enough to go blind. The next day, he'd be shot. He'd tell me he was having a sinus attack and, dunce that I was, I suggested an over-the-counter antihistamine.

Gordy was a man who knew no fear when it came to abusing his body. I used to make myself great malteds at home and bring them in, in a thermos when we shot. Gordy loved anything unhealthy, so I always made one for him. He dined on liverwurst sandwiches, several hot dogs, the malted, many Camel cigarettes, and brandy at happy hour. I warned him, timid coward that I am, about his regimen. Once, scouting an old age home, he surveyed the inmates and said, If I ever get that way, kill me. I didn't have to; he was working on it himself. Gordy looked like Beethoven. They were both geniuses in their chosen fields. Beethoven became deaf, the only thing a composer would dread, and Gordy, a cinematographer, started losing his eyesight. Nice deal, human existence. Full of delightful ironies.

Interiors opened and got some very good reviews. My feeling is critics are like all professionals: doctors, cops, lawyers, movie directors. Each profession has a few great ones, a few awful ones, and most fall into the middle; working stiffs who do a bread-and-butter job. The critics I've known have been nice people. Some have been interested in treating film as an art form, some have said, "I am merely a ticket buyer's guide." I was friendly with Judith Crist, who did nothing but encourage me right from the start. So did Gene Shalit. They both loved *Take the Money and Run* and *Bananas* and continued to be supportive. Their enthusiasm went a long way to getting me off the ground. I was friendly with Richard Schickel, a lovely man and bright critic who wrote well about the blacklisting era, about Bogart, and one of the very best books ever written about a show business personality, his biography of Kazan. And the friendships did not depend on them reviewing me well. Once, at a screening of someone else's film, Schickel, sitting in front of me, turned and said, "Sorry, I just didn't like *Interiors.*"

I had never read him on the subject, but it didn't matter for a second. I liked him. and that's all that counted. Although we rarely saw one another, I went back a long way with John Simon, who said to me once when I gave him a warm hello, "You're very forgiving." The truth was I always liked John and while I assumed he meant he had panned me in reviews, I wouldn't have read them and it never would have impeded my enjoying his company. For years, people used to say to me, "Oh, you must read what Vincent Canby said about your movie. He gets it all, and you'll love the review." But I never read him on my films. I knew from outside sources he was a fan, and I had a nice correspondence with him but it was not about my films, it was about Truffaut and Bergman and Buñuel and various masters.

I was pretty friendly with Kael, who was a lovely lady and fine writer and loyal to her friends, but she used to drive me crazy. I'd meet her sporadically for dinner at Trader Vic's, an exotic, very dimly lit restaurant. Breathless with energy as always, she'd pull out galleys of her review set to appear in the upcoming *New Yorker* and urge me to read it. I could never see the print well enough to read in the candlelight, but she was so proud and so enthused. I squinted and squirmed, but it was always tough going. If I had seen the movie I might very well have not agreed with her review. I told her I thought she had everything a great critic should have: an encyclopedic knowledge of movies, passion, great writing style, but not taste.

And so we argued all the time and the arguments boiled down to our personal likes and dislikes. She felt Altman was a greater movie director than Bergman. I very much liked Altman but felt Bergman's movies were greater. I was a paleface, she was a redskin. We'd argue. But I was impressed by her loyalty to friends and she'd ask me things like, "Can you get so and so a job catering your next film? He's a great caterer and needs the money." We had many an argumentative dinner, and she was another gifted lady who enjoyed her little libation. Often, by the time I got her back to her hotel, she had turned pugnacious from a medley of mai tais, and I thought she was ready to smack me if I couldn't see the greatness of some dreadful movie, now long forgotten but to her a masterpiece. She was also very funny and would come up with really witty lines. Like when she saw the movie *The Hindenburg* with George C. Scott and wrote, "Gasbag meets gasbag." I liked Scott, but she was a witty shark. And when she got it right, she was a joy to read. The reviews of *Interiors* didn't matter because a few days after it opened there was a newspaper strike.

In the case of *Manhattan*, my next opus, as Arthur Krim used to call them, I had seen Mariel Hemingway in the movie *Lipstick* and thought she was a terrific actress. Marshall Brickman and I had finished the scenario for *Manhattan* and felt she'd be perfect in it. She came in to meet Juliet and me, and as she had no disqualifying disfigurements or a police record, I hired her. She proved to be a wonderful actress and a lovely person. I got very friendly with her, and we went to the movies and museums and had dinner together a number of times. I played tennis with her sister Muffet, who was a terrific tennis player but in typical Hemingway fashion (not Ernest, the sisters) met me for tennis looking great in her outfit, and driving to the court she turned to me and said, "Oh—I forgot my racquet." As that would impede our game, we had to go all the way back to get it.

Mariel was staying in New York with her grandfather's widow, and when I picked her up, the apartment was decorated with leopard-skin rugs, tusks, marlin, and sailfish. I remembered my early childhood when my father took me fishing and we caught nothing, then stopping at the market to pick up some fresh flounder and proudly displaying them as our catch of the day. In thinking back on *Manhattan*, I have to say so much of it was good luck. If 80 percent of life is showing up, the other 80 percent, as Yogi Berra might've said, is chance. During the filming of that movie, we heard New York was going to have one of the most spectacular fireworks shows ever that very night. We dropped everything, ran to a friend's apartment in the Beresford, and prepared. Pushing our luck, we captured amazing footage that gave us the breathtaking opening of *Manhattan*.

Also, by sheer luck while the Philharmonic was recording the Gershwin; guys and women in heavy wool sweaters and galoshes were being conducted in the empty Philharmonic Hall by Zubin Mehta, there was a blizzard in the city. We quickly sent our camera operator up to my penthouse where he smuggled his film camera past the doorman and elevator operators (shooting was not allowed in the building) and from my terrace, got the most gorgeous footage of *Manhattan* blanketed in white. Pure chance in both cases, but I always felt blessed by the breaks that forever seemed to fall into place for me.

When the movie ended I had become very friendly with

both Michael Murphy and with Mariel. Mariel invited me to come and stay a few days at her home in Ketchum, Idaho, a short distance from where her grandfather had committed suicide. Ernest Hemingway was a hero of mine from the minute I began reading literature. I am one who shares Saul Bellow's estimate of Hemingway rather than John Updike's. I could pick up any book of his and turn to any page and read and the poetry of his prose kills me. The day he shot himself, either I called Louise or she called me to commiserate. It was shortly after we became lovers. We met for a drink and romanticized suicide. Her preference was to go by pistol shot, mine by placing my head in the dishwasher and pressing Full Cycle.

Now as I said, one of the cardinal rules of my life is: Never be anyone's houseguest. I wish I had heeded this personal axiom. But Mariel was so charming and so pretty and it was the whole Hemingway myth that was so enticing and so, on a freezing November day I found myself flying to Ketchum to accept the family's invite. I liked the Hemingway family very much. Her mother was sweet and pretty, her two sisters, Margaux and Muffet, were lovely, beautiful and energetic and her father was very nice. He was an outdoorsman, and in the family tradition his room was awash with fly-fishing equipment. I fly-fished as a boy, learning to fly-cast and even buying all the equipment to try and tie my own flies, but since all skills escape me, my flies were big, stupid globs of feathers and chenille that got huge laughs from all the trout that saw them. So here I am in Ketchum, Idaho, sitting down for dinner with this outdoorsy family, fresh from my midafternoon arrival.

Outside, mountains everywhere and swirling snow.

Hmm—do I really want to be here? I'm a guy who experiences anxiety if I'm not within striking distance of New York Hospital, and suddenly I'm eating quail Mariel's father had shot that morning. With each bite, the buckshot is dropping out of my mouth and clanging on the plate. After dinner they whisk me away for a long walk in the freezing, dark snow because Mariel's dad had some time ago suffered a heart attack and exercise was prescribed. The next day I was taken on a long hike in the blizzard-covered hills where my fashionable suede boots got drenched. Still I had many laughs with the hosts, and as I was going to Paris in a few weeks, I asked Mariel if she wanted to come. This panicked her, unbeknownst to me, and she wrote about it in her memoir. She and her mother talked it over; her mother was in favor but the prospect was too scary for Mariel.

Here's the only thing I disagreed with in Mariel's accurate account of my visit. She wrote that she declined my invitation and the following day I left. The implication being I left because of her refusal but no, I really liked the whole family very much and, as stated, I have remained on great terms with Mariel to this day. I left earlier than I had planned because when I arrived I was hit with a crushing piece of news that I tried being a little soldier about but couldn't. It was announced that I would have my own bedroom, but I would be sharing a bathroom with her father. Upon hearing the news, I blanched and quickly phoned my assistant, having her book a small plane to come fetch me back to Broadway. I hadn't had to share a bathroom with a male since I was twenty, marooned in Hollywood, and now I was forty, my youth and mental health long up the spout. I tried to tough it out, but after two days it became unbearable and even before Mariel passed on visiting the Eiffel Tower with me I was booked for an early exit. I needed the private plane, as there were no direct flights to Ketchum and getting there entailed connecting flights with all the accompanying rigmarole, and I am not a happy traveler.

Anyhow, I thanked them all for a lovely two days, and by ten that night was hunched over a plate of tortellini at Elaine's. No buckshot. No flavor, either, but I was back in Manhattan. I got to cast Mariel again years later in only a small part, but she told me close to filming she wanted to work and it was all I had open. As usual, she came through.

Manhattan was a huge hit. Huge by my standards, but it didn't earn more than the last *Star Wars*. Film companies have tried everything to jack up the grosses of my films, only to wind up sobbing bewilderedly. They've tried big openings, small openings, sophisticated ads, rotten commercial ads, trumpeting my name, downplaying my name, opening different times of year, pushing some big stars in the cast— all to no avail. The marketing wizards work their voodoo, assuring me with these ads on this day in these theaters, we will all soon be driving Maybachs. Then the film opens, drops violently dead at the box office, and the litany of excuses come: the weather, the World Series, the stock market, Purim. Meanwhile, nobody shows up at the box office.

And who is my audience, anyway? I've been asked that a million times. I don't know—impossible to handicap. I've had a solid worldwide audience and have had movies that did better in the single city of Paris or Barcelona than in the entire USA. *Manhattan* was a hit all over. When it opened I found myself on the cover of the *New York Times Magazine* section, on the cover of *Time* magazine for the second time. The movie was a hit all over Europe, South America, the Far East. I was hailed by *Time* as a comedy genius, which is to a real genius like Mozart or da Vinci, as the president of the PTA is to the president of the United States.

I didn't like the movie *Manhattan* when I cut it together. I offered to make a movie for free for United Artists if they'd scrap it and not release it. They waved me off as a crank. When it succeeded so strongly I was, of course, bewildered. Naturally, amidst all that adulation there was some backlash. Anything with so much praise has a hard time living up to the hype, and to me *Manhattan* fell far short. But not for most people, and it went on to win awards all over the world and it still plays everywhere today. It was not nominated for best picture by Hollywood, nor was I nominated for best director. Some said it was the Adcademy's revenge for my showing no interest in the Oscars when *Annie Hall* won, but I'm not a conspiracy theory paranoid and I don't find anything dicey about Academy voters being insufficiently impressed. I do know the Academy was a little miffed at me when *Annie Hall* won its award because I wouldn't let UA trumpet it in the ensuing newspaper ads. As I said, I was not into the whole award circus, and big ads announcing it embarrassed me. Don't you think that after two weeks the Academy called irate and said, "Why are you not saying your movie won four Oscars in your ads?" I couldn't care one way or the other, and I told UA that if it means so much to the Academy they could include it. I didn't mean it as any kind of statement but it was taken as such. I never joined the Academy despite their pressing me to join, but not for any other reason than I'm not a joiner. The only thing I ever signed up for in my life was the Cub Scouts when I was ten, and I hated it. I never learned even the most basic scouting skills like reading a compass, and to this day in order to locate true north, I have to start by first facing Zabar's.

I followed *Manhattan* with *Stardust Memories*, a film that I felt was a bit misunderstood. Naturally as the author taking some heat I'd feel misunderstood and I'm not a complainer, but here I did think people glommed on to the wrong aspect of the movie. My intention was to go inside the mind of a man who seemingly had everything; wealth, fame, a good life, but he was suffering from anxiety and depression and his wealth and fame meant nothing. Because of the style of the movie and that it was subjective through the protagonist's eyes, people made the same mistake with me that Marlon Brando once complained about. Marlon said in a TV interview, "People confuse me with the roles I play." And so with me. They thought the lead was not some fictional creation of mine and that I was disdainful of comedy, unappreciative of my success, contemptuous of my fans, and God knows what else. None of that was the case. I was humble, felt my fans had treated me very kindly, and enjoyed comedy. People sometimes said to me that I was successful and how dare I have my protagonist complain. I felt, yes, I'm very lucky. The character is lucky. I'm the first to say I have had more luck and success than I deserve, but I'm complaining for everyone who is not so lucky and even for those who work their way to the top and then discover that despite all their fame and fortune, the paths of glory lead you-know-where. In the opening scene of *Stardust Memories*, the dump is where winners and losers wind up.

I was also writing of the love-hate relationship the public has with its heroes or celebrities. One moment they want your autograph, the next they're ready to shoot you. Some months after the movie came out a devoted fan killed John Lennon, and I felt I had diagnosed things correctly. Didn't matter. I could stand all year babbling about what I intended and what I felt the audience should get out of the film. The reality is, they came away with something else, and most of them didn't like what they came away with. I was buoyed by some nice letters of support. I remember a note from Lillian Ross, whom I didn't know but respected, and one from Norman Mailer, whom I knew slightly and also respected. It remained Mailer's favorite film of mine throughout my career. Most people came away parroting the masses in the film telling me they preferred my earlier funny films. But you can't function as an artist if you're afraid of experimenting, and I had no intention of staying safely within what I knew I could do well. I intended to try and grow as a filmmaker, to try and deepen, to move to drama without giving up comedy but not to try and be a crowd pleaser. I had my own delusions of grandeur, and I resolved to always make the idea that interested me at the moment with no regard except trying to make a good movie.

And now, prepare for a little digression, a brief non sequitur. You'll think when I'm telling this, My God—what was he smoking? Nothing, by the way. I led the dullest off-screen life of any actor in film: a nondrinker, a nonsmoker, totally uninterested in any mind-altering experience. I was always wary of changing my perception and would not even wear sunglasses for that reason. To this day, I've never had a puff of marijuana. Even Jack Benny in his seventies told me he was eager to try it, and he did and he enjoyed it. But I never had any curiosity and would not join him. That's another thing about my alleged intelligence: my total lack of curiosity. I have no desire to see the Taj Mahal, the Great Wall, the Grand Canyon. I don't want to visit the pyramids or stroll through the Forbidden City. And I definitely do not want to be on one of those first rockets to outer space, to glimpse Earth from afar and experience weightlessness. The truth is, I hate weightlessness; I am a big fan of gravity and hope it lasts. I don't even wonder what all that steam coming out of the ground in Manhattan streets is about.

Nevertheless, in a moment of inexplicable lunacy, I decided to pause briefly in my meteoric rise to unmerited heights and become a great chef. Till then, my culinary skills were the equal of any citizen who could handle a can opener. I was an able man around a tuna fish sandwich, managed soft-boiled eggs with some aplomb, and I'd say my cold glass of water was the envy of any Cordon Bleu graduate. Being a bachelor, and when Jean Doumanian or similar companionship was not available for a meal at Elaine's, I could usually be found ordering Chinese takeout and wolfing it down, glued to my TV screen. What I'm getting at is that there came a day I decided to learn how to cook. But I didn't want to just learn to heat up Spam or make great Minute Rice. My Coleridge-like fantasy was to become a truly master chef. I would learn the secrets of culinary expertise and dine on ortolans and peacock tongues, even if only perched solo before Walter Cronkite.

And there would be ancillary perks. Clearly possessing the gifts of an Escoffier or a Gordon Ramsay would make the single man's road to seduction freer of potholes. The voluptuous blonde CEO I invited to dine, first charmed by my wit and a new pompadour I sported, modeled after Hokusai's *Great Wave*, would come over expecting to politely tolerate some possible version of lard and gruel thrown together by a lone inept bachelor; perhaps a defrosted Bird's Eye concoction or a thin soup of the variety served the guests of the Gulag archipelago. She would offer to take charge and show me how, in a jiffy, a feast was fashioned by someone who knew the ropes. But wait, what's this? What have I surprised her with? Coquilles St. Jacques, perhaps with a Chablis or Sauvignon. Or maybe baked camembert with a red Bordeaux. Or a blanquette de veau, and for dessert a clafoutis, done with cherries. Or, if she'd prefer, my tarte Tatin. Is that impressive enough? I think so. From there it should be an express ride to the boudoir to work off some of those calories in the sack.

Confident I would never again have to subject myself to my own spaghetti and meatballs, a dish rivaling library paste for consistency, my first move was to have my assistant phone Julia Child and say Mister Woody Allen wants a recommendation for a great cooking teacher. Private lessons, of course. Madame Child, whom I'd never met, was kind enough not to transfer the call to the FBI and obliged, suggesting a wonderful lady named Lydie Marshall. An appointment was made and Ms. Marshall showed up at my apartment. She scrutinized my pots and pans, my stove, the long white apron and toque blanche I doffed in anticipation, and, sensing she had a live one, phoned her accountant telling him it was okay to put the down payment on that sable coat she craved.

Each lesson would be three hours, and she would bring

the assorted ingredients with her. There wasn't enough time for me to grow a thin, Gallic mustache before our first lesson commenced. I would make homemade pasta, beef with béarnaise sauce, asparagus, lyonnaise potatoes, profiteroles, coffee, and madeleines. I can't remember much else except to say it was all stuff I'd either seen on menus at Lutèce or Grenouille, or read about in Proust. I gave her an ear-to-ear grin and, mispronouncing "bon appetit," dove in. Well, to cut to Hecuba, I lasted three lessons and was so crippled with exhaustion I couldn't stand erect as each session ended. I was too weak to eat the meals; I was panting and wheezing, and twice she asked if she should dial 911 and did I have any next of kin.

I had always been an athletic guy, and at that time I was playing a lot of tennis and could easily play singles for three or four hours with no signs of letup. But the hysteria and tension of cooking crushed me. I'm running all over the kitchen, the pasta dough is hanging on the back of the chair, drooping like taffy, the duck is actually on fire, I'm sweating from the heat of the stove, my hand is numb from whisking. I can't whisk anymore. My wrist is being damaged from whisking. It will kill my serve. And why am I whisking? I hate whipped cream. Meanwhile, if I stop stirring the béarnaise sauce it won't do its sauce thing. For some reason the crème caramel has come out indistinguishable from a hockey puck, and as I had never used a fire extinguisher before, I somehow managed to coat the branzino with a thick white foam. It was at that moment that somewhere Joël Robuchon and Daniel Boulud breathed a sigh of relief, sensing their reputations were safe from falling to a four-eyed interloper whose poached salmon had imploded. Sadly, I would continue to eat moo goo gai pan from cardboard buckets and reheat delivered pizzas. The women I invite over for dinner would be advised to stop off at Popeyes and bring their own nutrients. It may be a less suave segue into the kip, where I'm still trying to earn that first Michelin star.

When I regained my sanity, I made *Zelig*. I was interested in the documentary style for comedy since *Take the Money* but now had more experience. With a cinematographer like Gordon Willis and my willingness to shoot in black-and-white, which immediately limited the box office (some countries would not show a black-and-white movie, and even now black-and-white becomes a hard TV sale). *Zelig* was about how we all want to be accepted, to fit in, to not offend, that we often present a different person to different people knowing which person might best please. With someone who loves *Moby Dick*, for example, the protagonist will go along and find things to praise about it. With one who dislikes the book, the *Zelig* character will get with the program and dislike it. In the end this obsession for conformity leads to fascism.

I wrote the script and, waiting to begin preproduction, I wrote *A Midsummer Night's Sex Comedy*. The latter was only meant to be a celebration of the country, of the woods with its alleged magic, and to have fun with the love and marital problems of some amusing people.

I told United Artists I'd shoot them both at the same time. They liked the ideas, being gluttons for productivity, and I thought it would be easy. Particularly if you're a comedy genius—which it turned out I wasn't, and it was not easy. But the problem was not physical. It was no trouble shooting a few scenes from *A Midsummer Night's Sex Comedy* and then at the same or a nearby location, switching costumes and doing a scene from *Zelig*. The problem was mental. It was very hard to get emotionally wound up in one world and to switch to another. I had trouble handling the switching of psychic energy, committed to do one tale, and suddenly having to retool for other characters and plot. I vowed never to try it again.

A Midsummer Night's Sex Comedy did turn out very beautiful and magical, and nobody liked it or came to see it. *Zelig* had a much better fate, and the name Zelig has since entered the vocabulary, but is always used to designate a secondary property of the creation. It is frequently employed to denote someone who appears everywhere, at popular events, alongside the rich, the famous, a ubiquitous nonentity. But the primary meaning of "Zelig" should be when one searches for a word to describe one who keeps abandoning his position and adopting the new popular one.

In both movies I had a new leading lady, Mia Farrow. How did that happen? For that I must go back to give some mildly interesting exposition.

A few years earlier I had received a fan letter from Mia, who I'd never met and only read about. I always found her very, very beautiful. Mia reminded me of Louise, a good beginning. Her letter praised my latest movie or my work in general, I forget which. But it ended with a sentence I do remember and it was, "Quite simply, I love you." It was a very nice letter to get from a famous woman and a beautiful

213

one. I wrote a thank-you, and that concluded the matter for a few years. I finally met her when I was dragged to a small party in Hollywood by Sue Mengers, whom I was pretty friendly with. I had known Sue when she lived in New York, and when she moved to LA, she and her husband, Jean-Claude, hosted me graciously whenever I went out there. When we were all in Paris together, she took me for my first time to Maxine's and also on Christmas Eve to the Tour d'Argent, and I made that a little holiday ritual for years after with my friends. As a frequent dinner guest at her house in Beverly Hills, Sue was always trying to fix me up with one lovely movie actress or another, but for whatever reason it never seemed to work out. She was great fun and the stories about her are legend, though none will ever top her sizing up the crowd at a Hollywood party and referring to them as Schindler's B-list.

On this night it was a party that Mia happened to be at. We were introduced, made some polite small talk, the earth didn't move, and we went our separate ways. I met her once again years later in passing at Elaine's. She came in with Michael Caine, passed my table, we said hello, she got seated elsewhere, and I lunged back into my tortellini. Tortellini was one of the only things you could eat there and that tasted passable if one's demands for flavor were kept at a minimum. I often told Elaine that her food would have been turned down by the lost party on the Donner Pass.

Those were the few times Mia and I encountered one another. Now the New Year's parties. I was never a big partygoer. Mostly because I have my entering phobia. Once I'm in, I'm much better. Not great but better. I really need someone with me dragging me in, a tiresome business for mature adults, but try as I have, I have problems entering. So during Thanksgiving my friends Jean Doumanian and Joel Schumacher urged me to make a New Year's Eve party, and by hosting it, I would not have to enter. After much tergiversating, I agreed, especially since Joel said he would help. And help he did. He knew the best people for flowers, music, lighting, all the stuff that makes a great party. And a great party it was, I rented the Harkness House, the mansion once owned by Rebecca Harkness that became a ballet school after her death. It was spacious and grand, with a great hall of the type the king in Robin Hood movies eats a whole roast boar in and where a picturesque reminder of the deceased former owner greeted you on the first floor. That is to say, there was an urn with Rebecca Harkness's ashes in it, designed by Salvador Dali complete with fluttering mechanical butterflies.

One floor we made into a disco, another a socializing space; there was caviar, an oyster bar wherein I had to go find a dozen humans adept at shucking clams. There was wine and champagne and liquor, savories and sweet meats of every sumptuous description; there were tons of flowers and the men were elegant looking and the women decked out and quaffed, and all that was missing were the tumbrils waiting outside. Everyone was invited and everyone came. Everyone in show business, in the arts, in politics, in sports, in journalism, in society. In one group you might find the mayor talking with Walt Frazier, S. J. Perelman, Bob and Ray, and Tom Wicker. The group a few feet away could be Arthur Krim, Ted Sorenson, Bill Bradley, Liza Minnelli, Leo Castelli, Bob Fosse, Norman Mailer. It lasted all night, and at about 3 a.m. breakfast was served in the huge basement, and many people went down and had ham and eggs and coffee and more wine. I got credit for a Gatsby-like evening, but all the credit should go to Joel Schumacher and my assistants, who did the heavy lifting.

Vowing never to get involved in such an undertaking again, I was talked into doing one years later and brought it off, if perhaps not with the spontaneous brilliance of the first time, still it came close. Again toute New York showed up, and in among the giddy multitude was Mia with some friends. Sondheim, I believe, and Mia's pretty sister Stephanie. Again, Mia and I exchanged pleasant hellos as she vanished into the crowd. I was at that time dating Jessica Harper, the sexy, bright, and talented girl from *Stardust Memories*. A few days after the party, I get a note plus a book, a gift from Mia. She thanked me for the swell time and sent me a copy of *The Medusa and the Snail*. I sent back a note thanking her for the book and then made a casual suggestion that would eventually change the lives of many people. I said if you're free one day let's have lunch.

Now, as I say, I was a bachelor dating the female lead in my movie who was quite terrific and I liked her, but it was a casual thing; we were not in love or committed to each other. Jessica was adorable but she liked snorkeling, and the thought I might eventually come face-to-face with a stingray kept me up nights. Not that I had any designs on Mia. I didn't know her. What if she was one of those actresses into nutrition or astrology? What if her religion included handling snakes or she didn't like *The Bicycle Thief*? All I knew was that she was a pleasant beauty who crossed my path a number of times over the years in the most casual way. We agreed to meet at Lutèce the following week, as I was leaving for Paris shortly after. So I sat there and waited for her, and she showed up late looking like a zillion dollars and after lunch and wine we agreed to have dinner the night I came back from Paris. I grabbed the check, found her a cab, went home, and two days later I was at Maxim's in the city of light with Jean Doumanian. I had to be back in a week to do reshoots for *Stardust Memories*.

After a fun week, I came back and took Mia to dinner; my secretary arranged the date. "Woody will be back the ninth, can he pick you up at eight?" And that's the way I dated her for several months, I never phoned. My secretary always called and said, "Woody is shooting, but is eight thirty Thursday okay?" And she'd say yes. And off we'd go. She turned out to be bright, beautiful, she could act, could draw, had an ear for music, and she had seven children. Tilt. I found it amusing in a sitcom sort of way that I was slipping into a relationship with a woman with seven children, but at that point it was nothing more than another fact about her. Should I have twigged at all over the idea she had three biological kids and then adopted four more? Not really. It was unusual but hardly sinister. Maybe for a more perceptive person, it would have signaled something slightly more than unusual, but with that face looking back at me over candlelight one tended not to search for deal breakers. Besides, I liked kids and always got along with them. I never had any pronounced feelings about having any of my own. If, when I married Harlene or Louise, either had said they never wanted children, that would have been fine with me. If either had said, I want five children, that would also have been fine.

Kids weren't on my mind or agenda as a writer or

filmmaker but I was happy to be a father if my spouses so desired. I preferred girls but enjoyed boys, as my son Moses will attest to. I taught him baseball, basketball, took him fishing. I think I'm a clichéd father, addled in the eyes of my two currently college-aged daughters but loving and very dedicated to spoiling them. So Mia having seven kids caused me no anxiety. We'd just met, and her goals in life were different from mine, and she articulated them intelligently and convincingly. The flirtation with my leading lady in *Stardust Memories* faded gracefully, and I found myself beginning an affair with a beautiful movie star who could not have been nicer, sweeter, more attentive to my needs. She was not demanding, better informed than me, more cultivated, appropriately libidinous, charming to my friends, and, best of all, living directly across Central Park, so there was a major saving in carfare.

In retrospect, should I have seen any red flags? I guess, but if you're dating this dream woman, even if you see a red flag you kind of look in the other direction. And remember, I was not the most perceptive guy on the block, especially in matters involving Dan Cupid. In retrospect, the red flags existed every few feet, but nature provides us with a denial mechanism, else we couldn't make it through the days, as Freud teaches us, as Nietzsche teaches us, as O'Neill teaches us, as T. S. Eliot teaches us. Unfortunately, I was never a good student.

For instance: Shortly after we began dating, Mia announced she had purchased a country house in Connecticut. She said she needed a place for the kids when summer vacation came round, which I found completely understandable. She said she knew I was a city boy and if I had any problems with it she'd sell it. I knew she adored the country, but as someone who had always been two with nature, I hated the country. I don't mind it so much in the daytime, although I'm not thrilled about dew on my shoes, but in the evening when it gets dark and silent, I always expect to see a flayed hand come up from the lake or two red eyes at the window. Anyhow, I sensed our totally divergent tastes on how and where to live and spend time could eventually loom as a problem, and chose to ignore it.

A second red flag came up a surprisingly short while after we began dating, several weeks to be exact. Mia turned to me as we were seeing a movie, *My Brilliant Career*, and said, "I want to have your baby." Unused to requests any more aggressive than, Are you going to eat that last piece of herring, I was taken aback but fielded it like a graceful shortstop. I recall changing the subject to lawn mowers and put it all down to overdramatizing. After all, she was an actress and given to playing scenes.

Not very long after that—and again, I'm talking weeks here—at a Chinese restaurant, she suddenly suggested we get married. The suggestion caught me in mid-eggroll, and I thought maybe she didn't have her contact lenses in and was mistaking me for someone else. When I realized she was serious, I told her that beside the fact we had only been dating a very short while, I saw marriage as an unnecessary ritual. I had been married twice, as had she, and I learned over the years if a relationship works, it works, but a binding piece of paper doesn't help to reinforce one's love nor rectify a situation that has soured. I was happy to be in the relationship with her but, nothing personal, I just wasn't thrilled with the idea of memorializing it. Then I think I lapsed into Nixon's Checkers Speech and sang "Old Man River" from *Showboat*. Clearly she was visibly annoyed hearing my cop-out. She withdrew the offer petulantly and made some remark about me spoiling things, by which I imagined she meant, we met, dated, liked one another, and suddenly I was unwilling to progress. Her idea of progress was to run out and marry. But the swiftness of the proposal, such as it was, and her irritable reaction when I wasn't instantly up for it should have clued me in that I was dealing with a more complicated person than just this fragile, beautiful supermom.

The truth is it did shake me up at the time, but it wasn't so traumatic that I felt I should quickly pack and go into the Witness Protection Program. Should I have been flattered? I wasn't. We never married. We never even lived together, I never once in the thirteen years we dated ever slept at her apartment in New York. Apart from a small number of times that first year or two where she might stay a night at my place, we lived separately. The moment school ended, she lit out for Connecticut with her brood, and apart from a July Fourth weekend or a Labor Day weekend, I spent the summers alone in Manhattan. What kept us together was a very convenient and pleasant arrangement, which I will soon describe, but I was enumerating the red flags that I missed or chose to miss right from the start.

Here's another. Our backgrounds were solidly different. I had grown up in a lower-middle-class Jewish family. My parents, cousins, aunts, and uncles all had their quirks and conflicts, but they were within reasonable parameters. No violence, divorce, no suicide, no drugs or alcohol. Just whining and grousing about money and the doctor who did

Ruthie's nose job didn't take off enough, and maybe the guy who slices the sturgeon at Russ and Daughters should have done it. Mia's family was rife with extremely ominous behavior that swelled in the years I knew her. Drinking and major drug problems with siblings, criminal records, suicide, institution for mental troubles, eventually a brother convicted of child molestation and sent to prison. Every single Farrow cursed with flaws that ran the gamut from the Athenian stage to *The Lost Weekend*—except, it seemed, for Mia. I was amazed how she could grow up tiptoeing through that minefield of craziness and come out charming, productive, likable, and unscathed. But she hadn't been unscathed, and I should've been more alert.

In my defense, as we didn't live together, I had little knowledge of what really went on in her home. I knew nothing of the way she treated the children, the adopted ones in contrast to her biological ones. As Moses and Soon-Yi have described, she took great care to hide it from me as she did from the world. Later, I will detail some of that for you, and you will be taken aback. Another red flag: an unnatural closeness with her son Fletcher. Too close. That one even I could see, and while it seemed very odd and a tad creepy, her family relations were none of my business. She was not someone I was planning to marry or ever live with, so my take on this mother-son attachment was that it was her own affair. But it was clearly bizarre. I'd pull up in the car to pick her up for a date. She'd come strolling out of her apartment house, get into the Lincoln, and instantly grab the car phone to call Fletcher, whom she'd just left. OK, the kid has trouble separating. No one has more empathy with separation anxiety than me. But as weeks pass, she begins bringing him along now and then on our dates. The kid is laid down to sleep under the table at Elaine's while all the adults eat, drink, talk till midnight. I say, But won't he be too tired like this to function in school tomorrow? But if for any reason he might not want to go to school, she didn't send him. He was the uniquely favored child, and he called the shots.

A moment of conflict arose when I suggested she and I take a week and go to Paris. Only if we can bring Fletcher, was the reply. Otherwise, I'd rather not go. Of course, said more sweetly than I just wrote it. But won't the other kids resent the obvious favoritism? Selecting only him to take to Paris? Don't worry about that. Can we bring him? No, I said. This was meant to be the two of us going for a week or a few days. A grown-ups-only vacation. She wouldn't budge without the kid. P.S.: We didn't go. I went to Paris with Jean Doumanian. We stayed at the Ritz, strolled the Champs-Élysées, a pair of flâneurs, knocking back our Romanée-Conti. I had just been introduced to wine and I remember being a little drunk and viewing the Place de la Concorde lit up at night and it was so beautiful, and I shook my fist at Paris like a character in Balzac and said wistfully, "You old whore." Unfortunately, I was facing a lady tourist from Detroit at the time and she didn't appreciate it.

There were rumors about Mia I discarded because they were rumors. One was that she had behaved very badly with Dory Previn when Dory was married to André Previn; she insinuated her way into their household, became pregnant by André, and stole André away from Dory, causing Dory terrible mental suffering. Dory had written a famous song about how Mia had betrayed her called "Beware of Young

Girls," which I was unaware of. The truth is, I knew neither Dory nor André and was not about to jettison a new relationship over some rumor. It was only years later, when I was involved in a public custody fight with Mia, that Dory, whom I'd never met or spoken a word to, contacted me and told me the rumors were true and how deceitful Mia had been, and I must beware of her. She alerted me also to a song she'd written, the lyric of which referred to some encounter that went on between a little girl and her father in the attic. The song is "Daddy in the Attic," and the lyrics went:

And he'll play
His clarinet
When I despair
With my
Daddy in the attic

She told me Mia would sing it, and she was certain that's what gave Mia the idea to locate a fake molestation accusation she would make in the attic. But I'm not quite up to that yet.

Another rumor that I heard early on was that Mia's brothers had been sexually aggressive with the beautiful Farrow sisters growing up. The Farrow brother who is now serving years in prison for child molestation has said that their father had molested him and quite possibly his siblings. Moses says that Mia had told him she had been the victim of attempted molestation within her own family. Mia's father had a reputation as an unfaithful husband. Mia herself told me she caught him in the act with a famous movie actress. Mia had three beautiful sisters and three brothers. One brother died behind the controls of a plane. Another brother committed suicide with a gun. The third brother was convicted of molesting boys and sentenced to prison.

Now I know what you're thinking: What kind of boob am I? Given the profile I just rattled off, why didn't I bail, fake my own death, and start over in a situation with less potential for emotional combustion? I have no answer. I just know that a charming personality and big blue eyes have always been able to launch a thousand ships. So here was I, blinded by a bright actress with a drop-dead punim, putting my little four-chambered organ in her hands and telling myself that it was amazing how Mia escaped all the family bedlam. Whatever effort it took to control herself to hide things, to function, charm, she managed with great acting skills.

Her children were well-mannered and polite. Never a peep out of them. I got along with all of them, although I did find Soon-Yi a tad sullen. I took a particular liking to Moses, a small, part-Korean kid with black-rimmed glasses. I only learned much later by reading Moses's account of growing up in that household and Soon-Yi's sad tales, that Mia disciplined them all psychologically and corporally into submissive obedience.

For example, Moses writes, "I witnessed siblings, some blind or physically disabled, dragged down a flight of stairs to be thrown into a bedroom or a closet, then having the door locked from the outside. She even shut my brother Thaddeus, paraplegic from polio, in an outdoor shed over-night as punishment for a minor transgression." Mia has of course denied it, but Judy Hollister and Sandy Boluch, two women who worked in the house at the time, both corroborate the story exactly. (Moses's essay is devastating, and I advise you to read his blog for yourself.)

Moses back then was Mischa, but one day at a basketball game, watching the great Moses Malone play, Mia fell in love with the name Moses and changed her son's name.

I was fine with the change because I loved the name Moses and didn't care for Mischa. Mia always liked to change names. She changed Dylan's to Eliza, then to Malone, and she tried changing Soon-Yi's name to Gigi but Soon-Yi wouldn't go for it. Ronan was Satchel, then Harmon, then Seamus, then Ronan. I, on the other hand, always gravitated to naming kids after my African-American heroes. When Ronan was born, I named him Satchel, after Satchel Paige. I named the two girls I adopted with Soon-Yi Bechet, after the great jazz virtuoso Sidney Bechet; and Manzie, after his drummer Manzie Johnson. I've taken some criticism over the years that I didn't use African-Americans in my movies. And while affirmative action can be a fine solution in many instances, it does not work when it comes to casting. I always cast the person who fits the part most believably in my mind's eye. When it comes to the politics of race, I have always been a typical liberal and sometimes maybe even radical. I marched in Washington with Martin Luther King, donated heavily to the ACLU when they needed extra to push the Voting Rights Act, named my children after my African-American heroes and said publicly in the 1960s that I was in favor of African-Americans achieving their goals by any means necessary. Anyhow, when it comes to casting, I do not go by politics but by what feels dramatically correct to me.

Back to my personal life. For a while, the arrangement

between Mia and me seemed convenient for both of us. We weren't in love but we provided one another with reasonable companionship. Winters we dined out often, saw movies, worked together on films. Summers she would take the children to the country, and I'd be a summer bachelor remaining in Manhattan. I visited on July Fourth, gritted my teeth for the weekend amidst the mosquitoes and humidity and bees and ants. The kids all played in bathing suits, they swam and rolled around in the grass, and tramped through the woodsy foliage. I was always dressed in long slacks and long-sleeved shirts with my ever-present hat, and not one of the kids ever got a tick but I got Lyme disease.

In addition to July Fourth I visited for one other day, on Labor Day. So I saw Mia and the Farrow clan about three or four days every summer for some years. When they returned to the city, we'd start going out again, but by then she spent fewer and fewer nights at my apartment and since I never stayed at hers, the relationship didn't exactly deteriorate but mellowed into a relaxed dating one. It was still occasionally intimate but less so and going no place special. Over the next years, we made a number of films. Then, somewhere in among them, Mia explained to me she wanted to have more kids. It was unfathomable to me, since she had more than enough, but she explained in that sincere, highly intelligent way she has, that I enjoy making movies and she likes raising kids. When I pointed out that it seemed impossible to be able to devote sufficient time to raising so many children properly, she said I was wrong and knew nothing about raising children, since I only knew what I had seen my mother and aunt do. I, though skeptical, agreed she must know better than me.

She had once flown to Texas with Soon-Yi to adopt a Mexican infant but sent him back after a few days in her New York apartment for reasons known only to her. I also recall her adopting a little spina bifida boy who lived in the apartment for several weeks, but her son Fletcher found him annoying, so he was sent back. If there were other kids she adopted and returned I have no idea—as I said, I lived on the other side of the park. It was about that time that she told me that rather than adopt another child, she'd really like to be pregnant again. I looked over my shoulder to see who she was talking to, but she meant me. I didn't want to father a child. Not under the circumstances that existed. I spent no time with any of her kids except for Moses, not that I didn't like them, although ironically Soon-Yi couldn't stand me. Mia assured me I could participate in rearing a new child to any extent I cared to. If I wanted to be a hands-on father, great; if not, she'd raise it, and I would be the same free soul I'd always been. I'm almost too old as it is, she'd say plaintively. You know how I feel about motherhood. And you are under no obligation. After all, what's one added face living at my apartment when you come over? She was right—except she was wrong.

What followed was months of trying to impregnate her, a phenomenon we could not seem to make happen despite trying everything short of me donning feathers and doing a fertility dance. As time passed we continued to work together and made a half-dozen films, which I'll touch briefly on later. Finally, throwing in the towel, she gave up and adopted a young baby girl that she named Dylan.

I was totally indifferent to the whole enterprise, caught up in moviemaking. Still, I figured, if it made Mia happy, fine. But that's not quite how it worked out. I quickly found this tiny baby girl adorable and found myself more and more holding her, playing with her, and completely falling in love with her, delighted to be her father. After a year or two I fussed over her and Mia said, "Boy, you were really ready for fatherhood." I was still playing chess with Moses and plenty of sports. He had asked me to be his father, and I thought he was a great kid and agreed. I didn't legally adopt him at that point, but as he'll tell you, I was his father in every substantial way. And now there was an added treasure. I found myself bolting out of cabs stuck in traffic so I could race to Mia's home and get there before Mia put Dylan to bed. As she grew, I took her to preschool and picked her up, as the school was closer to where I lived than where Mia lived. It was a new, pleasurable dimension in my life, a sweet kid I could hug and tell stories to and try perhaps in vain to teach Cole Porter songs. I was a very loving father without really being a legal father. But it never occurred to me I needed a piece of paper. Mia seemed okay with my enthusiasm. She even wrote when I finally did adopt Dylan what a wonderful father I was to her and how much Dylan adored me.

And then one day Mia announced she was pregnant. I naturally assumed it was by me and the wolfsbane had finally kicked in; and despite her suggesting Satchel was Frank Sinatra's child, I think he's mine, though I'll never really know. She may have still been sleeping with Frank, as she hinted, and may have had any number of outside affairs, for all I know. As I said, we lived apart. The news did not throw me, as I was enjoying Dylan so much and the thought of another child was actually exciting. I wrote a script for Mia with a pregnant character so she could act it as she began showing. I called it *Another Woman* and had the great pleasure of working with Gena Rowlands and, too briefly, Gene Hackman. It was my first film using Sven Nykvist, Ingmar Bergman's cameraman. Sven was a big, likable talent who had had an affair with Mia in the past, and we all worked well together. Mia's acting was excellent, and it would be even better in my least-seen film, *September*, where even my good friend Joel Schumacher said, "I saw it and thought, why would you want to make that picture?"

Well, I wanted to, because some years back I had seen *Uncle Vanya* made into a movie in Russian and thought it was such a beautiful piece of work by Andrei Konchalovsky, I wanted to do something like it. The problem is that one never figures on a confounding intangible so although I did all the things Chekov might have done, I left out an essential unquantifiable ingredient—genius. Chekov automatically infused his work with genius, something that you can't learn or control, and so even if someone like me does all the right things as a dramatist, the sauce does not thicken. Still, as my kick is in the making of a film, it was great fun to play at being a Russian dramatist.

Mia was wonderful in both those films, and I always felt she never got her acting due. Many years back Pauline Kael had called me and said, You know who you should work with? Mia Farrow. I had nothing Mia was right for at the time, but it seemed like a reasonable thought and eventually it came to pass, as the author of the King James Version might put it.

My relationship with Mia, as I said, had mellowed into a pleasant one, less passionate but still carnal on those occasions when the planets formed a syzygy. And then suddenly it took a rather ominous turn.

Here's my theory—and mind you, it's only my take on matters. See what you think. Very early on, as I had described, Mia turned to me when we went to the movies and said, "I want to have your child."

Now it was years later, and she had finally struck pay dirt, impregnated as she was by yours truly. From the moment this natal Mega Ball was hit, she turned off me like Diane Keaton once did to oysters in New Orleans. Keaton, who previously adored oysters, was standing in a bar with me and happily expunging an order of Gulf Coast bivalves when suddenly she realized what she was about to put in her mouth. Dropping it back on its bed of crushed ice, she never ate another in her life. And in such unabridged fashion, Mia turned to me and said that she would not be sleeping at my house ever again, that I should not get too close to the upcoming baby, as she had questions about our relationship continuing. The key she had given me to her apartment years ago, she now wanted back. Though I grasped that over the past years our relationship had become more serviceable than all-consuming, still, this came as a sudden shock— particularly because since Dylan's appearance on the scene, I had come over to Mia's apartment more frequently to visit Dylan and often used the key.

I even came up to the country to visit more often after Dylan was born. I would have preferred to stay put in town, as the life bucolic affected me like chloroform and I could never get used to the sound of a moth hitting the bug zapper. It was like Lepke getting the chair. The truth was I made the drive to the country almost every weekend to play with Dylan and Moses, whom I had strong feelings for. I tried rekindling my boyhood love for rod and reel to help scotch the ennui up there, but I couldn't swing it. Still, I did teach Moses to fish and managed to fly-cast, happy I hadn't lost the old knack of placing my Royal Coachman somewhere up in the trees. Cement baby that I was, I screwed things up at Frog Hollow because when Mia bought the place, her good-sized pond was brimming with frogs who ate mosquitos and kept the place mosquito free. I, thinking I was doing her a favor, stocked the pond with bass. Who knew the bass would eat the frogs, and there was no one left to eat the mosquitos?

But all of that was before Mia's pregnancy. Now she wanted the key to her apartment back, and when I did come up weekends, she had become cooler and indifferent. My theory, which I've longwindedly come around to, is that I served my purpose knocking her up and had become irrelevant. I had once written a sketch where Louise and I play spiders. She is a black widow and I impregnate her and, as in nature, she then kills and eats me. Gee, I thought, reacting to Mia's behavior, you don't think—? When I made the trip to Connecticut to visit, Mia, who used to greet me, now rarely stopped whatever activity she was involved in to say hello.

The relationship, always civil, continued to ebb away in ever larger chunks, and in the city as well. The routine devolved into the following: I rise, about five thirty a.m. and walk across Central Park to her house by six thirty. I would have breakfast with Dylan and Moses and return home, dropping Dylan at school. I was Dylan's responsible parent, as was testified to in court by a teacher at Brearly. She swore I was the only parent who ever came to the parent-teacher conferences, while Mia didn't seem interested enough to show up. The teacher explained that only I attended all discussions of Dylan's marks and periodic reports on how she was doing. I would take Dylan to school, go home, and work. I would not see Mia all day unless we were filming, which was only about eight weeks a year.

The rest of the time I'd write at my penthouse and then go over to Mia's apartment at about six to sit with Dylan and Moses when they had dinner. I'd stay for another little while, maybe some chess with Moses, or make up tales to amuse Dylan. Then I'd say good night to Mia, who usually had retired early to her room, and I'd go meet my friends and we'd go to Elaine's for dinner. Every so often Mia and I might go out to dinner, but it had become increasingly rare. When Satchel was born, things took an even darker quantum leap. From his birth, Mia expropriated Satchel. She took him into her bedroom, her bed, and insisted on breast-feeding him. She kept telling me she intended to do it for years, and that anthropological studies have shown positive results from tribes where breast-feeding goes on much longer than on the Upper West Side. Years later, two very professional and perceptive women who worked in Mia's house, Sandy Boluch and Judy Hollister, the first as baby-sitter and the second as housekeeper, described numerous incidents. Sandy reports seeing Mia sometimes sleeping in the nude with Satchel (now Ronan) a number of times till he was eleven years old. I don't know what the anthropologists would say about that, but I can imagine what the guys in the poolroom would say.

Of course it was a little late for red flags by then. But here's not a red flag but a skull and crossbones that was hoisted loud and clear, and I was either too thick or too preoccupied with second-act problems to notice: Mia did not put my name on Satchel's birth certificate when he was born. Why would she leave it off? Why exclude me after all that heartfelt nonsense about wanting to have my child? Was he really not mine? Clearly I was being escorted out of the picture long before our dramatic breakup. Mia has tried to get around this scam by saying as we were not married, the hospital required that I sign a separate form. But she is not being truthful when she says she presented one to me which I gave to my lawyer and never returned. Clearly that makes no sense. I would have been happy to sign on as Satchel's father. I was looking forward to his birth, was in the delivery room holding Mia's hand when he popped out, named him Satchel, and would push later to be the legal father of Dylan and Moses. But Mia never told me it was required nor gave me any form to fill out. If she wanted me to be his father and gave me a form, she would have said, Hey—where's the form I gave you?

Anyhow, Mia was delirious with Satchel. She monopolized his time, and short of me forcing the issue, which could have led to some sort of custody proceeding where my position was quite vulnerable, he was rarely available. I say vulnerable because I had no legal claim to Dylan and Moses, and I could easily lose them if I pressed too hard for access to Satchel. I had my hands full trying to work around Mia's unnaturally obsessed behavior with our new son, which was worse than her lunacy with Fletcher. Fletcher by now was showing some academic problems, the result no doubt of his mother's willingness to let him go to school or stay home as he had wished.

As Satchel would get older and display high intelligence, he would eventually usurp Fletcher's position as the favorite. Mia had little parenting time left to spend on Moses and Dylan or any of the other kids. But then, they were adopted kids, and both Moses and Soon-Yi described the second-class citizenship of the adopted children. Fletcher and Matthew were both biological, and she adored them. Sascha, Matthew's twin, she favored least of the biological children and could speak derisively about him often. Once when he overheard her from the next room, he wept. As Soon-Yi pointed out, Mia enjoyed adopting, loved the excitement, like one buys a new toy; she liked the saintly reputation, the admiring publicity, but she didn't like raising the kids and didn't really look after them. I felt peculiar when it was designated to me to go before the press to try and downplay the embarrassment when some of her kids were busted for stealing. It is no wonder that two adopted children would be suicides. A third would contemplate it, and one lovely daughter who struggled with being HIV-positive into her thirties was left by Mia to die alone of AIDS in a hospital on Christmas morning.

I was, as my shrink pointed out, mainly a sponsor in the household. I had employed Mia for ten movies, hired her sister, hired her brother, hired her mother, given her a tax-free gift of a million dollars so she could better support all these poor kids, not just mine. Finally, I decided in a moment of clarity that not being the legal father to Dylan and Moses was just not acceptable. For years, I had assumed full responsibility for both of them as their father. They were by now my children, too, and if I was ever to voice my disapproval with the weird raising of Satchel, which I knew would cause Mia to erupt, I needed the legal clout of paternity for the other two. Interestingly, for someone who always wanted me to father her child, Mia was suddenly very cool to the idea of me adopting Dylan and Moses when I broached it. (At that point, I was completely unaware that I had been left off Satchel's birth certificate.) But Dylan and Moses loved me. Typically, one early morning I went to Mia's apartment, scooped up Dylan and Moses while Mia was forever alone with Satchel in the bedroom, doors shut, other kids left to their own devices. I took Dylan and Moses to my cutting room where I edit my movies. They could play while the editors and I cut. They loved the attention we all gave them, and playing with all the movie equipment and ordering food. Sometimes I would take Moses and Dylan to my apartment, and we'd play games or I'd do some magic tricks for them.

As time passed I tried my best to include Satchel in my parenting, but he was always harder to see. I saw him mostly evenings when I'd come over after work. Satchel was always very cute and smart, and Moses was as cute as they come, and until then, I always found little girls cuter than little boys. Probably because I was a little boy and grew up among little boys and knew that little boys grew up to be those creeps who used terms like "In my view" or "At this particular point in time," or telling you, "You have a nice portfolio." The boys I knew got into fights, started fires, played hooky, and got bad marks, while all the girls at P.S. 99 were clean and sweet and never gave a middle finger to any teacher and they all had such neat penmanship. Between being raised in a family of affectionate women with a close relationship to my older cousin and a good one with my younger sister, it's no wonder I've felt particularly comfortable directing women over the years. So many of the people I work with are women. My producers, editors, doctors, lawyers, assistants. But I've always had great affection for Moses and Satchel, even though I was forewarned not to get too close to Satchel.

And so I pushed Mia with the idea of me legally adopting Moses and Dylan. She was very wary, and it took her a long time to agree. But then one day she agreed. Don't know what prompted the change. Maybe she did the math in her head and saw some advantage in me becoming financially responsible for both of them. Maybe she wanted to keep things going on a low flame for work reasons, or possibly she wasn't as possessive regarding those two kids since they were not biological. Sometimes I think if you asked Mia then, she might very well have said she loved me, but if so it was delusional. If she loved me, she had a funny way of showing it; no intimacy, not much dining together, no traveling, no more house key, no interest if I visited in the summer, in fact a bit of an annoyance, civil but not warm, planning her future whether I fit in or not—I can go on. If Dylan and Moses hadn't existed, before Satchel was born I never would have gone over to her apartment anymore. There would have been no reason to.

The air was out of our relationship. Our lives had grown apart. We were social companions on those occasions where there'd be a dinner, an event, but after the event she'd go home and I'd go home. At one point, before Satchel was born, I wondered if maybe moving in together might work, since I visited twice daily to see Dylan and Moses, but neither of us really had much enthusiasm for that idea and it faded fast. I guess I thought living with Dylan and Moses would be fun, and maybe even Mia and I'd grow closer. I had learned nothing from my fiasco with Louise, and the reality was neither of us really wanted to live together. After a few weeks of speculation and even going through the motions of checking out some huge apartments, we both mercifully let the idea drop. With the birth of Satchel, she made it clear what a foolish fantasy the possibility of any deep relationship with her would have been. Anyhow, for reasons only God would know, she agreed finally to the adoption, and I became the legal dad for Dylan and Moses.

And now, before I get back to my movies, let me fill you in on how Soon-Yi and I went from two people who never particularly liked one another to a couple now married over twenty years and still passionately in love. Soon-Yi never knew her father in Korea, and her mother either couldn't afford to or didn't want to take care of her. She remembers herself as dirt poor. Rural life was a nightmare for Soon-Yi as a tiny child, and she ran away from home at age five and wandered the streets of Seoul like the urchins in Buñuel's *Los Olvidados*. She ate out of dumpsters and once was starving so badly she picked up a bar of soap from a trash can and tried to eat it. She was taken off the streets by nuns and wound up in an orphanage.

She spoke well of the orphanage to me. The nuns were kind to the kids. Then one day Mia showed up and adopted her. This was years before I knew Mia, but Soon-Yi remembers it well. Soon-Yi had no say in the matter. One would think of this as great good fortune but Soon-Yi, then seven, did not. She took an instant disliking to Mia, who showed up, plucked her from a life and friends she had gotten used to and liked, and showed no warmth nor empathy. Mia then took her out of an environment she had bonded with and on a tour of other orphanages, where Mia browsed for new orphans like one goes through the remaindered bins in a bookstore. Failing to find a human she fancied, Mia moved on. She took Soon-Yi to her hotel room and plunged her into a bathtub and left her there, alone. Soon-Yi had never been in a bathtub before, spoke no English, and didn't know what was going on. Mia was strict and impatient with a fierce temper. Over time, she tried to teach Soon-Yi English, not the easiest thing for an orphan to pick up overnight at seven. Mia would awaken Soon-Yi in the middle of the night to drill her and yell at her for not learning fast enough. Soon-Yi had trouble with English, and Mia would grow angry and frustrated. Later, she would punish Soon-Yi's inability to learn to spell faster by holding her upside down, dangling her, and threatening to put her into an insane asylum if she didn't learn quicker. At that point, Mia and her husband, André, were not getting along, and they had screaming fights that would wake Soon-Yi and terrify her.

Mia regarded Soon-Yi as hopelessly stupid. I recall once she spoke to me contemptuously of her soon after we met, saying Fletcher at four had a better brain than Soon-Yi at nine. Not really knowing any of the kids at all and assuming Mia was a supermom, as the press made her out to be, I listened in distracted agreement. But as I would later learn, Soon-Yi was not just a diamond in the rough but round cut and flawless. Nor was Mia a supermom or even a fit mom, and she never bothered to get to know her adopted daughter.

Mia never attempted to develop her. They started off living in London for the first two years in a lovely house (Soon-Yi took me to see it years later, and it was truly lovely) in a town about an hour out of London. Mia never had any interest in Soon-Yi, as she alone among the children had the temerity to challenge Mia's cruel authority. Despite the proximity to London, Mia never once took Soon-Yi to a show or a museum. This indifference in raising her continued in New York, where they moved eventually, and lived for years. On no single occasion in Manhattan did her mother ever take her to a movie, a show, a museum, or even for a walk in Central Park. She got no basic education, as Mia moved the kids around to suit her filming schedules. They got read to a bit but not much else. After London, Egypt, Bora Bora, Colorado, Los Angeles, Martha's Vineyard, all with no steady education, they settled on the Upper West Side, and Soon-Yi and her siblings were placed in some lightweight play school and then abruptly plunged into Ethical Culture, a high-end, competitive, and demanding school. Predictably, all the kids there had to be transferred because none could handle it. But Mia and Soon-Yi were always at odds. Like the other adopted girls, Soon-Yi was made to do chores, really her mother's responsibility. When my sister visited Mia's apartment because of the interaction, she thought Lark, another adopted daughter, was a servant and was surprised to hear she was family. Mia was indifferent to the real needs of the adopted kids.

Moses relates this harrowing tale: "Most media sources claimed my sister Tam died of 'heart failure' at the age of

21. In fact, Tam struggled with depression for much of her life, a situation exacerbated by my mother refusing to get her help, insisting that Tam was just 'moody.' One afternoon in 2000, after one fight with Mia, which ended with my mother leaving the house, Tam committed suicide by overdosing on pills. My mother would tell others that the drug overdose was accidental."

Years later in high school when Soon-Yi broke her ankle playing soccer, Mia didn't even bother to take her to the doctor but only told her to go by herself and not to get X-rays, as they cost too much. A high school girl in great pain from a broken ankle, Soon-Yi made her way to the doctor's office by herself on a bus and was frightened to allow the doctor to x-ray her ankle. Finally, the disbelieving doctor phoned her mother and insisted. She got the X-ray, but going against Mia's orders meant punishment, often being hit.

Soon-Yi saw this happening all around her. Mia didn't care enough to take Moses to the doctor or emergency rooms, and so Lark or Soon-Yi had to do it. Soon-Yi had to take her brother and little sisters to school on various buses every day at a very young age; she had to do all of Moses's therapy massages on his palsied leg nightly. Mia was proud to advertise herself as a mom willing to adopt a child with cerebral palsy, but the dedication and work involved fell to the other kids. When Soon-Yi went to look at colleges, Mia had no interest, didn't go with her, and let her go alone. Finally her friend's mother was so appalled by the neglect, she went with Soon-Yi to look at the schools. Mia never even bothered to attend her adopted son Thaddeus's graduation. According to Moses and corroborated by both the housekeeper Judy and the babysitter Sandy, she made

Thaddeus wear heavy iron leg braces for public appearances rather than his lighter plastic ones because the lighter ones were worn under the trousers and would not be seen by the press photographers, and Mia wanted it publicized that she adopted the disabled. The iron braces were visible to the camera, as they were worn outside the trousers. Thaddeus was the one she locked in the outdoor shed overnight. Is it surprising he committed suicide with a gun ten minutes from his mother's house? Mia acted surprised at Thaddeus's suicide, but the truth is he had attempted suicide six or seven years earlier by overdosing on medicines and had to be rushed to the hospital to have his stomach pumped.

I offer this background because when Soon-Yi went off with me, it was not simply a case of some ungrateful orphan betraying a kind and loving benefactress who had changed her life from rags to riches. And Soon-Yi's personality is large; she is not a shrinking violet. (She had to have some moxie to hit the streets and fend for herself at five. Could you? I couldn't. I was still being sung to sleep at five.) Soon-Yi was the one adopted child who stood up to Mia and incurred her wrath. Consequently she was hit—hit with a hairbrush, hit with a phone—and once Mia hurled a ceramic rabbit at her, barely missing her head. The tchotchke shattered into a million pieces in the room. The kids told me they loved it when I took Mia out to dinner and they were rid of her, free for a breather. A number of times Soon-Yi's sisters secretly came to me and asked if there was any way I could spring them from having to go to the country on the weekend as it meant chores for Lark, cooking, cleaning. It meant baby-sitting work and boredom for Soon-Yi, who wanted to be with her friends like any other teenager.

Soon-Yi and I had no interest in knowing about each other. I thought she was a quiet, boring kid, and she thought I was her mom's patsy. All that was missing was a ring through my nose. When we discussed it years later, I explained in my defense that whenever I came over to the apartment or visited the country house I saw no signs of turmoil or tyranny. Soon-Yi said it was a totally different ball game when I was not around, and that I was foolish to think Mia ever loved me, as she always had great romantic interest in her friend and neighbor, Mike Nichols. She was crushed and depressed when he remarried rather quickly after his divorce from Annabelle, his wife. Soon-Yi had me down for an unperceptive Ignatz who served Mia as a high-profile significant other and kept her career moving.

At any rate, for years I never gave Soon-Yi a moment's thought. I was too busy working. I acted in a film directed by Paul Mazursky called *Scenes from a Mall*. I heard it was a god-awful movie. I did it for two reasons. The first was the money, but the more important second reason was because I had great respect for and wanted to work with Paul Mazursky. I found him to be great fun to be around, a terrific storyteller, fine director, and nice man. I got to work with Bette Midler, whom I liked. We shared the same birthday along with Richard Pryor. (Means nothing unless you're a horoscope loon.) Bette was fun and nice, and she had a tiny little daughter who grew up to be a fine actress. I used Sophie in *Irrational Man* and even lengthened her role because I thought she had a real acting talent. Mazursky had just come off an Oscar-winning project, but with me and Bette, for whatever reason, the movie rocketed directly into the bathroom plumbing. And I didn't think we acted badly—but who knows? I never saw it.

And after that, I was busy directing *Shadows and Fog*, a film I knew was destined for commercial doom but you can't let those things scare you or you'll keep doing safe middle-of-the-road projects. My movie was set in Germany in around the twenties or thirties, and Carlo Di Palma shot it in black-and-white. Santo Loquasto built the biggest set ever made at the Kaufman Astoria Studios in Queens and the whole picture, the exteriors and interiors, were all shot indoors. That's how the Germans often did it in the UFA days, and I wanted that look. It was an existential murder story, and you should have seen the faces of the Orion suits at the first viewing when the lights came up. They expected a conventional serial killer story, but a comic one. Instead, they got my personal take on life and death employing a grim but hopefully amusing metaphor. To say the movie tanked at the box office would be describing it through rose-colored glasses. It's not a bad idea but you have to be in the mood for it, and marketing tests showed it did not appeal to homo sapiens.

After that I shot one of the best films I ever made— in my opinion. I decided when I finished writing *Husbands and Wives* that I'd shoot the movie predominantly handheld and obey no rules of filmmaking. I'd cut when I felt like it, not worrying about people facing the right direction, I'd jump-cut and go for the opposite of pretty or well-made.

It came out to be a good film, I thought—and I'm not easy on my work. It was somewhere on the project, either the writing, the preproduction, or the shooting, that things started to warm up between Soon-Yi and me. Earlier, I had

243

taken her to a basketball game as I had season tickets. Once or twice I remarked to Mia how reclusive Soon-Yi seemed and maybe she needed a shrink. Mia said, "Why don't you go for a walk with her or take her to a basketball game? You're always looking for someone to go with."

It was true. I owned four season tickets to Madison Square Garden and sometimes had no one around who shared my interest. I finally asked Soon-Yi if she liked basketball. She liked it well enough to say yes, probably figuring it was free popcorn. And so I did take her to a game and, awkward as it was, I confronted her about the fact that we never got along and said it seemed that she didn't like me. She assured me that it wasn't so much that she didn't like me but thought I was a featherbrain, her mother's lollipop, sleepwalking through an embarrassing hustle obvious as the Turk con. Clearly, she had no trouble volunteering her candid opinion of me, and I resisted the temptation to pierce her superior judgment with my rapier wit. She felt her mother had treated me like a veritable cat's paw, and I was a consummate sap for not getting it. I soon learned she and Mia didn't get along, and life at their home was quite different when I was not present. I began to realize this was not an empty young woman as Mia had painted her but quite an intelligent, feeling, perceptive one. It was the start of a friendship that would slowly grow over time and climax with the preposterous realization that we cared a great deal about each other. It took a long, long time to move from square one to this mutual caring, but it would happen and surprise us both.

Still, despite an unexpected nice time at that first basketball game, I was too busy to even think about anything but movies. In spite of her mother calling people and insisting Soon-Yi was "retarded," she graduated from college, got her master's at Columbia, worked, and raised a family, but that all comes later. Meanwhile, Mia and I were still droning along thanks to that reliable all-purpose waterproof adhesive, Inertia. As much as I nosed around trying to see if I could pick up on the darker side of Mia's behavior, apart from her obsession with Satchel I never saw her beating anybody or throwing any fits. It was OK for me as I liked seeing my kids, however limited, and working, playing jazz. My little jazz band, which Soon-Yi likens to Ralph Kramden's Raccoon Lodge, was great fun.

If I had met any interesting women, I was very ripe for the plucking, and there came a time down the line when Soon-Yi, in town from college, was going to accompany me to a basketball game again. I looked forward to seeing her, catching up, exchanging intimate confessions and laughs. As we chatted at the game, I found I was enjoying her company more than I should have. I asked her about her mother saving her, and wasn't an apartment on Central Park West and a country home and a private school a much better deal than an orphanage? No, she said. She preferred the nuns.

By now the Knicks were losing, and my attention was needed on the court to jinx the other team. I took her home, dropped her off in front of her apartment building, and sped off into the night, thinking that I'd had a really nice evening for the first time in a while and she was an amazing young woman who had been through a lot. Most of what she said about her mother caused me to twig on the early red flags, which billowed feverishly in the turbulent winds of retrospect, if you'll excuse my bid for a National Book Award.

All I know is I took her to another basketball game and despite that famous photo in which it looks like we're holding hands, I never took her hand. First, I didn't have that kind of relationship with her at that point—and if I had, I never in a million years would have done anything in public, much less in the brightly lit, packed arena of Madison Square Garden. My death wish did not extend that far. We chatted and had another very nice time. As we had gotten on the subject of movies, I asked her if she knew the movies of Ingmar Bergman (always searching for that perfect woman into Swedish films). She did not, and as I waxed euphoric over his work, it was decided I would set up a screening of *The Seventh Seal* for her at my screening room. This was me being romantic—*The Seventh Seal*.

I have a screening room where I edit my movies. The editor and I edit the movie, then go into the other room and screen it, hate it, return to the editing machine and reedit it. Now, who can say I'm not a fun guy? A young, attractive girl in from college—what could be more enjoyable than seeing a black-and-white film set in medieval Scandinavia dealing with the plague, death, and the emptiness of life? She was game, even eager to see it. And so we decided I'd screen it some afternoon when she'd be in town.

Cut to sometime later. I'm shooting *Husbands and Wives*, and on a Saturday when I'm off, Soon-Yi comes in from college and I screen *The Seventh Seal*. Bergman's film ends, and we're alone in my screening room and I'm giving my pedantic lecture on Kierkegaard and the Knight of Reason and she's listening dutifully, trying to keep her eyes open, and quite smoothly if I do say so myself, I lean in and kiss her without knocking over anything. I brace myself for a bolo punch, the specialty of Kid Gavilan, the immortal ex-welterweight champion. But it doesn't come. Instead, she is complicit in the osculation and, to the point as always, says, "I was wondering when you were going to make a move."

Make a move? Gimme a break. I'm still in some version of a relationship with your mother. True, for the past years we've just been going through the motions, but what are we getting into? But it was of no use. We were attracted to one another in a way that would end up in a long and great marriage, and here are the awful details of what ensued.

While I was filming the movie *Husbands and Wives*, Soon-Yi and I started an affair. An affair that began the next time she came in from college. Passionate from that day on, it has resulted now in many happy years and a wonderful family. Who would have predicted? I only knew she was not the nonentity her mother had dismissed and written off. How wrong Mia was. Here was a sharp, classy, fabulous young woman; highly intelligent, full of latent potential, and ready to ripen superbly if only someone would show her a little interest, a little support, and, most important, some love. We spent a few afternoons walking and talking, delighting in each other's company and, of course, going to bed.

We were sitting around my apartment one weekend afternoon, and I had been given a Polaroid camera for a present from someone who didn't know I had no interest in cameras. People always gave me Polaroids thinking they were so easy to work, even I could do it. I joked about me and any kind of gadget, and one thing led to another with storm clouds gathering outside my penthouse window.

At the very early stages of our new relationship, when lust reigns supreme and we couldn't keep our hands off each other, the idea arose that we do some erotic photographs if I could figure out how to work the goddamned camera. Turned out she could work it, and erotic photos they were, shots well calculated to boost one's blood up to two twelve Fahrenheit. Anyhow, you probably read the rest in the tabloids. Mastermind that I was, I sequestered the photos in a drawer—but as it turned out, not all the provocative little snapshots.

A number of them I had brilliantly put on my fireplace mantel as the Kodak squeezed them out. The mantel was eye level, maybe a soupçon higher, so when this epic photo shoot was over moments later, the ones on the mantel remained there, out of sight and out of mind, while the remainder were safely salted away. They say if Napoleon had been a few inches taller, the history of Europe would've been radically different. Well, if I had been an inch or two taller, just able to see over my fireplace mantel, carnage on a par with the Napoleonic wars might not have occurred in Manhattan. Yes, a number were right up there for the casual browser to enjoy, but I lived alone. Still, I am not the kind of guy that can bring off an affair. Too much of a schlepper. Would Clark Gable or Cary Grant leave such incriminating photos right out on the mantel? Only a bumbler, all thumbs, a Jerry Lewis. True, I had a housekeeper who cleaned and dusted, and she might have discovered them while searching for fresh items to break, but I'm sure that, being French, she would have shuffled through them with continental sophistication and merely given me a Madame Claude wink. The life-changing glitch came the following day, when Satchel was brought over to my apartment, as he was each week to have a private session with a child psychiatrist to address some personal issues. Sometimes Mia would bring him to these meetings.

Invariably she'd sit in the living room reading while he was taken by the shrink to another part of the fairly large penthouse to go over his problems. After an hour he'd be marched back in to his mother. Anyhow, this Monday the boy was a minute or two late ending his treatment, and his mother impatiently wandered into the other part of the house to see what was keeping him and her eyes roamed over the fireplace mantel where she discovered the group of Polaroids that would be heard 'round the world.

Of course I understand her shock, her dismay, her rage, everything. It was the correct reaction. Soon-Yi and I thought we could have our little fling, keep it a secret, since Soon-Yi wasn't living at home and I lived alone like a bachelor. I thought it would have been a nice experience, and probably Soon-Yi would eventually meet some guy at college and enter a more conventional relationship. I didn't realize how attached to one another we'd already grown. It had started slowly, but once it hit it was the real thing. Were it not for the discovery of the photos, who knows how long the burned-out, convenient regimen with me visiting the kids at Mia's apartment would have lasted? Of course, sooner or later one of us would've been gone as it was definitely over in spirit, if not routine. Soon-Yi said her mother had expressed wishes she could've moved on to some other man years ago. As stated, Mike Nichols was a frequent fantasy. Did I leave the photos exposed to bring the enervated relationship with Mia to a head on purpose? Was it my way of causing a breakup without really realizing it? It was not. It was simply a blunder by a klutz. Sometimes, a cigar is just a blunder by a klutz.

Psychiatrists say in times of crisis one becomes who one is only more so. The day Mia discovered the affair, she called all her kids together and spared them nothing. After explaining that I had raped Soon-Yi—which led Satchel, aged four, to tell people "my father's fucking my sister"— she called people and told them I'd raped her underage, retarded daughter. She then locked Soon-Yi in her bedroom, hit her and kicked her, and she and André cut off her college tuition. She then phoned me in the middle of the night several times to tell me Soon-Yi was awash in guilt and thinking of committing suicide. She's a good actress, and when you're awakened at 3 a.m. and a hysterical woman is telling you someone is suicidal, it's unnerving. Soon-Yi was of course not allowed to use the phone, and this was pre–cell phone days. On the advice of a well-known psychiatrist neighbor, Mia was persuaded to send Soon-Yi to a reputable head doctor. Once out of the house, Soon-Yi called me and said of course she was not suicidal and didn't regret a second we'd spent together, but Mia had her locked up and was violent periodically. Sidebar: Mia hit her with a phone.

When Soon-Yi described it in an interview she did years later with *New York* magazine, the magazine asked her if there were witnesses. I thought, right—in the bedroom of Mia's apartment, there were pedestrians, construction workers, a bus tour of out-of-towners, the Mormon Tabernacle Choir, there's always a big turnout in Soon-Yi's bedroom. The magazine, not looking for trouble, watered down Soon-Yi's account and wrote Mia slapped her. But she hit her with a phone. Sidebar to the sidebar: Daphne Merkin, who wrote the story on Soon-Yi for *New York* magazine, relates how Ronan phoned the magazine prior to the story coming out and pressed them to drop it. They wouldn't but he pressured them, and so they softened it in a number of places in ways that might not offend the Farrows. Example: Daphne and I saw each other for a lunch perhaps once a year if that, but the magazine made up that we were close friends, so it appeared she could be prejudiced in my favor. And I already gave you the watering-down of the being hit with a telephone. They also had planned to put the story on the cover but dropped it after the phone call from Ronan. Is this not the quintessence of hypocrisy when Ronan writes a book critical of NBC for trying to kill his story on Harvey Weinstein? But, I guess whatever works.

OK—why didn't I just say to Soon-Yi, Bail and come to live with me? Because visitation and custody of my children was a real issue, and on a lawyer's advice I had to be very careful till that issue was resolved. I was trying to balance Soon-Yi's problems with my own, with Dylan, Moses, and Satchel, whom Mia had possession of, complete control over, and a willingness to use them as pawns if and when necessary. I advised Soon-Yi to "hang in," which translated means I have no idea how to handle this yet and can only say when Mia tries to hit you, duck.

All this was taking place over just a few short weeks. After Soon-Yi had an introductory session with this very fine New York psychoanalyst, Mia was asked to meet with him. The doctor only needed one session with Mia to see what an unhinged and dangerous woman she was and instantly intervened to protect Soon-Yi. First, he asked me to put money in the bank to ensure Soon-Yi's college education. Of course I did. She'd be able to return to Drew despite her mother's cutting off her tuition. The psychiatrist felt it was urgent Soon-Yi should get away from her mother. Fortuitously Soon-Yi's brother had worked at a summer camp, and Mia began insisting Soon-Yi get a job there. It was in Maine, and Mia felt she would be safely away from me, whereas Soon-Yi's shrink thought she would be safely away from Mia. The fact was, however, Soon-Yi and I loved one another and we spoke on the phone, and the camp told Mia. It wasn't long before Mia was raging more volcanically than ever, and Soon-Yi hated the camp and the freezing nights in Maine. She came back to New York, not daring to go home, and moved in with a friend whose mother had always been more of a caring person to Soon-Yi than her own apathetic mother.

She put Soon-Yi up for a while, and it wasn't long before we were back together. We didn't want her to live with me because I was enmeshed in negotiations for visitation or custody of the kids, and it would have been impossible to maneuver in court if we were living together. Mia knew we were in love, and while lawyers postured and threatened I saw the kids in the most meager, distorted way. I did have a legal claim—but more potent than a legal claim, Mia had possession. Fantasies of kidnapping them, gathering up Soon-Yi, and sailing to the South Seas to live on mangoes and coconuts crossed my mind, but just taking them to the Papaya stand on Eighty-Sixth Street was more practical. It was around that time Mia made that infamous, chilling call to my sister. She told her, "He took my daughter, now I'll take his."

What she seemed to mean was that knowing how much I loved Dylan, she was embarking on a plan to see to it I would not be able to see her anymore. Dylan's feelings wouldn't matter. The loss of her father, whom she loved, wouldn't matter. She would be used to exact revenge. Mia's ugly plan would take some doing, but was it already forming in her mind? Another vituperative call, this time to me, ended with "I have something planned for you." I joked that placing a bomb under the hood of my car was not a proportionate response. She said, "It's worse." She was so raging and incoherent on those vicious calls, which would come any hour of the day and night, that I'm surprised she was in control enough to plan a strategy more complex than ringing my bell and running.

Attempts to deescalate the situation did not work, and I guess it's easy for me to say as she was the hurt party, but where she took this rage crossed the line from understandable to unforgivable and then to unconscionable. Not only was it malignant to me but horrendous for poor Dylan, who had just turned seven and was too young to have any perspective. Nor was she caring of any effects on her prized son, Satchel, who was taught to hate his rapist father from the age of four. Moses was already a teenager and not as easy to manipulate. Though past the vulnerable age of brainwashing, his loyalty at that point was ambivalently to his mother. I vainly kept trying to employ reason; our relationship had fizzled, we had not been intimate for years, Soon-Yi was not a child but a college student, she was clearly not retarded, not underage, yes it was messy but couldn't we try and solve the mess I admittedly caused by calming down and trying to explain things to the kids who would certainly be better off if talked to properly and not inflamed or frightened? Isn't crying rape a little hysterical? Does it help to tell people she's underage when she's not? And why threaten to "take my daughter"? Should the kids be used to wreak vengeance? Do you really want to deprive Dylan of her father to punish me? Are there no limits to your vengeance?

And what is this awful thing you have planned for me? Is there no way we can cool this down and do what's best for the kids? About my love of Soon-Yi, Moses said, "The kids recognized it as unorthodox, but the relationship itself was not nearly as devastating to our family as my mother's insistence on making this betrayal the center of all our lives from then on."

I visited Mia's country home one early summer Saturday to see the kids for a barbecue. This was a temporarily negotiated right. I, of course, didn't sleep in the same room as Mia but on a different floor in a different section of the house in a guest room. Whatever festivities or frankfurters occurred, I roamed around trying to enjoy my few moments with Dylan, Moses, and, if possible, Satchel. I returned to my room to find a note Mia had pinned to my bedroom door. It read: "Child molester at the barbecue. Molested one daughter, now after another." I knew Mia was fond of telling people I had molested her underage daughter when in fact Soon-Yi was twenty-two, and of course our love, which has resulted in a marriage of over twenty years, was hardly molestation. Remember this ugly note, she pinned to my door, was prior to any suggestion of abuse. Was she laying the groundwork for what would be a frame-up? I assumed from the note she was mentally out of control, and it never occurred to me I was being set up for a false accusation. Who thinks that way? A few weeks after the looney note, still prior to any allegation, she phoned Susan Coates, Dylan's doctor, and said, "He must be stopped." Doctor Coates warned me about it and testified in my behalf at the hearing. In hindsight (which I'm good at), it's obvious a false accusation of molestation was to be her worse-than-killing-me plan.

So August 4, 1992, I float up to Connecticut to see my kids as haggled by our lawyers. It's an uneventful after-noon. Mia goes out shopping while I watch a little TV with a room full of people all warned to keep an eye on me. (Read Moses's account. He was there.) I wander to the pool alone while they continue to watch, I make a phone call or two to kill time. Soon, Mia comes back. It is determined that I will stay over in her guest room, and Mia and I will have dinner later to discuss more details of custody and visitation. Soon, the sun goes down and night falls in the country, and I check to make sure Mia casts a reflection in the mirror. We go to have a quick bite to eat in town. The atmosphere is, shall we say, frosty. All that's missing is me turning my back and her emptying the contents of her ring in my drink. Talk is sparse but civil. Nothing brilliant from me, no Joan Crawford moments from her. Back to the house. Me to my isolated quarters, nodding off while clutching the fireplace poker in the event Dick or Perry should show up or even Mia, who I recalled had given me a hostile Valentine's card with an actual, terrifying kitchen knife stuck viciously through the heart. Next morning I rise, have breakfast, spend an hour with Dylan and Satchel while they deliriously check off every toy in a catalog they would like me to bring next time I come up. It was a great morning for the three of us. Who knew it would be the last? Anyhow, I go back to the city, I resume my life, mosquito free and mercifully on concrete. No more bearded fescue for a while.

The next day I went for a scheduled visit with Susan Coates, Dylan's shrink, who I was conferring with to try and navigate the waters and do what was best for the kids. She broke the news to me that I was being accused of molestation and she had to report it. It was the law.

I was dumbfounded and couldn't believe it. I thought the whole notion was preposterous. I said no problem, report it. Coates would testify that unlike actual predators I made no attempt to dissuade her from reporting it. That was because I hadn't done anything and assumed no sane person would take the idea of me molesting anybody seriously.

What had happened was that during my visit, while Mia had gone shopping, after explaining to everyone that I had to be watched carefully, all the kids and the babysitters were in the den watching TV, a room full of people. There were no seats for me, so I sat on the floor and might have leaned my head back on the sofa on Dylan's lap for a moment. I certainly didn't do anything improper to her. I was in a room full of people watching TV midafternoon. Alison, the nervous babysitter for Mia's friend's children—prompted by Mia to be hypervigilant—reported to her employer, Casey, that at one point I had my head on Dylan's lap. Even if so, it was utterly harmless and totally appropriate. No one said I molested Dylan, but when Casey phoned Mia the following day and said her babysitter reported my head was on Dylan's lap, Mia ran to Dylan. According to Monica, the nanny, she said, "I've got him." The head on the lap would over time somehow metamorphosize into my molesting her in the attic, but that reenactment of Dory Previn's song scenario would come later.

At that point, the thought I might need a criminal lawyer would never have blipped anywhere on my radar scope. I had a domestic lawyer who was up and back with Mia's lawyer often, but it never occurred to me for a New York second that a totally nonexistent event, obviously made up by a woman who deeply sought vengeance, would turn into an international cavalcade, an industry that would cost millions and millions of dollars and touch many lives.

Incidentally, I had been the victim of a false accusation once before when I was in my twenties, and if the Mia one was March Hare time—get this: I'm twenty-five. I'm working as a comedian. Suddenly, I get a call from my manager that a woman is suing me. She claims I'm Ferdinand Goglia. Who, you ask? Ferdinand Goglia, her long-lost husband. Suddenly, I'm being served papers by Mrs. Goglia. She saw me on TV, my manager says, and claims I'm her husband who abandoned her. You must be kidding, I reply, while cumulonimbus clouds gather just above my head. No, says my manager, she says Ferdinand, a garage mechanic, always made the same jokes as you did when she saw you on TV and he has ducked out on her and you're him with the same glasses and you owe her a bundle of back alimony. (I told you this was nuts. I'm Ferdinand Goglia?)

Meanwhile, as the screwball suit is for real, the flag over at Becker and London, my attorney's firm, gets thrown and my salary starts ticking away. I have to go to court to defend myself. Believe it or not, I have to prove I'm not Ferdinand

Goglia and that I was never married to Annabel Goglia. It seems outlandish. I can tell my lawyer is wondering if it's possible the woman is telling the truth. Could I have been married to her under a different name and did I skip out? my lawyer asks Jack Rollins. My manager calms my lawyer down, assuring him I am not the lammister spouse here accused, but even he is operating on faith. For all Jack Rollins really knows of my past life, I could be a deceptive deadbeat. So what saved me after months and much precious specie doled out to my legal beagles? Only that the woman was truly loony tunes, and when I showed up in court (trying not to dress in anything like I imagined Ferdinand Goglia would wear), she failed to show. We came with all the evidence we could muster, and it was finally deemed by the court I was not Annabel's ex, who was much older than me and who fled her and no wonder. She was batty, and thank God she never resurfaced.

So, back to my latest surreal adventure. Try and imagine where I'm coming from here. I never laid a finger on Dylan, never did anything to her that could be even misconstrued as abusing her; it was a total fabrication from start to finish, every subatomic particle of it, no different from I'm the Goglia character. The sheer illogic seemed to me dispositive. I mean, it makes no sense why a fifty-seven-year-old man who has never been accused of a single impropriety in his life, while in the midst of a contentious and very public custody fight, drives up to the hostile environment of the country home belonging to the woman who hates him most, and in a house full of people sympathetic to her, this man, who is thrilled as he has just recently found the serious love of his life, a woman he'd go on to marry and have a family with, would suddenly choose that time and place to become a child molester and abuse his seven-year-old daughter whom he loved. It defied simple common sense. Especially since I had been alone with Dylan many times in my apartment over the years, and if I were actually a fiend, I had ample opportunities to act like one. Yet it makes perfect sense for the angry woman who had announced she would take away my daughter and had a plan worse than death for me, to resort to the single most common cliché of custody warfare, accusing the spouse of abusing the child.

And yet, despite the obviousness of it all, it soon became clear that this bubbe-meise, which never occurred anywhere in space-time and had now swung into ham-fisted action, would not vanish but would blossom into, as I said, an industry. Did it not look suspicious to anyone that it was Mia who brought the molestation idea to Dylan? Dylan did not come to her mother and say she had been touched. Mia came over to Dylan and suggested it to her. Dylan denied it. Mia needed to get her to change her denial. She took her to the doctor, in search of something she could use as evidence. The doctor asked Dylan if she had been abused. Dylan said no. Mia took her "for ice cream" and returned to the doctor's office, where the seven-year-old had somehow changed her story.

We see this pattern repeated over and over, as Moses has so vividly described. That is, being coached, threatened, even beaten, to learn to recite false stories as Mia dictates them. Moses's harrowing account confirms this. "One summer when the wallpaper was being redone," Moses writes, "I was getting ready to go to sleep, when my mother came over to my bed and found a tape measure. She gave me a piercing look…and asked if I had taken it, as she had been looking for it all day. I stood in front of her, frozen. She asked why it was on my bed. I told her I didn't know, that perhaps a workman had left it there. She asked again and again. When I didn't give the answer she wanted, she slapped my face, knocking off my glasses. She told me I was lying and directed me to tell my brothers and sisters that I had taken the tape measure. Through my tears I listened to her as she explained that we would rehearse what should have happened. She would walk into the room and I would tell her I was sorry for taking the tape measure, that I had taken it to play with and that I would never do it again. She made me rehearse it at least a half-dozen times. That was the start of her coaching, drilling, scripting, and rehearsing—in essence, brainwashing."

Mia then subjected Dylan to taping her naked over a period of a few days to try to get her to tell the story Mia had made up. And failing to create a tape that convinced anybody—in fact, it backfired and showed up Mia's mail-fisted coaching technique—in desperation, she allowed material that only she had possession of to magically find its way up to Fox News. A self-serving though not very maternal exploitation of her naked seven-year-old.

Moses recalls, "It was [the nanny] Monica who later testified that she saw Mia taping Dylan describe how Woody had supposedly touched her in the attic, saying it took Mia two or three days to make the recording. In [Monica's] testimony she said, 'I recall Ms. Farrow saying to Dylan at the time, "Dylan, what did Daddy do…and what did he do next?" Dylan appeared not to be interested, and Ms. Farrow would stop taping for a while and then continue.' I can vouch for

this, having witnessed some of this process myself. When another one of Dylan's therapists, Dr. Nancy Schultz, criticized
the making of the video, and questioned the legitimacy of
the content, she too was fired immediately by Mia." Again,
common sense: Why would a mother subject a seven-year-
old daughter to a prolonged naked taping of what, if true,
would be a traumatic experience, except to create a spec-
tacle in an attempt to harm the father? So isn't it obvious
what was going on? Did it even need an investigation?

And yet it had not one but two major investigations.
One by the Child Sexual Abuse Clinic at the Yale–New
Haven Hospital, whom the police used to look into such
matters, and one by New York State Child Welfare. Unlike
so many women who complained of sexual misconduct
only to have their complaints swept under the rug and not
taken seriously, Mia's accusation was taken most seriously.
It would be followed up on by the law, investigated by a
few groups of experts, including the most renowned one in
the country, the above-mentioned Yale–New Haven Child
Sexual Abuse Clinic whom the police hired. I quote their
written conclusion:

"It is our expert opinion that Dylan was not sexually
abused by Mr. Allen. Further, we believe that Dylan's statements on videotape and her statements to us during our
evaluation do not refer to actual events that occurred to her
on August 4, 1992...In developing our opinion, we considered three hypotheses to explain Dylan's statements. First,
that Dylan's statements were true and that Mr. Allen had
sexually abused her; second, that Dylan's statements were
not true but were made up by an emotionally vulnerable
child who was caught up in a disturbed family and who was

responding to the stresses in the family; and third, that Dylan was coached or influenced by her mother, Ms. Farrow.

"While we can conclude that Dylan was not sexually abused, we cannot be definitive about whether the second formulation by itself or the third formulation by itself is true. We believe that it is more likely that a combination of these two formulations best explain Dylan's allegations of sexual abuse."

Is this a good moment to point out the reason Dylan was taken by Mia to see a pediatric shrink long before any of this occurred was that Dylan had serious problems telling the difference between reality and fantasy? I mean, how could her mom have an easier mark to convince she was abused? A little girl, just turned seven, who has been in treatment because under normal circumstances she has problems telling what's real from what's fantasy, is taken from a loving father forever, placed in the hands of her out-of-control mother during an emotionally confusing crisis, suggested to by her mother that she was abused, then her denials are finessed over years of contact with only one parent and she is taught, led over time, to believe she has been molested. I did not suggest this story of Mia coaching. It was a conclusion the Yale investigation brought up.

In addition to the Yale investigation, the molestation accusation was dismissed by New York State Child Welfare investigators who examined the case scrupulously for fourteen months, and came to the following conclusion. From the letter received on October 7, 1993, I quote: "No credible evidence was found that the child named in this report has been abused or maltreated. This report has, therefore, been considered unfounded."

But prior to these reports coming out, a custody hearing was set up in court. There are still people who think the custody hearing was some kind of trial and somehow I beat some imaginary rap. There are still loonies who think I married my daughter, who think Soon-Yi was my child, who think Mia was my wife, who think I adopted Soon-Yi, who think that Obama wasn't American. But there was never any trial. I was never charged with anything, as it was clear to the investigators nothing had ever occurred.

What followed over the next months was a feeding frenzy and a dumb waste of money, mostly mine. Psychiatrists were interviewed, pediatricians, private detectives were hired, publicists had their day, the tabloids cleaned up. The custody hearing went before Judge Eliot Wilk, who hated me from the minute he set eyes on me, and who could blame him? From his perspective a wonderful, beautiful mother who adopted disabled children trusted a slimy, scheming boyfriend, a roué who seduced her daughter thirty-five years younger than him, and exploited the poor college student for pornographic photos. All that's missing from his picture of me is a dungeon in my basement where I kept co-eds chained to the wall. One could understand Judge Wilk's first impression, an impression he would never rise above despite all evidence to the contrary. Wilk was a political liberal who at one time had a photo of Che Guevara on his wall. I later discovered he was not quite the noble protector of women he played at for Mia's approval. In fact, if trying to take sexual advantage of a woman based on the superior inequality of one's position is harassment, Wilk would be sweating it out before the #MeToo bench. He and I did not like each other and neither tried to hide it, which was not to my advantage in a battle where he is the decider. I didn't endear myself to him when I was quoted in the press saying, "This case needs a Solomon, unfortunately we got Roy Bean."

Not long after the custody hearing Wilk died of a brain tumor, which was ironic as I was asked early on in the proceedings, by a magazine, if losing the custody of the children wasn't the worst thing that could happen to me, and I said no, the worst thing would be getting an inoperable brain tumor. This honest reply did not sit well with the righteous, who felt I was casting doubt on my devotion as a parent. Nevertheless, I wasn't lying. Then what happens? The poor judge gets just that. A fatal brain tumor. I hated the judge but felt bad when I heard he was diagnosed so tragically. Harsher ones around me were less moved by his plight and quipped it was the only time in his career justice was actually served. I couldn't bring myself to see it as a proportional response by fate despite all the trouble he had caused.

The public also jumped on me when in discussing my love for Soon-Yi, I said the heart wants what it wants. They found it selfish, but few if anyone realized I was simply quoting Saul Bellow quoting Emily Dickinson, not actually describing a philosophy of my own. Anyhow, Wilk's irresponsible mischief extended much beyond my experience with him. A child shrink told me the worst cases of suffering for kids he dealt with inevitably came from bad judgment in the Wilk court. Another weeping mother told me Wilk had ruled against her because she had to postpone a court date to attend her child's birthday and he wouldn't hear of it. Another woman told me he ruled for her but refused to ever enforce his ruling, so it was as if she'd lost the case. Finally, the gifted still photographer Lynn Goldsmith told me this story. She had been before Judge Wilk in a case where he ruled in her favor. A day later he showed up at her apartment unannounced and tried to sleep with her. When she resisted and pointed out he was married, it did not matter. He persisted. She finally got rid of him. Talk about exploiting one's status. But that's the kind of man I was at the mercy of. Still, when the Yale investigation concluded that Mia had likely coached Dylan and no molestation had taken place, I felt he should've at least taken a fairer look at things. Clearly though, he was profoundly disappointed in the results of the investigation and squirmed to find some face-saving angle, finally criticizing Yale for destroying their notes. As it turned out, that was Yale's and FBI's standard procedure to protect privacy, and one can only imagine if Yale had concluded I molested Dylan, the fact that they destroyed their notes would have been a nonissue, and he would have had the report reprinted in gold leaf editions.

The police case was headed by Frank Maco, who hired Yale. Dr. Coates, Dylan's shrink, thought the Connecticut Police were anti-Semitic, a card I never liked to play. While she was in Connecticut being interviewed, one of the police told her, "Miss Farrow did what she should have done when the girl was abused. She rebaptized all the children." Poor Maco must have been crushed when Yale concluded no molestation took place. To go to court with such a high-profile case would've made his career, but not if he lost it, and when reality set in, he sadly had to grasp that any fantasies he might have had of using the Farrow case to advance his dreams of glory were out the window. He kept the case open for months, all during the custody hearing, which served no purpose except as a big help to Mia's side. But why? What was in it for him to hurt me? When the aforementioned Sandy Boluch and Judy Hollister worked in Mia's house at the time, they individually described how Maco would show up unannounced now and then, reeking of cheap cologne (their words), and that Mia would dress up and make up and go out to lunch with him. This was apparently Maco's idea of conducting an impartial, unprejudiced investigation.

No question it was curious when Maco finally dropped the case and said he could have pursued it but didn't want to upset Dylan. A number of lawyers told me that was not very ethical, and there was an article in the *New York Times* that agreed, calling Maco's behavior a violation of my civil liberties. That trying to keep alive the question of my innocence or guilt (though it had been concluded there had been no molestation) was a gift to Mia is undeniable. But let's be honest—you really think he finally closed the case because he didn't want to hurt Dylan? This excuse by a clown who subjected the poor seven-year-old to police interviews, who never said anything about Mia taping her naked, and never squawked when Supermom dragged Dylan to a doctor who knocked the poor kid unconscious with an anesthetic so she could have her probed vaginally in search of any morsel of evidence, but of course nothing was found. I feel reasonable people might disagree that it was concern for Dylan that caused District Attorney Maco to let his case fade away.

The truth was, Maco was a sad schlemiel who I believed

would have given his right arm and both of Dylan's to prosecute had he the slightest chance of a win. Of course, when
the very investigating experts you yourself hire come back
and conclude nothing ever happened, that the girl was very
inconsistent, told the investigators at one point she was not
molested and not in the attic with her father, and appeared
to be perhaps coached by her mother, the chances of a
conviction lose a certain gale force. He had curried favor
with Mia, who could charm the most sophisticated men
much less a buffoon who might have fantasized he would
be her knight and savior. And finally, if you don't believe
me, here's what Judge Wilk wrote regarding Maco's claim
that he had cause to prosecute: "The evidence suggests that
it is unlikely that [Allen] could be successfully prosecuted
for sexual abuse."

During the court procedure, I was so naïve. I assumed
if you perjured yourself you went to jail, but it didn't
seem to matter when people were exposed in court as liars.
Mia would swear under oath I was and had been seeing a
psychiatrist because of inappropriate relations with young
girls. When that was completely disproven, there was no
penalty for lying. One person told of Dylan grabbing my
thumb on an occasion and sucking it. (Moses says in all his
years around us both he never once saw anything like it.
Of course he didn't, because it never happened.) Nevertheless, even that fabrication is a far cry from the lie Ronan
concocted when he wrote years later that I would force my
thumb into her mouth. How about when Mia's myrmidons
contacted Stacey Nelkin and asked her flat-out if she'd lie
and say she was underage when we went out. Of course,
she wouldn't.

Here's one amusing highlight: Mia's team comes in and accuses me of recently using call girls for illicit sex. Anything to paint me as a sleazeball. I deny it; they claim they have proof. I still deny it but I can see my lawyers look at one another, wondering if I'm being honest with them. The bad guys send their proof. Photocopies of a credit card with my name on it for a number of escorts and massage virtuosos. I hold to my denial, and everyone is now really giving me the fish eye. Turns out upon closer investigation, it's a different Woody Allen. Some poor guy from the Midwest was in New York and treated himself to a brace of hookers. Who dreamed there was another Woody Allen? I must remember that next time I get a request to do a benefit.

Where was I? OK, the liberals I always had great admiration for disappointed me. Murray Kempton had been an idol. He came one day to cover the hearing and shellacked me in his next column. He excoriated me for having a battery of lawyers to Mia's one or two. But I needed the child custody lawyers, plus I also was being accused of a criminal thing—molestation—so I needed my criminal lawyers. But he made it sound like I was this rich, powerful guy with lots of money and many lawyers versus this poor, betrayed mother. I wondered why he didn't look deeper into the fake molestation charges and why he came down on me so hard simply because I couldn't remember the exact name of the shoestore where I took my kids to buy them shoes. He really had it in for me, and I recalled that some years back he had liked my *New Yorker* pieces and wanted to do an interview with me. I was flattered and said OK, but I did not want to do an interview for the *Post*, as it was at the time a particularly awful tabloid. We went up and back over it. He said it's who he wrote for. In fact he was a fine, crusading liberal but I didn't want to contribute in any way to the *Post* in those years, so I held firm and passed on the interview. He waited a long time to get even but he did get even and then some. Gloria Steinem was another journalist I really admired who railed against me. No one seemed interested in pursuing what was at least a possible miscarriage of justice. Steinem simply accepted the accusation as true, and insightful as she has been over the years, here she was wrong.

Another amusing moment in the courtroom was Alan Dershowitz screaming at a lawyer, "Perjurer! Perjurer!" from the witness stand. The issue was that my lawyers had accused Dershowitz of saying he could make the whole case go away for seven million dollars. Four lawyers in a room testified he made that offer. He denied it furiously, his mother looking on proudly in the courtroom as her son performed. But I understood it and have always said openly that I did not think it was the shakedown my lawyers thought it was, but an attempt to keep both Mia and me from getting into a messy public conflict. I recall him saying the issue should not go to court, it should be settled quietly, sparing us both mud slinging publicity. He and Mia calculated my kids' school expenses for their lives through college, three kids, support, private schools, college. Anyhow, his adding machine came to seven million skins. But I wouldn't settle. I said I don't care about bad publicity. I never abused Dylan and I'm not settling for a dime.

I was not afraid of the truth and was not going to buy silence. I couldn't care less about my reputation. I was ready to go to court and declare with total honesty that I never abused anyone in my life, and I was ready to defend that statement publicly. Let Yale investigate. Let New York State investigate. I welcomed a closer look by experts. I took a lie detector test from someone the Connecticut Police had the highest respect for, Paul Minor. He was the chief polygraph examiner for the FBI from 1978 to 1987. I passed easily, but when we asked Mia to take the same test, she refused. I knew I had truth on my side, which I now know is no assurance of anything, and those William Steig cufflinks my aunt Molly bought me for my bar mitzvah, which depicted a man with a spear through his body and the caption "People are no damn good," was an insight that trumped Anne Frank's.

Resigned to the fact I would need a top child-custody lawyer and an experienced criminal lawyer, and despite being a total novice in these areas, I wound up with two strong professionals: Sheila Riesel and Elkan Abramowitz. Elkan is a tall liberal Democrat who had headed the Criminal Division in the U.S. Attorney's Office for the Southern District, had served as assistant deputy mayor for the City of New York, and also as special counsel to the Select Committee on Crime for the U.S. House of Representatives.

He agreed to see me, and I spieled out the whole story. He instantly said the strategy of not talking to the Connecticut police should now be reversed. He felt my story was so clear and consistent that he would go there with me and I should tell it to the police. My previous lawyers had kept me from going and, I must say, with good reason. We had agreed to be interviewed by the Connecticut police when they requested it as long as there was a stenographer there to record the interview. Maco did not want any record of it. This did not exactly inspire trust among our team, so we didn't go. Elkan, however, after hearing my whole story felt it was so clear I was innocent that we should go. I went, they asked questions, I answered. They were polite, in no way hostile, no good cop–bad cop nonsense.

I do recall one creepy moment the following week. They asked if I'd give them a hair sample. I didn't have that many to spare but felt I could manage a few strands and suggested the gray ones. I was fingerprinted—just like the criminals I'd grown up fascinated by. And then they sat me down to yank a few hairs from my head. Because I was a celebrity, they let me know they were pulling the hairs out gently— giving me an "easy one," was the way it was put. And as I sat there, for the first time I realized what it would be like for a noncelebrity, a poor person, a black man. He wouldn't get this special treatment; his hairs would be yanked out mercilessly, with no regard for his pain. It was the real world I was coming in contact with, and though it's real for everyone, it's more real for some than others.

During the hearing I was informed about a very hot underground source. A private eye with underworld connections who could get the inside skinny on anyone, uncover any unscrupulous mischief planned against me, and bring my opponent's case to its knees. He came to my apartment, and I gave him the now tedious tale in all its detail. I gave him my opponent's phone numbers, daily habits, anything I could be helpful with. He left. That was the last I ever heard from him. Was he a con artist? A double agent? Did I turn him off with something I said? He didn't do anything to harm me, just vanished.

During the maelstrom of the custody hearings, two professions exposed themselves as surprisingly disappointing.

One was private detectives. After all, I had at one time considered becoming one. Entranced as I was by Sam Spade and Mike Hammer, I saw myself having my own office, feet up on the desk, fedora cocked back, shoulder holster, beautiful secretary with a crush on me while I solved crimes way ahead of the bumbling police. The reality that I would have been beaten to death or turned up in an alley with bullet holes through both eyes hadn't occurred to me.

The dicks I met and dealt with were nothing like Bogart or William Powell. They were mostly overweight ex-cops with a few old friends on the force allowing them minimal access to information an energetic high school freshman could secure. The thought of them tailing someone without falling down a manhole or solving a crime more complex than jaywalking was ludicrous. As for the dynamite blondes, the idea of Veronica Lake heating up over some paunchy shamus who couldn't score with a nymphomaniac on a desert island using Spanish Fly made me laugh. Much money spent, little bang for my buck.

The other losers were the child psychiatrists. How intimidated they felt by Mia. A few whined to me in private that they had to toe the line or they'd be fired. One child shrink phoned and begged me not to let him be called to the witness stand, as he was so terrified he couldn't sleep nights. Another, who was no help, complained he could not get Mia and Satchel to separate, and the first step of treatment was to get her into the other room. One shrink plaintively asked me if I could possibly help get his son into the movie business because the boy lacked direction. All the shrinks walked on eggshells with Mia, enabling her to prevent me from having any contact with my kids. The one seeing

Dylan in Connecticut was taking his marching orders from Mia, as his daughter had been hired by her as some kind of assistant. Judge Wilk, who was supervising the case, found nothing wrong with any of this when I pointed it out. But then this is the same guy who read the Yale report and still concluded there was no evidence that Mia had coached Dylan. This despite Yale's prolonged meticulous investigation versus his total zero investigation. What was this guy smoking? And why was he twisting and wriggling to find some way to help Mia?

During the hearing the Yale report was finished up, and the investigators summoned both Mia and myself into their office to read us the results in person. We sat there as they read their conclusion:

"Dylan was not abused by Mr. Allen." Her statements had "a rehearsed quality." They were likely "coached or influenced by her mother."

Moses says, "Those conclusions perfectly match my own childhood experience: coaching, influencing, and rehearsing are three words that sum up exactly how my mother tried to raise us."

Mia rose in a rage. She is given to rages, as Moses described, Soon-Yi described, and the Yale report confirmed. She stormed out of the room. I said good-bye, anxious to get back to New York. While exiting I chatted for a second with one of the investigators, who told me that Dylan had been very inconsistent and even said at one point that I had never molested her and she was never in the attic with me. Shortly after Sandy Boluch started working in the Farrow house, she saw Dylan crying and asked her why she was crying, and the child said, "Mommy wants me to lie." A short time later Dylan had been rewarded with a new doll previously denied to her.

Despite the obvious prejudice of Wilk's reaction to the Yale report and his duplicitous, face-saving comments, it has held up as a valid, extensive, and correctly concluded report. The investigation took six months, every conceivably relevant person was interviewed, Dylan nine times, me, Mia, kids, babysitters, maids. Then, suddenly, Maco's and Wilk's dreams of playing hero to Mia went up in smoke. The custody hearing ended, and like Maco, Judge Wilk scrambled to write a summary that could do the most damage to me. The best he could come up with in his effort to torpedo the report was the following, "I am less certain . . . than is the Yale–New Haven team that the evidence proves conclusively that there was no sexual abuse." Of course, Wilk based his conclusion on never having done any investigating whatsoever, just wishful thinking, whereas Yale–New Haven had investigated the case minutely for months.

If Wilk had sat in on a typical Yale investigating session, he might have seen one like the one I will describe to you. Get this picture. Mia and I are both sitting before three experienced, professional investigators in a New Haven office. Mia insists I molested Dylan, claiming poor Dylan was so upset by the abuse that she instantly went running into the next room and into the arms of her sister Lark, who she would go to for comfort. Mia described in detail how Dylan embraced Lark, shaken by the experience, and poured her heart out to her sister, who calmed her. I, cagey fox that I was, listened carefully to Mia dramatize the story to the investigators, and waited to play my ace. I said, "You're telling me Dylan was so traumatized she fled weeping into the embrace of Lark?" Mia stood her ground, rubbing in the child's need for succor by her older sibling. "Why do you ask?" the investigators queried me. "Because," I said, rising like Lincoln ready to do his bit about no full moon, just a waning moon that night. "Because," I explained, "Lark was not in Connecticut when you alleged that happened. She was in New York, so how could Dylan have run and embraced her?" An awkward silence filled the air and Mia, scrambling for a reply and thinking on her feet, says, "I know Lark was in New York at the time but Dylan embraced her spiritually." This was the kind of tap dancing I was up against, and while it may have played to Judge Wilk and Mia's base, it did not fool the investigators.

As regards the salacious question which people always ask me: Was there ever any canoodling between Maco and Mia, or Wilk and Mia? I find that hard to believe, but I tend to be naïve in such matters. In *Double Indemnity*, when Fred MacMurry and Barbara Stanwyck were kissing each other hotly in the bedroom of his sleazy apartment as the screen faded to black, I thought it was so that we wouldn't see them dye Easter eggs. I had contempt for Maco and no respect for Wilk, but that's all I can say. I must argue, Wilk mandated a stupid, vindictive, and harmful visitation plan for me and the kids. I will explain it; see what you think.

First off, no visitation at all with Dylan. Why was that fair or good? For me or her? Despite the investigation concluding there was no molestation, I still can't see her. Thanks to Wilk, the kid is totally cut off from her father, completely under the aegis of her implanting, coaching, naked-taping mother, and I never get to have any contact with her. And so, I never was able to speak to Dylan after that ruling. Between the court edict and manipulation, not a single word or note has been passed or been allowed between us since she was seven. This was a brutal blow to me, a cruel deprivation for Dylan, but the successful culmination of You took my daughter, now I'll take yours.

Dylan told the Yale probers, My mommy said Daddy did a bad thing but I still love him. Dylan and I had bonded deeply, and Mia's plan to take my daughter took a great toll on me and no doubt on a child just turned seven who lost a father she was very attached to. I adored Dylan and spent as much time with her as possible from her infancy on. I played with her, bought her endless toys, dolls, stuffed animals, My Little Ponies. In those days F.A.O. Schwarz was a kid's paradise, and they used to let me in early before it opened so I could shop for Dylan and Satchel. As a boy, my father had a millionaire friend from Chicago who would visit New York on business now and then and always wanted my father as his driver. My father would drop everything to chauffeur Mr. Lorenz. Once he took my father to F.A.O. Schwarz and said, Buy your son anything you want on me. My father got me a complete realistic cowboy costume including two six-shooters. I was about seven and thrilled. I looked great but got my spurs caught in the bedspread, crashed, and broke a lamp. Once, when my father hit his number, he went to F.A.O. Schwarz and bought me a huge Lionel chemistry set because I showed an interest in science. Worried about my safety, he called his druggist friend and read him the list of every chemical and asked which ones were dangerous. He flushed the dangerous ones down the toilet, leaving me half a set. I still managed to create an orange dye and dyed my mother's dark brown beaver coat orange. For some reason, this upset her and she tried killing me with a salad fork. I put that scene in *Radio Days*. I remember her chasing me around the house, brandishing her shoe. I thought they were going to have to hose her down like in *The Hairy Ape*.

Speaking of shoes, incidentally, once Dylan had her heart set on the ruby red slippers Dorothy wore in *The Wizard of Oz*. I stayed up until midnight having the costume department of my movie make her a pair so I could leave them on her bed and she could discover them when she woke up in the morning.

I was crushed when Mia's plan worked, and the judge shilled for her to make sure I would not get to see Dylan. For a year, I had dreams about her coming back to me but every waking attempt I made to see her, to write to her, to talk to her, was thwarted. When she got a little older and I imagined she would realize how she was being used, I wrote her, just sweet, affectionate, brief letters asking how she was doing. No commercials for me. The letters were all intercepted by Ronan and I received curt, evasive answers that began, "I told Dylan about your letter and she is not interested." (In Hitchcock's *Notorious*, another unnaturally creepy mother-son relationship plays out. Claude Rains and his mother have Ingrid Bergman in their house, and they're slowly poisoning her as Mia was doing to poor Dylan's mind. They disconnected Bergman's phone so she couldn't have contact with Cary Grant. Finally, he goes over and rescues her, but that's the movies. In real life, if I tried what Cary Grant tried, I couldn't get past the doorman.)

I finally wrote Satchel and said, "Do you always open your sister's mail and read it?" No answer except he wrote back that if I really wanted to help out, I should send money.

I already was supporting them generously by law, but if Mia was right about Satchel being the son of Frank Sinatra, then I was really being bilked.

One of the saddest things of my life was that I was deprived of the years of raising Dylan and could only dream about showing her Manhattan and the joys of Paris and Rome. To this day, Soon-Yi and I would welcome Dylan with open arms if she'd ever want to reach out to us as Moses did, but so far that's still only a dream. Anyhow, you think that was a wise judicial decision, given the options available? I think it was not only deliberately cruel to me, but also catastrophic for Dylan, as you will later see.

As far as Satchel went, I was allowed supervised visitation. But why supervised? No logical reason. "Supervised" means a hired person, often different each week, must attend and be present during the visits. What for? If no molestation ever took place, what are we talking about? (Not that I was accused of laying a finger on Satchel, although at one point the written record shows that Mia was so disconnected, she tried to sell the notion I may have molested both of them, but when it didn't fly with Satchel and Dylan was more vulnerable, she concentrated on her.) But why must I be supervised? All it does is confirm to Satchel his father is to be feared, a threat. But I loved him and wanted to see him. So I was faced with accepting Wilk's only route to visitation, and every week, after hearing from his mother I'm a rapist and a monster, the poor kid is packed off to ride an hour and a half to New York from Connecticut to be with the predatory old man.

The psychiatrist on the case said custody should go to the parent who does not poison the children against the other parent. Bear this in mind when you now read what was written by a dissenting appeals court judge who felt the visitation rules for Satchel and me were too restrictive. His opinion comes from two eyewitness accounts by two experienced professional custody supervisors, Frances Greenberg and Virginia Lehman, both independent social workers who were charged with supervising the visits with Satchel in New York.

They reported their findings to one of the appeals judges, J. Carro, who wrote: "There is strong evidence in the record from neutral observers that Mr. Allen and Satchel basically have a warm and loving father-son relationship, but that the relationship is in jeopardy, in large measure because Mr. Allen is being estranged and alienated from his son by the current custody and visitation arrangement. Frances Greenberg and Virginia Lehman, two independent social workers employed to oversee visitation with Satchel, testified how, 'Mr. Allen would welcome Satchel by hugging him, telling him how much he loved him, and how much he missed him.' Also described by both supervisors was a kind of sequence that Mr. Allen might say, I love you as much as the river, and Satchel would say something to the effect that, I love you as much as New York City...then Mr. Allen might say, I love you as much as the stars, and Satchel would say, I love you as much as the universe. Sadly, there was also testimony from those witnesses that Satchel had told Mr. Allen, 'I like you, but I am not supposed to love you.' That's when Mr. Allen asked Satchel if he would send him a postcard from a planned trip to California with Ms. Farrow, Satchel said, 'I can't [because] Mommy won't let me,' and on one occasion when Satchel indicated that he wanted to stay with Mr. Allen longer than the allotted two-hour visit, 'Satchel did say he could not stay longer, that his mother had told him that two hours was sufficient.' Perhaps most distressing, Satchel, 'indicated to Mr. Allen that he was seeing a doctor that was going to help him not to see Mr. Allen anymore, and he indicated that he was supposed to be seeing this doctor perhaps eight or ten times, at the end of which he would no longer have to see Mr. Allen.' In contrast to what apparently is being expressed by Ms. Farrow about Mr. Allen to Satchel, 'Mr. Allen has been reported to say only positive things to Satchel about Ms. Farrow, and conveys only loving regards to Moses and Dylan through Satchel.' "

My God, what more does anyone need to see regarding what was going on in the Farrow home after Judge Wilk turned both children over to Mia exclusively? Are the two independent social workers' testimonies different from the constant brainwashing Moses witnessed? So after months of Mia poisoning the five-year-old, the brainwashing takes. Professional supervisors are hard to find and expensive, and part-time monitors come and go. Young women, maybe college-aged, maybe a bit older, show up at Mia's each visitation day. Mia preps them for their encounter with me. Given their instructions to other babysitters to keep a close watch on me and armed with one or two nasty things the judge had to say about me, she sends our son, groomed to despise me, on this journey to Manhattan hell. It would be as if I gave the supervisors the Yale report to read before she met Mia. They'd look at her with very different eyes.

Naturally, as time passes the kid enters my apartment with the supervisor, carsick, belligerent, raging with ambivalence,

having been taught I'm Moloch in Ralph Lauren cordu-
roys. Then comes the stiff, unnatural awkward mess of a
supervised visit. Meaning that instead of a father and son
spending some nice time doing something together, there's
always a third person right there to be sure I don't rape
the poor kid. Not only that, if I take him for lunch or ice
cream, there's a third at the table with us. I can't take him
for a walk without the supervisor or to a basketball game or
movie without me springing for an extra ticket. Most of the
girls who supervised were nice; a few were kind and could
see the ugly unfairness of what was happening and tried as
best they could to leave us alone. A few were stupid and had
been intimidated by Mia's poisonous briefing. They gave
me a hard time on the visits, acting as insipid martinets.
After a year of this nonsense I put an end to it, realizing it
was not bringing Satchel closer to me but was pushing him
further away.

This is what's out there in matrimonial court. Guys like
Judge Wilk. Capricious men with the power to regulate
families. On several occasions, I was stopped in the street
by strangers. Sad men begging me to help them see their
children who were taken from them in custody rulings. One
wept. Like I could intervene. Like I'm a celebrity, so I must
have some juice. Meanwhile, I was supervised myself and
Mia given free rein over the children. And what awfulness
went on under her twisted rule. Moses was there when this
little episode—which, as Blanche would say, "Only Mr. Poe,
Mr. Edgar Allan Poe"—took place.

Listen to Moses, who was there and described things:
"After Ronan finished law school, Mia had him undergo
cosmetic surgery to extend his legs and gain a few inches in

height. I told her I couldn't imagine putting someone through the ordeal for cosmetic reasons. My mother's response was simple, 'You need to be tall to have a career in politics.' It was, of course, a long and painful process for Ronan, who had his legs broken a few times and reconstructed to lengthen them. The insurance company didn't see the medical necessity and refused to pay for it. Of course, Mia and Ronan tell a different story but that's what happened." The covering story handed out about Ronan's knee problems, his walker, and months of reconstruction was based on his actual contracting of a disease while working abroad. This was supposed to account for the surgery, but Moses was present during much of the painful process. Meanwhile, Mia might put Ronan through this leg-breaking barbarism to satisfy her plans for his future, while I'm the one the judge sticks with a monitor.

Yes, Wilk punished me, but he left two children in sole possession of a woman capable of some dicey behavior. The children become pawns and are deprived of a loving parent, taught to fear and hate their father. Poor Dylan grows up with the fake story relentlessly drummed into her that she was abused. Same with Satchel. Kids of seven and four, easy pickings, totally dependent on only their controlling mother.

I did not dislike Mia's lawyers. Court is an adversarial place, and one gets angry at the rotten tricks and nasty accusations, but the lawyers are hired guns and Mia could have easily hired mine and me hers. I had two terrific lawyers, Sheila Riesel and Elkan Abramowitz, and they presented a winning case. But while the molestation nonsense was seen through by the experts, when it came to the Wilk matrimonial court, Sheila Riesel found herself in a boat race. I liked Alan Dershowitz. I believe he tried to find a way to minimize the damage to our reputations, but he didn't know Mia well enough to know she was an extremely troubled woman, a convincing actress, whose word couldn't be counted on. Maybe I should have said something when Mia forged a friendship during the hearings with Wilk's court clerk, who drove her home from the courthouse many nights. Was that cricket? Certainly it was an unfair conduit to the judge. Anyhow, too late to lock that barn door.

People who followed the newspaper accounts often came away saying, All show business people lead crazy lives. He's nuts and Mia's no better. They're both insane. Many viewed it as, "He says—she says—" and accorded our conflict a false equivalency. The real truth was that it was, "She says,"—and not just "He says," but "Every single investigation of the facts also says what he says." It was not simply a dispute between two balanced positions, but between one already determined valid and the other closely scrutinized and found to be false. Nevertheless, it didn't matter to the public, and why should it? There were much more pressing things to pay attention to in the world than the tabloid adventures of a couple of strutters and fretters and their slapstick passions.

So now back to Soon-Yi and me hiding reclusively in my penthouse. We stayed in to avoid the paparazzi surrounding the building, we took our nature walks in my large roof garden amidst the abundant, beautiful, overgrown foliage. My penthouse was what I had fantasized as a boy. From my afternoons in the darkened cinemas, where I stared at all those 35-millimeter gods and goddesses drop ice cubes into glasses of scotch and throw open the French doors to the terrace, revealing Manhattan. For years, I had been living in an apartment that could have been a film set high above Fifth Avenue. I put in large, nearly floor-to-ceiling glass windows, and my views of the city were truly stupendous. I saw fabulous sunsets and during electrical storms gigantic bolts of lightning sometimes stretching from the George Washington Bridge to the Battery. The loud thunder clap would be preceded by a majestic flash over Central Park West, over New Jersey, over eternity. Once I saw a bolt of lightning flash in the western sky and make a perfect circle, a huge letter O.

Once my building was hit by lightning, the railing on my terrace, to be exact. The whole building shook as lethal blocks of stone broke off the side and crashed down to Fifth Avenue. Only the intense downpour kept pedestrians from walking on the street and so no one was hit. The block was roped off for months after, while the building was repaired. Though the lightning hit twenty floors up, workers in the basement felt 930 Fifth rock.

Many a time after, as I sat at my all-metal Olympia portable and wrote during electrical storms, I was nervous a bolt would smash through the glass and strike my type-writer barbecuing me as I pounded out a puckish satire of contemporary mores. Snowstorms and blizzards were a different experience but equally awesome. To wake up on a winter morning and see every inch of Central Park blanketed in snow; the city, silent and empty. And maybe a red fire engine would race along against the perfect white. So much depends upon a red fire engine against the snow in Central Park beside the white chickens. Close. The same great buzz occurred when April happened and you could see the trees budding. At first ever so slightly, and the next day a bit more. Then a few more days and boom, green is everywhere and spring has come to Manhattan and in Central Park you see blossoms and petals unfolding and the air smells of nostalgia and you want to kill yourself. Why? Because it's too beautiful to handle; the pineal gland secretes Unspeakable Melancholy Juice, and you don't know where to put all those feelings that are stampeding inside and God forbid at that point your love life is not going too well. Get the revolver.

Fall is a different matter entirely but no less emotional. To me, it's the loveliest time of the year. See, summer in New York is bad news. It's hot, muggy, everyone's away, and yes, you can move around with less traffic but it's dull with all your friends gone and everything kind of sticky and humid. Anyhow, comes fall and the town starts percolating. New Yorkers return from vacation, the weather cools off. When I was a kid in Brooklyn, the summers were a godsend because it meant no school and I could play ball all day and hit the movies. It was fun, but even then, fall meant all the cute girls were back from camp, and although the nightmare of books and classrooms loomed, at least there would be some sigmoid anatomy to hasten the blood. I never ever went to camp, hated the idea, and tried it just once for a day. Touted to be Shangri-La, I signed on as a junior counselor, rode the train upstate, sized up the situation immediately, and called my father to come get me. Always on the lookout for trouble, he got his pal Artie, a burly enforcer with a jake leg, and armed with guns they drove up to spring me from this sweet little Jewish summer camp. Needless to say, there was no shootout.

Finally, when you looked out the window of my penthouse and saw those leaves change color it was both stunning and sobering. Stunning because the reds and yellows in nature outdid all the tubes of pigment no matter how inspiringly the painters combined them, and sobering because the leaves soon died and fell in typical Chekhovian fashion and you knew you would one day dry and drop; the same stupid, brute ritual would overtake all your own sweet little neutrinos and what was that about? On the other hand, it's all perspective. To a human, the fall-colored leaves are gorgeous. To a red or yellow leaf, I can guarantee they find the green ones lovelier.

So here I am, this guy with a Cedric Gibbons penthouse, on the twentieth floor in New York, but something Metro-Goldwyn-Mayer doesn't tell you or ever shows up in their movies is that penthouses leak. None of those expensive terraced apartments, where the skyline is thrilling and Robert Montgomery removes a cigarette, taps it on his case and smiles at Carole Lombard and, unlike me, doesn't forget to open the flue when there's a roaring fire in the fireplace, ever leaks. I lived in my rooftop aery for thirty-five years and it never didn't leak. I had in engineers, I tore up the garden and redid the roof, I caulked and put in copper pans, and yet when it rained, out came the buckets because when I say leaked, I don't mean a few disconcerting droplets—I mean the buckets filled up fast and I had to repaint every year.

Still, it was like being in love with a great and beautiful exasperating woman. Like Louise. The highs trumped scrambling to place the pails to catch the rainwater, and I'd probably be there still if Soon-Yi and I didn't have children and needed more space. And when Soon-Yi and I created our brouhaha and we were the desiderata of every paparazzi, we holed up for weeks in the penthouse and took our strolls in the very large roof garden and it was exactly the kind of "you and me against the world" that in a movie makes people fall more and more in love, which it did. As far as marriage was concerned, neither of us had any great need to formalize our relationship. We both felt that no contract is worth the paper it's printed on if the parties are not happy. We loved each other and there was no need to resort to legislature. We would definitely not wed, and that was that. And then we married. Why? Not for romantic reasons but strictly financial. I adored Soon-Yi and knew I was much older and could drop dead at a moment's notice. If I did, I wanted her to be legally protected to get all I owned automatically with no hitches. As the law provides for a wife to simply take over her husband's everything upon his death, I insisted.

As practical as our reason for marrying was, the wedding was very romantic. We decided on a quiet, secret wedding. Just my sister, one or two friends. We decided to marry in Venice, a town we both loved. The mayor would marry us secretly in an office in his building. No one would know. All arrangements were made secretly. On a cold dark December day in 1997 Soon-Yi, my sister, and close friend Adriana Di Palma, widow of my late cameraman Carlo Di Palma, strolled through the streets of Venice while I, like James Bond, counted to five hundred, then, dousing the lights, peeled out secretly from our suite at the Gritti Palace and took a gondola, silently gliding through the canals and backwaters to arrive at the same building from a different direction. Brought separately into a secluded room, the mayor married us. Unobtrusively Soon-Yi and I departed separately, left the building unnoticed, and, taking different routes, met back at the hotel. When we entered our suite the phone was ringing. It was Page Six from the *Post*. They'd heard we were in Venice and just got married. I looked under the bed before we consummated the marriage. We honeymooned two days later at the Ritz in Paris, and by then the secret had become headlines. Soon-Yi and I were husband and wife. It had little effect on the stock market, although Xanax went up ten points.

As I looked back on my film experience with Mia, apart from *Husbands and Wives* when everything blew up, I would have to say it was an interesting one with creative ups and downs. Things had exploded with Mia the last week of filming *Husbands and Wives*. Naturally the air was full of tension, yet we completed the shooting, gritting our teeth and both being very professional. Mia did not exactly relish the thought of working with me, having just discovered I was having an affair with Soon-Yi. I didn't relish Mia phoning people telling everyone I had raped her underage, retarded daughter. *Husbands and Wives* was the last movie Mia and I would make together.

We began thirteen years earlier with *A Midsummer Night's Sex Comedy*. I had always wanted to do a movie that paid homage to the joys and beauty of the country. Don't ask me why. I hated the country. But the idea of magic and the music of Mendelssohn caught my fancy. And so we built from scratch the home the story takes place in. We filmed in the woods on the Rockefeller Estate up in Sleepy Hollow. I was hoping to do for the country what I tried to do for Manhattan in New York movies: show it with love. The fact I didn't love it didn't matter. After all, I was an artist, a creator, a weaver of dreams, a schlemiel in over his head. Mia was excellent, and I loved working with José Ferrer, whose literacy and cultivation from Shakespeare to jazz impressed me. How many actors can you hire for a role that requires singing a Schubert *lied* who actually knows one by heart and can sing it? We saw the perfect house for the story in a book on architecture. It existed somewhere in the Midwest. We copied the Victorian exterior exactly and rebuilt it on the Rockefeller estate in Pocantico Hills.

After the movie came out, we got sued by the owner of the original house for stealing his design. I think we won that one. Meanwhile, when the film wrapped, someone bought our house. They transported it to Long Island, did the interior according to legal building codes, and they live there to this day, hopefully happily. I made *Zelig* simultaneously and have described the emotional strain of switching hats all the time. No one came to see *A Midsummer Night's Sex Comedy*, but *Zelig* was much more successful. *Zelig* was much easier to film as the goal was to make it look like a documentary with period footage. The sex comedy, on the other hand, took place on one single day but was shot over three months, and keeping the lighting consistent as the seasons changed was a real feat. We kept painting brown leaves green.

Next up with Mia was *Broadway Danny Rose*. My range as an actor is, shall we say, limited. I can play an intellectual, which I resemble physically, but as I've said, it's truly acting. I look like a bookworm so I can be one on the screen; I'm believable as a college professor, maybe a shrink, a lawyer, an educated professional. But because of who I am naturally, I can also play a lowlife. I can be a small-time crook, a bookie, a street weasel. Danny Rose was a streety guy, an uneducated loser, a small-time hustler.

In those years, I used to take Mia to Rao's, the great Italian restaurant that needs no introduction. Let me describe it this way: A couple from Texas phoned and wanted to make a dinner reservation. They were coming to New York and heard how fabulous the food was. Frankie, who ran the place before his sad, untimely death, said he could give them a table in fourteen months. Mia and I often talked about her playing a character like Annie Rao. Annie and Vincent cooked and ran the joint. Annie was a fabulous character, with her stacked up blond hairdo and dangling cigarette, her New York City style of talking, her roast peppers. Oh, and her ever-present sunglasses. So that was Mia in *Danny Rose*, and it was very different from the usual Mia Farrow, and she did a damn good job. That was a fun picture to make, and I got to work with some great acts. Alba, the bird lady, had all these talking birds and gave one to Mia, and damned if it didn't speak beautifully.

Nick Apollo Forte played the goomba act that Danny handled as a small-time manager, and Nick did a great job. I auditioned every singer for that part from Jimmy Roselli to Robert Goulet and filmed a number of them. I couldn't decide between a lot of possibles so I called in my north star, Keaton, and showed her the screen tests and she said, Nick Apollo's the one, and that's all I had to hear as my faith in her taste never faltered. And Keaton was right. He was a natural. He was a lounge act from Massachusetts who came from one of those Italian families—fishermen, as I recall. He'd tell me stories about how they fished for a living by throwing dynamite in the water and when a multitude of dead fish floated up, they had their catch of the day. Nick never did a movie before, and I thought he'd be overcome with humble gratitude when from all those fine singers we'd chosen him for a leading role, but he said, You want me, you gotta take my drummer—oh, and I wrote a song I wanna use. We took the drummer, who was fine. The song Nick "wrote," "Agita," about a nervous stomach, we used and it was great. P.S.: We got sued for it because some guy claimed Nick stole it from him. Don't know how it ended.

My next movie with Mia was *The Purple Rose of Cairo*. I consider it one of the best films I ever made, and coming off *Danny Rose* gives you a good idea of Mia's range and how she got better and better picture after picture. I originally cast Michael Keaton, a wonderful actor, in the Jeff Daniels role but there were two problems. Michael seemed so contemporary on the screen I was having trouble buying him as a thirties character. Add to this he had just become a father and the baby was keeping him up all night, and he'd understandably come to work bleary-eyed. It's hard to tell an actor you're replacing him because natural insecurity always convinces them it's because you don't like their acting. We replaced Michael with a new find of Juliet Taylor's, one whom she urged me to check out and I resisted out of laziness, shyness, self-destruction, whatever, but the minute Jeff Daniels came in and read, our spirits rose. We knew we had hit the jackpot. Here's a truly meaningless piece of trivia: We had filmed a bit with Michael Keaton, including a long,

291

overhead night shot of the abandoned amusement park in the story. The tiny, dark figure skulking around is not Jeff Daniels but Michael Keaton. We figured no one could tell and why stay up all night in the cold and spend a fortune to reshoot a cumbersome scene? Anyhow, I told you it was trivial. Jeff lived up to our fondest hopes and has gone on to have a fine acting career on stage and screen.

I never test-screen my movies. I am not interested in collaborating with viewers to make my film. Once I hand it in, it's done. The film company can test-screen and have cards filled out if it helps their marketing strategy, but don't tell me about it because I'm not interested nor am I changing anything. So UA tested *Purple Rose* in Boston and I got a nice call from one of their executives who said it went well. I thanked him for his thoughtful call. Then he said, very gingerly, you know if you could end it more happily it could really make some money. By that he meant that if Mia and Jeff Daniels got together somehow like, say, the mermaid and Tom Hanks in *Splash*. I explained very politely that was not going to happen and he very graciously dropped the subject. I had final cut, but have never had to pull rank and have always had good relations with studios and distributors.

Once, when Harvey Weinstein was distributing *Everyone Says I Love You*, a film he bought for a lot of money, he saw, hated, and asked me to take out the word *motherfucker* from the rap song. I explained that I wasn't going to do that. He said if I would just cut that one word the movie, a musical, could play Radio City Music Hall. I said I understand, but I don't make films to accommodate movie houses. Incidentally, despite what was printed in the newspapers, Harvey never produced any movies of mine. Never backed me. He only distributed a few already completed films and distributed them well. In addition to Harvey's skill at distributing, he had an eye for offbeat, artsy movies and presented a number of them. Still, I would never have allowed Harvey to back or produce a film of mine because he was a hands-on producer who changed and recut a director's movie. We never could have worked together.

As far as having my movie open at the Radio City Music Hall, I had experienced that once before and didn't like it. It was not a film I directed but only wrote, *Play It Again, Sam*. It did not do well there and was pulled after two weeks and put into a small east side art house where it did very well. Also, I didn't think the projection at Radio City was that great. I had the same disappointment with the projection at the Ziegfeld. The throw was just too far to get a really vivid, color-saturated look. In the end, since I refused to make the cut Harvey requested, *Everyone Says I Love You* was not allowed into Radio City. It played elsewhere and did okay. Just okay. And so *Purple Rose of Cairo* opened with the sad ending and it also did okay.

Originally I had the idea that Mia would play a devoted movie buff who loses herself from her sad life by going to the movies (c'est moi), and eventually one of the characters in the film she watches, on seeing her every day in the audience, talks to her and comes down off the screen, and they have a romance. I wrote the first fifty pages and found I had nowhere to go with the story, so the fifty pages lay in my drawer for months. Then one day it occurred to me: The real live actor who plays the screen character who talks to Mia comes to town, and with two identical men, the fictional one who came off the screen and the actor live from Hollywood coming to town, many possibilities open up. The script suddenly flowed, and I made one of my favorite pictures.

After that, Mia and I did *Hannah and Her Sisters* together. I had originally written the lead male role for an American. I had a chance to get Jack Nicholson, who wanted to do it but was going with Anjelica Huston whose father, John Huston, was trying to get *Prizzi's Honor* going and if he got it off the ground, Jack would be obliged to do it rather than *Hannah*. And it came to pass Huston did get *Prizzi's Honor* made, and I lost any chance for Jack and turned to Michael Caine even though I had resisted using an English actor. Still, I'd rather have a great actor like Michael and sacrifice the character being American. The end result was Jack Nicholson won an Academy Award that year for Best Actor and Michael Caine for Best Supporting. Dianne Wiest also won an Oscar for her work in *Hannah*.

Wiest is another friend and won two Oscars in my films. She's one of our greatest actresses, and even in a movie like *September*, which failed to charm audiences here— though I'm told played well in Zanzibar—Dianne was great. *Hannah* we shot in Mia's actual apartment, and she was compensated by the crew doing renovating work after the movie was over. I got to direct Lloyd Nolan, a treat second only to directing Van Johnson because both were in so many movies I watched in Brooklyn movie palaces growing up. Lloyd had cancer when he made *Hannah*, and while it necessitated him resting between calls to the set, his performing energy never let down. On *Hannah*, I also got a chance to work with Mia's mother, who did a good job and was also a great storyteller. Maureen O'Sullivan as a young woman was startlingly beautiful. And hot. Tarzan was a lucky tree dweller. Maureen told me when she was in *A Day at the Races*, she had a little letch for Groucho but never told him of it. Consequently, he never pitched her. Years later, I never mentioned it to him because missing out on a freebie like Maureen could've caused him a coronary.

One of Maureen's many lively tales is when she was a young, upcoming actress and Garbo hit on her. She evaded it, as she tells it, and passed when Garbo's assistant said, "Miss Garbo would like you to come to her dressing room."

Lee, Hannah's desirable sister, was played by Barbara Hershey, a wonderful actress. I had always wanted to work with Barbara, who was magnetic on the screen, and I had offered her the role Janet Margolin eventually played in *Annie Hall*. I was disappointed when she turned it down as I was very taken with her acting depth and felt she could make a great contribution to the script Marshall Brickman and I had written. Finally, I got to work with her, and as if her acting talent was not potent enough, she was delicious to behold and gave new meaning to the word *eros*. Michael Caine told me you get the feeling if you just go up to her and touch her, she would have an orgasm. And here I'd been shaking hands with Max von Sydow every morning.

Sometimes I couldn't get my mind around the fact I was directing the knight from *The Seventh Seal*. In that great film, Max's character wants to perform a meaningful act before he dies. He protects a family going through an ominous woods during a storm with Death lurking. I tried to think if I had ever performed any meaningful act in my life, but besides flagging down a cab in the rain for an old lady on Sixth Avenue, I couldn't think of one. *Hannah* opened to a great reception, and there were some who wanted to change the Pulitzer rules so they could give it an award, but screenplays didn't qualify. The whole awards thing is so out of control. Award shows are obviously fun for people to watch. And of course, they can be very lucrative for the ones who produce them, though they pay nothing to the stars who get honored. I'm thinking of the Golden Globes or the Kennedy Center. Even the Oscars. At least for a Nobel, you realize a couple of shekels. But many awards are given only if the winner agrees to show up live to accept it. If not, they give it to someone who will show up. Obviously, it has nothing to do with genuine achievement and everything to do with exploiting a big name who wants an ego massage. Is it any wonder in his later years if you wanted to honor Orson Welles, he'd charge you?

In *Radio Days*, Mia did a special job. She performed broad comedy plus she sang. Her son Fletcher was in the film looking so handsome. *Radio Days* was based loosely on my childhood. Very loosely. Hire great performers and get out of their way. That was always my directorial secret. That and knock off at five. Dianne Wiest, Julie Kavner so terrific. And that Cole Porter cameo by Keaton. I loved making that film, and Jacqui Safra was so funny in the movie as the student in the speech class. He was also the very funny man on the stationary bike in *Stardust Memories*. And the role of the Masked Avenger, a radio hero played by Wally Shawn. I first was introduced by Juliet Taylor to Wally Shawn for a part in *Manhattan*. He played Keaton's ex-husband, whom she's always describing in these overpowering and sexually aggressive terms, and Wally's persona is not like that. He's quiet and thoughtful, naturally amusing. When we shot his scene in *Manhattan* the crew couldn't stop laughing. He's a great actor and a wonderful playwright, and he wrote this movie *My Dinner with Andre*, a two-hander, and the director, Louis Malle, asked me to play the man opposite Andre Gregory, but I just didn't have the professional dedication to memorize the long speeches. Anyway, in the end Wally played the role and so much more brilliantly than I could have.

Mia's range was very flexible. She could play the dopey cigarette girl in *Radio Days*, switch in the film to the affected gossip columnist and then give the performance she does in the film that followed, *September*, a drama that asks the question: Can a group of tortured souls come to terms with their sad lives when directed by a guy who should still be writing mother-in-law jokes for Broadway columnists?

Here, as I said, I wanted to do something Chekovian; one set, people in a country house, conflicting and confusing emotions. I structured it so it could all be shot indoors in a house on a set Santo built, with terrific actors all caught up in seething anxious emotions. It would evoke an end-of-summer, melancholy mood, and I would be hailed as a tragic poet and perhaps have a sandwich named after me at the Carnegie Deli. For one of the male leads I hired Chris Walken, whom I had worked with before on *Annie Hall*. He played her crazy brother. Chris is one of our finest actors, and when things were not working out I looked for the reason in the wrong place. I studied his performance to figure out the problem, but I should have been examining the writing. Always look at the writing first when something's not working. As the days passed, Chris was becoming more and more uncomfortable in the part. Finally in the nicest, most gentlemanly way, he quit, assuring me he thought I was a brilliant director who had a great future once I beat the problem of delusional self-worship. We parted on good and friendly terms, but I always regretted letting this great actor down. I replaced Chris with Sam Shepard, whom I liked very much. Sam was never comfortable saying my words and, being a fine writer, preferred to change my speeches all the time. I never minded this, and to this day I never mind when an actor prefers to put things in his or her own words, as long as the point of the scene is made.

Anyhow I got along well with Sam, and we talked jazz a lot, as his father played drums. Sam had a very low opinion of me as a director and publicly said Robert Altman and I knew nothing about directing actors. I ran into him and we talked about it, always friendly, always frank, always on good terms. When Sam's father died, he left behind boxes of jazz records and Sam sent them all to me as a gift. He was a terrific guy and yet another actor I let down. I wondered if drama was not my métier, and perhaps I was more at home with knockabout characters wearing bulbous rubber noses and brandishing pig bladders.

September starred, among others, not only Mia but her mother. Now I told you what a good, lively storyteller she was in person, and I assumed her humor and energy would translate onto the screen for the flamboyant, narcissistic character she was playing: a selfish ex-actress in a household of lesser exciting mortals. Anyhow, it didn't. When I finished shooting, glued it together, and saw what I'd wrought, it was Chekov all right—Moe Chekov the plumber.

No amount of imaginative editing could save it and I decided in a moment of grandiose dementia to shoot the entire movie over. This was not as Erich von Stroheim as it sounds since the budget was low, the set was standing in the studio and I could probably do a new version in six weeks and still not exceed the original budget. I told Orion Pictures of my decision and as long as I didn't spend more than they had originally given me, they were fine with it. As actors move on to other commitments, I was forced to recast. Mia's mother had been a major disappointment, and charming and outgoing as she was in life, she could not rev up the energy to do the self-obsessed lead character. Since I was dating her daughter, I did not look forward to bouncing her, and there were no excuses to help save face. She was just bad in the role.

God bailed me out and she took ill, not seriously, but enough so that she became unavailable, and I replaced her with Elaine Stritch. Suddenly, the role took a big uptick. Stritch was a knockout. She was brilliant, strong, funny, great to work with, and as she had married an English muffin mogul, I received cases of English muffins every Christmas for years after. Like Maureen Stapleton, Stritch was a pleasure to tease and insult, and each of them topped me and sent me limping off from their bull's-eye deliveries. I loved the way you'd take Stritch to dinner at a classy Manhattan restaurant and she'd put all the rolls in her purse for midnight consumption. But as great as she was, she couldn't save me from my writing, and despite wonderful performances from everybody, *September* floundered. I had replaced Sam Shepard with one of my favorite actors, Sam Waterston, and Dianne Wiest was her usual great self. Mia, too, gave me one of the best performances of her life in a futile cause.

And so after proving I was not Chekhov, I set out to prove I was not Ingmar Bergman. I made *Another Woman* and even used Ingmar's cameraman, Sven Nykvist. Like Sisyphus, I push the boulder of serious drama up the hill and the satisfaction is in the trying. Unfortunately, the boulder keeps rolling back and crushes not only me but also my investors who don't know from Camus and prefer to quote the late, great Jack Rollins—"Funny is money."

I had the idea a long time ago that one could overhear talking through a heating vent in an apartment. My first take on it was that it was a shrink's office and I hear a lovely girl's most intimate thoughts and needs in life, and as I am playing an amateur magician, I contrive to meet her and form a relationship and make all her dreams come true since I know them. This is an idea I used in this comic romantic form years later with Julia Roberts in *Everyone Says I Love You*. But years before, when I was going with Mia and she was pregnant, I was trying to solve three problems: to write a story based on overhearing someone, to create a role Mia could play while pregnant and showing, and to finally establish myself as a great master of European-style drama.

I came up with an idea that fit two of the three criteria, and the premise was not a bad one if a bit pretentious and mismanaged. I wanted this woman (played superbly, of course, by the great Gena Rowlands) to be leading an unsatisfying cold life. I wanted her to shut out everything in her life that is now unpleasant and frightening, and too painful to deal with but eventually the truth comes through the walls, through the vent. It was a nice idea, and in more skillful hands could have worked better. I gave it my best shot, got to work with Gena and, in a small role, Gene Hackman. I also got to work with Sven, who was among the numerous illustrious men Mia had had a romance with previously. I recall when I first dated Mia I was so overmatched. She was beautiful and had grown up among Hollywood royalty. She knew everyone in movies from Bette Davis to Katharine Hepburn to Charles Boyer, and I'd take her for dinner up at Rao's and first we'd see a Bergman film and she'd tell me about her romance with his brilliant cameraman, Sven Nykvist. On the car radio en route to dinner the Mozart symphony was being conducted by her ex-husband André Previn, a musical wunderkind, and she knew all the great classical artists, Daniel Barenboim, Vladimir Ashkenazy, Itzhak Perlman, Pinchas Zukerman. Meanwhile I'm sitting there hoping to impress this beautiful blonde somehow. Then at Rao's the jukebox is playing Sinatra—for me, a god, for her, yet another lover, an ex-husband; a million stories and anecdotes about Frank, his family, Palm Springs, Vegas.

Who did I know? Mickey Rose, who I wrote *Take the Money* and *Bananas* with, who played third base when I played second, and who left cans of tuna fish around town. I knew Marshall Brickman, a funny guy who walked the streets with me, confounded as I was over how a woman with a pretty figure instinctively knows to turn her head away when you're driving by in a car trying to see her face. And David Panich, who had a different loaded gun within easy reach in every room of his apartment because he suspected an imminent Nazi uprising. She knew Comden & Green and Steve Sondheim. I knew Keaton, her sisters, her Grammy Hall, and George the boarder, who refused to roll the dice in Vegas because he believed each person has just so much luck in life and he didn't want to use up any portion of his at a crap table. But I babble. The movie proceeded, and to me the only significant part of it was that shortly after, Mia had Satchel whom she carried on the set during the next film.

After *Another Woman*, I participated in a movie called *New York Stories*, which was three short films, each by a different director. Francis Coppola did one, Scorsese did one, and me. Suddenly I'm involved with these two great filmmakers. There's a photo of the three of us outside the Plaza Hotel, and it should be captioned, "What's wrong with this picture?" Two of my all-time favorite moviemakers and my short comedy piece in amid their offerings. I've met a number of great directors, and while I can't say I ever got close to any of them, I did enjoy the brief time I spent with each.

I dined with Bergman and had a number of long phone conversations where we just gabbed. He had the same insecurities we all have, that he'd show up on the set and suddenly be seized with panic because he wouldn't know where to put the camera. He was, I felt, the best filmmaker of my lifetime, and he had the same fear I had. If he doesn't know where to put the camera to make the most effective shot, how would I ever know? But somehow, despite the anxieties, we manage always to find the right spot—or at least he does. Bergman invited me to his island a few times but I always ducked it. I worshipped the guy as an artist, but who wants to take a tiny plane to a Russian-owned island where there's just sheep and get yogurt for lunch? I'm not that dedicated.

I met Truffaut. At Sue Mengers's house. He and I were both taking language lessons from the same guy, him to learn English, me to learn French. Consequently, each of us only knew a few words of the other's language. We were like ships passing in the night. The great language barrier reef. But he liked my movies, and needless to say I was crazy about his. I worked briefly with Godard, met and dined with Resnais, spent much time with Antonioni, who was a great friend of Carlo Di Palma's and a cold, superb artist. Humorless, but brilliant. He told me he had an idea for a comedy which he told to Jack Nicholson because he wanted him for the role, and Nicholson howled. Antonioni said, "You think it's that funny?" Nicholson said, "No, I'm laughing because you think that's a comedy."

I met Tati, who advised me to save my money lest I wind up in the old actor's home, where he had just come from visiting a friend. I never met Fellini, but we had a nice long phone conversation. Picture this: I'm in Rome for promotion of some silly opus of mine and I'm at the hotel. Things are hectic with interviews and press, and the phone rings. My assistant gets it and says, It's Fellini. Having never met him or said a word to him, I figured it was a faker. I told her to brush him. She did. Moments later, he calls again. It's Fellini, she says. I say, Get a number, I'll call him back, figuring I'll verify it's Fellini's phone number before I do. He's calling from a street phone, my assistant tells me. Now I know it's a scam, so I say, Dust him. Five minutes later he calls again and now I want to get rid of this pest for good, but he gives his home phone number to my assistant and says call him tomorrow morning. Now I'm starting to feel a little nervous because I'm thinking, Have I brushed one of my film idols? One of the cinema's greatest artists? Could that have really been Fellini and was I terribly rude to him?

But why would he be phoning a schnook like me whom he's never met, and from a phone booth?

Anyhow, it turns out, when I checked with the Carlo Di Palma, it was him, so as I was leaving Rome early, I made sure to phone him before I left, naturally waking him up. So I find myself on the phone with a very sleepy film genius. Of course, I'm embarrassed and turn stoplight red. We had a long talk. He liked my movies (or faked it well for a guy just awakened) and felt our backgrounds had a lot in common. When I left there, I vowed to call and see him next time I came into town, but by then he had died, perhaps sensing I was serious.

They're all gone. Truffaut, Resnais, Antonioni, De Sica, Kazan. At least Godard is still alive, but he always was a nonconformist. The whole scene has changed and all the guys I wanted to impress when I was young have faded into this abyss that seems to be out there. It's about here I start to wallow in weltschmerz but in an effort not to panic the reader, I'll get back to Scorsese and Coppola and the three short films we did.

Mia was the lead female in mine, and I played the male lead. Sven shot it. It was cute, and I held my own contributing a tale about a hectoring mother who vanishes at a magic show to the relief of her son only to reappear over Manhattan in the sky and bully him as a public embarrassment. Mia played the shiksa who dumps me and I wind up with the more parentally satisfying Semite, Julie Kavner. A good time was had by all. Except the people who put the money up for the picture. I think it was Disney, and I think it proved once again that anthology movies are not good bets at the box office.

Enter *Crimes and Misdemeanors.* Or as cute little Moses used to call it, *Crimes and Mister Meaners.* Again trouble in the script. The film has two halves, a dramatic half and a more comic, satirical one. The murder half with Marty Landau went great and was a pleasure to shoot. Marty came in to read for the brother of the role he eventually played. He read the script and said he wanted to play the murderer. We said (the *we* is me and Juliet Taylor), "You think you can?" Like all actors he said yes. And he could and he did. Of all the actors I ever worked with, Marty read my dialogue exactly the way I heard it in my mind, every nuance and inflection on the money. Later I learned he grew up a few blocks from me, so we both spoke the same way.

I regretted that I had two interwoven stories. I felt it all should have been Marty's story expanded and my story dumped, especially when I got off on the wrong foot. In the movie where I play a documentary filmmaker who is doing a "worthy" documentary on old-age homes as opposed to the lucrative garbage TV shows my brother-in-law is turning out which make him rich and respected. Not too far into shooting, I noticed my half of the interwoven plot was like a bite from the tsetse fly. It caused slumber. My brother-in-law was played by Alan Alda, whom I worked with several times. Whatever you need to make a character interesting and a scene work, Alan not only delivers but also adds much more of his own that elevates the film. He's always real whether you need a villain, a romantic lead, or a comedian. A wonderfully gifted actor.

So after shooting tons of material of me and Mia at an old-age home, we scrapped that idea, and I decided the documentary I'm making should be about the egotistical character Alan is playing. As soon as that expensive plot reversal came to me the movie took off, although if I had it to do over I'd still eighty-six myself and make a longer film about the Landau half. Mia was very good as the beautiful TV worker seduced by Alan Alda's phony fame and success. I got to work with Anjelica Huston, a treat whom I later worked with again. She was very powerful as Marty's emotional mistress. I'd seen her in movies before and fully expected her to be great, and she was. She was much taller than me, and when I kissed her in the second film we did together I made sure she was seated. But she could play comic scenes and romantic scenes and play the unraveling victim whom Marty has bumped off, all beautifully.

The film had personal meaning for me because half was dramatic, and I confirmed for myself I could handle serious material. So much for that well-meaning magazine that had once described me as "an anonymous little giggle merchant." When *Crimes and Misdemeanors* finished, I had the following idea and it came to me thusly: Jean Doumanian had always been big on alternative medicine, which I was not a fan of. She visited a Chinese acupuncturist all the time who gave her herbs and vile potions to swallow—for a plump consideration. I had it down as vintage quackery, a hustle on a par with three-card monte. She was always washing her vegetables in vinegar and knocking back a noxious beverage out of the opening scene of *Macbeth*. If it wasn't bubbling, it should've been.

Well, there came a time when I began to suffer from a rather harmless curse but an annoying one. Chalazions, little bumps on the eyelids that drove one crazy and needed to be soaked endlessly or popped with a needle. I won't bore you with the details, but after months and months of me trying to get rid of this plague by conventional means, Jean said to try her doctor just once. He's magical, she said. He will rid me of my affliction. I couldn't bear the thought of succumbing to her silly mumbo jumbo, but with the passage of time and more suffering, I said I'd give it one try. Especially when she said he would come to my house and I didn't have to walk up the rickety stairs to his Chinatown office and pass the dead ducks hanging splayed in the ground-floor windows. And so, to my chic Fifth Avenue penthouse one Saturday comes Jean bringing an Asian gentleman, looking hoary with wisdom and direct from Central Casting. I laid my sob story on him and he looked at my eye.

"Gland is blocked up," he said. I agreed. "Needs pussycat whisker."

"Pardon me?"

"Whisker of pussycat," he repeated, and opening a silver case which held several pussycat whiskers, he extracted one. I tried to keep from dialing the bunco squad then and there as he approached me. Deftly, he inserted the whisker in my tear duct and swabbed it back and forth and I sat there calmly, trying not to lose my composure and press the panic button.

"Finished," he said, pulling it out. "All better."

I laid his fee on him and he exited. Only thing missing was the sound of a gong. Of course, I was not better, and when I told my eye doctor the story, he said, Don't ever let anyone put anything, much less a cat's whisker, in my tear duct. And that is how I came to write *Alice*.

Suddenly I'm directing Keye Luke, who I sat enthralled by as a kid watching him play Charlie Chan's number one son. *Alice* was pretty to look at; a triumph for Santo Loquasto. Poor Santo, this design genius, who I always stick with insurmountable problems and no money and he takes the no money and surmounts all the problems and his work is stunning. Example: I am doing a movie that takes place in New York, in Jersey, in Los Angeles, in small towns across America, on Hollywood studio lots, in hills, across farmland—all in the 1930s, all period signs, cars, buildings, stores, and I stick Santo with a tiny budget—and oh, I don't want to leave Manhattan, not for a single day. I'm not up to it yet, but if you haven't seen *Sweet and Lowdown* with Sean Penn, check it out. Santo accomplished all of the above, and he made Alice look very pretty. And there was that little red hat we grabbed off a counter at Bloomingdale's.

Jeff Kurland, our costume designer, had the same problem as Santo. No money to work with, but please give us a cast beautifully costumed from the 1920s, '30s, or '40s. The dresses, the gowns, a hundred extras to go with the sailors and soldiers, a different hundred to go in the nightclub scene with the gangsters and showgirls. By the way, you have even less money because we needed more to spend on extra Danish for the catering table. But he did it. When it came time to shoot there were all the principals and extras dressed in 1920s clothes with cloche hats and flapper skirts, guys in their raccoon coats. Jeff had a great sense of humor, a funny character who was one of the few people I liked to have around when I cast and when I saw dailies because his feedback was meaningful. He was good to agree and disagree with, and his buoyancy was a welcome relief from the hangdog gloom that originated with me and trickled down to my loyal gandy dancers. On *Alice* I first worked with Alec Baldwin, who respectfully kept calling me Mr. Allen. I first noticed Alec in *Married to the Mob* and said who is that guy? He's amazing. And amazing he's remained. Alec is really quite a phenomenon when you think of it. He plays both ends of the spectrum superbly. He can be as dramatically powerful as you like, as slyly amusing, as romantic, as broadly funny and all first-rate. *Alice* seemed to me an okay picture. It's a definite notch below *Citizen Kane*. If you go in liking me as a human being, you could enjoy it. If you think I'm in the wrong racket, this will confirm it.

At this point in my life I paused, however briefly to act in another person's movie. Jeff Katzenberg asked me if I would act opposite Bette Midler in a film Paul Mazursky was going to make called *Scenes from a Mall*. It paid a lot but the real pull, as I mentioned earlier, was Mazursky. He had just won an award for *Enemies, A Love Story*, and I liked his work in general. We met to discuss it. He was nervous, he confessed, meeting me. Why, I'll never know. He was a fine director, a good actor, a terrific raconteur, smart, and well-read. I was a quiet, polite, decent filmmaker but no Kurosawa, no actor of real reputation, that I should inspire nervous tension in anyone, much less Mazursky. I think I may make people feel awkward because I feel awkward so I inadvertently put them at sixes and sevens. I was certainly willing to put myself in Mazursky's hands and obey the director. It meant flying to California, and Jeff Katzenberg, knowing I didn't like leaving Manhattan especially at forty thousand feet, said he'd provide me with the Disney plane. I'd never flown privately before, and I asked if that meant after the shooting in California they'd take me back home.

Katzenberg laughed and said of course. I always liked Jeff Katzenberg, got along well with him, and found him to be a film executive of his word, usually an oxymoron in Hollywood.

And so I flew to California on the Disney Gulfstream, a G-2 if I'm not mistaken, and all the flight safety instructions regarding seat belts and life vests came over the loudspeaker from Mickey Mouse. How unsettling, I thought, there's a rodent at the controls. Mazursky worked the opposite of me. He rehearsed around a table, then on a floor with tape marks, then at the actual locations. He planned every single shot and knew exactly what he was going to shoot each morning. I, by contrast, never rehearsed, never planned anything, often had no idea what I was shooting till I came on the set and was handed the pages for the day. Sometimes I didn't even own a script.

This was contrary to how Gordon Willis worked, but we liked each other and both kind of compromised our instinctive way to work, with me doing most of the compromising. With Carlo Di Palma it was a different story. Carlo was a great photographer but totally undisciplined and he was like me; he liked to come on to the set and feel the light, mosey around, and eventually his gut told him where to go and what lights to use. So we'd both arrive, Carlo and I, Carlo sipping his morning cup of beer at seven a.m. and I'd mosey and he'd mosey and I'd say, "What scene is that again?" And the meter would be moseying at a hundred fifty grand a day and finally I'd feel what I wanted to do. Carlo would get it, maybe suggest a tweak—as opposed to Gordy's "I'm not making that fucking shot, it's pretentious." And somehow we all made movies together.

Mazursky had us in stitches all through rehearsal with his repertoire of funny stories, all beautifully delivered. He wanted me to wear a ponytail for the role as was fashionable among some Californians then. I didn't want to, but he was the director and I wanted him to be happy and call all the shots. I wore the ponytail.

I liked Bette and the more I got to know her, I liked her even more. Bette was forever talking character and motivation with Mazursky, who seemed to enjoy the constant analysis, which I found a waste of time. Mazursky handled it beautifully. I sat, tuned out, with a newspaper reading the sports pages. When it came to act, Bette was really terrific. And she was terrific not because of the endless palaver over subtext, backstories, and motivation. She was terrific because she's terrific. She wakes up terrific. She doesn't need all the conversation. And we had fun acting together, and I was my usual pleasure to work with because I did anything and everything Mazursky told me to do and even everything Bette told me to do. I showed up on time, hit my mark, and obeyed orders.

I never saw the movie. I heard it was not very good. My guess is Bette and I were okay and Mazursky was a fine director and it failed because of weaknesses in the script nobody picked up on. Maybe I'm wrong. Maybe with the Lunts it would have worked, but I got the pleasure of working with Mazursky and Bette, plus a big payday, plus the awesome experience of being flown privately by Mickey Mouse, a screen personality I'd modeled my personal wardrobe after. When I landed in New York I vowed I would never fly any other way than privately again and never have. How a nonentity like me could make such a pricey vow and have it come true is a tale for the museum of chutzpah.

Then, in an effort to top my lowest box office record and alienate as many fans as possible, I decided I wanted to make a one act play of mine called *Kleinman's Function* into a movie called *Shadows and Fog*, a black-and-white existential little tale that takes place in Germany one night during the 1920s. Everything would be shot indoors on a set, even the many exteriors. One only has to study the fundamentals of bankruptcy law to envision the box office potential. So Santo Loquasto set about building the European city, which was, to its time and for all I know, still the biggest set ever built at Kaufman Astoria Studios. I found working in a studio for months claustrophobic, and I longed to be outside shooting in the streets. Brian Hamill, the still photographer and a friend who did many pictures with me, and I used to love to shoot on the streets of New York. We loved checking out the passersby and all the great women. A lot of those women would stop because they knew Brian. He had photographed them or dated them. I got mostly male panhandlers.

Brian's brother, Pete Hamill, was the first to rally to my side in print when the false accusation hit. His other brother Dennis, also a journalist, has defended me against the al-legations over and over. The Hamills were no-bullshit street Irish from Brooklyn and know phoniness when they see it. They were quick to get what was going on, and Dennis has been quite passionate on the subject in the *Daily News*. Getting back to my movie, the downside of being out in the streets shooting is when the weather's cold, the traffic's noisy, and the passing multitude hard to handle. It made me long to shoot in a studio with its controlled lighting and sound. But in the studio, I felt trapped. Over the years loved ones have said I'm a chronically dissatisfied person, and it's true I'd always rather be where I'm not at the time. I mean, let's say it's a beautiful fall Sunday and I'm walking on the Upper East Side, maybe in Central Park with Soon-Yi, and it's just lovely. So I'm thinking, My god, wouldn't it be great to be in Paris right now or Venice? The fantasy that I'd be happier elsewhere extends to romantic notions of owning a beach house, strolling the beach, watching the crashing waves and staring out over the horizon, my head awash with intimations of a cosmos that's a little more user-friendly.

In reality, many years ago I did purchase this dream beach house right on the Atlantic in Southampton. I spent two years and a fortune fixing it up before moving in. I planted trees, I picked every carpet, every stick of furniture, every molding, finial, and screen door. I chose wallpaper and tiles. I made it the most beautiful house one could imagine. Finally, it was ready to live in. I went out there with Mia and her kids on a beautiful fall Saturday morning. The kids swooned. I walked the beach, the stars came out. I fell asleep to the gentle sound of the waves lapping on the shore. The following day I drove back to Manhattan, sold the place, and never returned. Who wants to hear waves lapping on the shore when you're trying to sleep? Two years in the making, one night and I knew walking the sandy beach and staring over the ocean at the horizon wasn't for me. Frankly, I didn't even like the horizon, although I never really got close enough to it to check it out.

I remember a similar occasion once when early in our relationship, Mia had dragged me to her house on Martha's Vineyard on an exquisite fall day. Alone and isolated, I stared out her window at Lake Tashmoo, while she made the fatal mistake of putting on the second movement of the Sibelius Violin Concerto. As I listened in the quiet autumn beauty of the vineyard, the unbearable strains of Sibelius transported my soul to Finland, Sweden, Norway, the fjords, the vast ice floes, and long, dark winters, and I experienced an intense longing for a chopped chicken liver sandwich, obtainable only in the vicinity of Fifty-Fourth Street.

The filming of *Shadows and Fog* came off without a hitch except for the movie. The executives gathered in my screening room to see it for the first time, a ritual usually followed by either exaggerated euphoria or polite insincerity extolling my prowess as a filmmaker. When the lights went on after the screening ended, the four or five suits sat immobile as if they had all been paralyzed by curare. With visions of their investment ebbing to black like a fade-out, they finally stirred and managed to give voice to a reaction. The most lucid amongst them piped up with, "Well, you certainly surprise us every new film," the words bunching up in his throat. The next move would have been for one of them to produce my contract from his pocket and run it through the paper shredder. Certain they were educated men, I expected a mix of philosophical observations followed by a discussion of the obvious existential motifs of the film. Instead I discerned what sounded like Hebrew imprecations, and a few of them had to be restrained. I thought I heard Eric Pleskow, an Orion head, say that he lived nearby and owned a machete. While the critical response to the film was reserved, there was no truth to the rumor the projectionist at the movie house rushed to the sea with the print and hurled it in. If I recall correctly, there may have even been a rather supportive review in the *Poultryman's Journal*. Not wanting to throw good money after bad, Orion opted for a limited ad campaign comprised of a few discreet curb stencils.

I made my final movie with Mia, *Husbands and Wives*, and as you now know, before the shooting ended a series of Polaroids discovered in my apartment would change the course of western civilization or, if not that, my predicted life span. The movie was one of my favorites because I paid no attention to the art of filmmaking. I couldn't care less about all the rules of jump cutting, screen direction, or anything else that gives a film its polished look. Much was shot handheld, lots of improvising. The end result was a movie with some energy and great performances by everybody. As I never see my movies after I finish them, I haven't seen it in years. Whether I'd still be as high on it as I was then, I don't know. And I don't want to find out.

I took you through the details of the to-do wherein Mia embarked on an Ahab-like quest for revenge. How did I get through the ordeal?—and it was an ordeal. Falsely accused, hideous press, enormous legal expense. I spent millions trying to see my daughter, Dylan, to get a less biased judge, couldn't swing it. Meantime, Mia went to another court to try and have my adoption of Dylan and Moses voided, but that judge, a woman, saw through her immediately. After a few weeks in court it became painfully obvious to Mia this was not a judge she would be able to con, and so she quietly folded her tent and receded. As for me, apart from not going out in public without a fake nose and glasses, I simply went about my business and worked. I worked while stalked, vilified, and smeared. Being innocent, I felt, It's not my problem. Let them carry on. I'm not going to sacrifice precious work time over a bad call savage hordes are dining out on. Playing second base in the PAL as a boy, I had gotten some bad calls from umpires and I lived. So this was yet another. I'd get through it. The trick was to accept the bad calls and move on.

I played jazz every week, never missing a session. I wrote and put on a play off-Broadway in an evening of one-acters along with David Mamet and Elaine May. I did a movie, I toured Europe with my jazz band, all the while an ostrich when it came to reading or hearing any of the nonsense about my private life. And by *ostrich* I mean I never ever read or saw a single thing about me for the year or year and a half the onslaught went on. Knowing I'd be smeared, I limited what I read in the paper, confining myself basically to the cargo arrivals. All over TV were talking heads, experts of all sorts exchanging theories and misinformation about an event that never took place. Confidently, they paraded their insights and told it like it was. I quickly gave up on news and talk shows, watched sports and movies and, as always, worked. Wrote.

The obviousness of the false accusation, I knew, would become clear to any who cared to pursue the matter in detail, and the whole thing would eventually straighten out. There were still ones out there who didn't get it, who, despite all logic, for one reason or another didn't seem to want to get it. Nothing could stir them from the idea that I'd raped Mia's underage backward child or married my daughter or molested Dylan. I had faith that in due time, common sense, reason, and the evidence would descend upon even the most phlegmatic mouth breather, but I also picked Hillary to win.

Meanwhile Soon-Yi and I adopted two girls at their birth, a Korean and an American. And by the way, before they just hand over two children, especially girls, to a man who's been accused of child molestation, two separate judges check you out pretty thoroughly to make sure they're not gifting two infants to a predator. Because the allegations upon the judges' scrutiny were so clearly unfounded, we had no problem adopting. I'm happy to report both girls have grown up unharmed by their alleged demonic father and are both in college, and the judges' decision to sanction the adoptions proved sound. After having vowed to live in the penthouse forever, we moved because with our first child and a nanny the penthouse was too small. We moved into a grand mansion on Ninety-Second Street, a twenty-thousand-square-foot stunning mansion, which was not too small, but too big. The living room (at least we thought it was the living room) was a huge ballroom that we filled with furniture, sofas, conversation areas, a piano; there was a billiard room, bedrooms, kitchens, two elevators—God, it was enormous.

Later, a lady who had been raised in the house and who now lived on Fifth Avenue, Mrs. Douglas Dillon, the widow of the ex–secretary of the treasury, asked if she could walk through it to have a nostalgic look, and of course we said yes. Only then did we learn her family had kept the enormous living room empty, doors shut, and only used it for large parties when they'd put up tables and chairs. Meanwhile we'd have friends over and peregrinate all over the room going from one conversation area to another, trying to employ the space. We lived there a few years and moved out. We then lived two years in a ratty sublet, which had formerly been a rendezvous pad for two illicit lovers till the man murdered the woman's husband. The Long Island contractor who beat the poor spouse's head in as he slept. The lurid press. The TV versions. You must've heard of it.

Finally, we found the perfect house for us and, being more experienced than when we left the penthouse, we knew what we needed and what we didn't. A house is very different from an apartment. With an apartment in New York you have many more conveniences, but in a house you're autonomous. You can work on it how and when you please, and you don't need board approval for every move you make. You don't wake up one morning and look out your window to find scaffolding's been put up and will be blocking your view for three months. Or the water will be turned off all day so we advise you to fill up some pots.

Or, most of all, if you're in a co-op, the president and his henchmen have to approve the person you've finally found who wants to buy it. These indignities don't obtain in a house. You're on your own for better or worse, and while there's no doorman to get you a cab when it's five below zero in January or shovel the snow so you don't get sued when some stroller fractures his pelvis in front of your sidewalk because you were too fatigued to clear it, you don't have to ride up and down in an elevator with some tenant who took a bath in Replique and pretend her Pekingese isn't creepy. We have the most beautiful, lovely, perfect town house you can imagine, built over 125 years ago with lots of original detail, many fireplaces, and a sweet garden. Every morning I clump down the stairs, mysteriously hung over since I don't drink, open the blinds on the ground floor, and there's New York City in its Runyonesque vitality. If I'm lucky with the weather, it's gray and misty, and in my mind, I hear the strains of "Street Scene" by Alfred Newman and I tell myself I actually own a small piece of this legendary island. Then I think of the taxes on the property and my arthritis sets in. In *Annie Hall*, I had to decide on which block to have Annie and Alvy live, and I picked a block I thought was tree lined and photogenic, the most beautiful on the Upper East Side, and now I live there, right across the street from where Annie Hall lived.

So Soon-Yi and I continued with our lives, she now a mother, aggravating appropriately over every little hiccup in our daughters' daily routines and seeing to it they grow up adept in art, French, and music, and me teaching them how to figure the point spread. I continued making motion pictures, thinking the ordeal of false accusation had been laid to rest forever by all the investigations, which were definitive and unanimous. Little did I know—once smeared, always vulnerable. Originally I had planned to make *Manhattan Murder Mystery* with me and Mia, but relations had since curdled into Roquefort cheese, and of course it was obvious we would never work together again. Mia surprised everybody by wanting to do the movie, and threatened to sue me if I didn't use her in the part. This, after swearing to the world I raped, molested, both Soon-Yi and Dylan. I guess acting was in her blood.

Anyhow, I hired Keaton and she flew east, and it was like old times. For me it was a totally self-indulgent movie. I grew up loving murder mysteries where the lead characters snapped off the one-liners, where the comic was cowardly and amusing and his leading lady was more adventurous and got them into trouble. I loved actresses who could not only stand up and trade one-liners with their male partners but often squelch them, and Keaton could always top me. It's one of the best films I ever made, amusing, good story, good gags, unpretentious, and it massaged my need to be in one of those films I was weaned on. Keaton and I played a sophisticated twosome living in Manhattan and sinking deeper and deeper into a mystery. There were no existential themes, no tragic climaxes or messages to chew over. It was strictly an airplane read. By now you've probably figured I'm not one of those directorial geniuses whose set is always alive with passion, with crises, temperamental outbursts. Probably because my nature is quiet, and I am writer and director and control the whole works, and we never hire actors who are trouble no matter how brilliant they are.

Anyhow, if I had to name a time of my life that was happy, I guess I would say those next years. I adored Soon-Yi, and despite the huge amount of flack I got for pursuing her, it was worth every second of it. Sometimes, when the going got rough and I was maligned everywhere, I was asked if I had known the outcome, do I ever wish I never took up with Soon-Yi? I always answered I'd do it again in a heartbeat, and the most satisfying achievement of my life is not my movies but that I was able to liberate Soon-Yi from a terrible situation and provide her with an opportunity to flower and realize her potential, and she would never have to eat a bar of soap or long for a hug or get hit with a phone again.

Since Mia and I had not been the lovers the public imagined, I had been very ripe for a more meaningful relationship. It could have been some actress, a secretary, a dental hygienist who liked Swedish movies. Of course with my flair for seppuku, it was Soon-Yi. So, yes, my loving her did not conform to Robert's Rules of Order, but we've both adored every second of our twenty-five years together. I remember when she was very young and I first spoke to her and asked her what she wanted to be and she said, A boss. And I said, A boss of what? And she said, Doesn't matter as long as I'm the boss. I don't want to say which of us actually calls the shots, but let me put it this way—I'm the one that gets an allowance. She runs the house, raises the kids, and plans our social life. We travel and have spent long periods abroad, Paris, Italy, Spain, the French Riviera, summers in London, Newport, sounds good.

But the age difference, you say. What do you talk about? Everything. For instance, I may ask, As someone underage who's been raped and is retarded, what are your views on the economy? And if she's too young to know who I mean when I bring up Weegee or Leo Durocher, I fill her in. And do we fight? Soon-Yi will be the first to tell you in over twenty years of marriage, and the many disagreements we've had, I have never once been right on a single issue. When I first started going out with her, she said a very sad thing to me. She said, "My whole life, I've never been anyone's top priority." I, who had been the top priority of a large, extended family, the apple of many loving eyes, tried to put myself in Soon-Yi's place and decided to make her my top priority. I decided I would dote on her, wait on her, spoil her, celebrate her, never deny her anything she wanted, and somehow try and make up for the horrific first twenty-two years of her life. She has no problem with this arrangement, allowing me the privilege of indulging her every whim around the clock. Out of a necessity to stay alive in the streets at five she has grown up hypercompetent, while I can't figure out how to use a swizzle stick. Yet she respects me as someone who can be funny, if nothing else, and considers me some kind of savant—I forget the full term.

What do we do for fun? For pleasure? For pure enjoyment, I guess I'd say Soon-Yi, when not overwhelmed bringing up two girls, whose provenance is unknown to us but it's clear there's bloodlines to the Jukes, she likes to read, go to the theater, museums, movies, to shop, to hunt down bargains, sample sales; the sheer joy of getting a five-hundred-dollar item for one hundred sends her through the roof, so some day I expect her to come home with a tractor we don't need because it was marked down. As for me, I enjoy going to doctors, having my blood pressure checked, posing for X-rays, hearing that I'm fine and the dark spot on my white shirt is from my ballpoint pen, not a melanoma.

Here's a typical day. It used to include taking the kids to school, but now that they're in college the roles have reversed and I need them to help me get the picture back on the TV after I've somehow lost it into the ether.

Soon-Yi and I get up together early, around six thirty. We eat breakfast and do some exercising. She is very exercise minded, and over the course of the week between the treadmill and yoga class and Gyrotonics and exercise class and Pilates she's fit as a Navy SEAL. I do the treadmill and pull rubber bands to maintain a build equal to any Giacometti sculpture. So Soon-Yi and I exercise and then she does family business, the kids, their schools, summer work plans, the household help, checking all the bills, return calls, sets up our dinner dates. She reads pretty much the whole *New York Times*. Soon-Yi and I are constantly clipping articles for one another that we think will be of interest or funny to read. I write, and then we have lunch together and see if we can find a fresh topic to quarrel over. I write after lunch, and she either has more domestic stuff to do or, if she's got free time, she goes to a museum with a friend or maybe a film, or maybe we take a walk. Later, she puts on the earmuffs airport workers use to block out jet whine and I practice my clarinet. Frequently we meet friends at a restaurant, or if we stay home she reads and I watch sports on TV or *A Streetcar Named Desire* if it's on Turner Classic Movies.

Streetcar is the finest work of art in my lifetime, and I never miss it when it's on. Problem is, the film version is so definitive that any production pales by comparison. Same trouble with the movie *Born Yesterday*. The ultimate version was done with Judy Holliday and Broderick Crawford. I found her the greatest screen comedienne ever. Maybe if Elaine May had made more movies. Diane Keaton is, of course, right up there with the best of them, but I must say, contrary to popular taste, I enjoyed but didn't go crazy over Carole Lombard. Again, it's not that I disliked her, but I didn't laugh at her. I found Eve Arden kind of funny and Alison Skipworth and Marie Dressler. For whatever reason I never laughed at some of the more highly touted female comic stars. Of course, Jean Harlow was great. But listen to me babbling. Sorry. And so, after Soon-Yi and I got together and the mushroom cloud settled, and I was enjoying a real marriage, a real love relationship, for the first time in my life, I continued to make films, which I will touch on till this paradise was once again invaded by fresh madness.

I wrote *Bullets over Broadway*, which I consider one of my best films. I wrote it with Doug McGrath. If it wasn't for Doug I never would have written it. I don't like to collaborate, but with ones like Mickey Rose, or Marshall Brickman, who were good friends and authentically funny human beings, it can be fun. Marshall is particularly bright, demanding, and full of funny ideas and great lines, and our collaborations came off quite well. So I decided to write a screenplay with Doug McGrath, another funny and very astute friend. Writing with someone mitigates the intense loneliness. Doug married my former assistant, Jane Martin, who had worked with me for over a decade. The two of them are close friends of Soon-Yi's and mine. They're both very witty, as is Soon-Yi, and with my flair for physical comedy, our dinners can get quite lively. I came to Doug with several ideas to do together. My personal first choice was a political satire with the idea for *Bullets* lower on the list. I favored the political idea, and since I was the senior, older, more experienced writer I tried to use my seniority to push him into saying he agreed with me that the political satire was best. But he didn't. He sparked to *Bullets* and maintained his conviction. The gangster backs the show, but the playwright must use the gangster's girlfriend. To me, it sounded a little hackneyed. Still, I succumbed to Doug's rabid confidence, and as it turned out, I'm thankful I listened to him.

As usual, Juliet helped me get an amazing cast: John Cusack, another actor who is incapable of a false moment, Jack Warden, Jennifer Tilly, Chazz Palminteri, the fabulous Dianne Wiest, Harvey Fierstein, Mary-Louise Parker, Jim Broadbent, Tracey Ullman, Rob Reiner. My God, with that cast how can you miss!? Every single one of them came through. Dianne Wiest won her second Oscar for me, and Carlo's photography and the sets and Jeff Kurland's beautiful costumes. I was proud of that movie. I even got a chance to work with Alan Arkin, a great actor whose scene had to be cut because that section of the movie was running too long. I can't believe I had a chance to work with such a terrific performer and I was forced to cut his scene.

Same thing happened to me with Vanessa Redgrave on another film. I may be the only director that cut Vanessa Redgrave out of a movie. Obviously not because of her acting but because of my inept writing. On that score I replaced John Gielgud. Can you imagine that? One of the greatest actors in the world. He was the original narrator for *Zelig* but he was too grand, too stentorian. It killed me to have obtained him to do it and then to have to replace him. It turned out he and Ralph Richardson were big fans of *Interiors*, which went a long way to reinforce my megalomania. And while we're on the subject of replacing actors: I have to hold the record for the most unusual replacement when I got rid of Ruth Gordon, who was just too difficult to work with, although we wound up good friends and dined together numerous times years later but, get ready—I replaced her with Geoffrey Holder, the tall, black, dazzling calypso dancer who you will admit looks nothing like Ruth.

The truth is it didn't matter what the magician in a scene in *Everything You Always Wanted to Know About Sex* looked like as long as the character was exotic. Ruth was exotic, her acting exciting and flamboyant. When it turned out neither of us could compromise over her costume, I searched for another flamboyant, exotic type and Geoffrey fit the bill. Ruth and I parted friends, exchanging insincere hugs. Years later, Mia would bring Ruth, whom she worked with in *Rosemary's Baby*, and her husband, Garson Kanin, together with us for assorted dinners at the Russian Tea Room. I found them both superb company, full of great stories about great people and the stories had great punch lines. Garson advised me, as Somerset Maugham had advised him, to write everything down because you forget things. It was good advice I did not heed very carefully, and I'm sure I have forgotten a lot of the most interesting things that ever happened to me—unless I haven't, and this is it, folks. I do write down movie ideas but then only a few words.

Anyhow, years later *Bullets over Broadway* was made into a musical in the theater. Susan Stroman did a fantastic job of staging it. I had been reluctant to let them adapt it at first, but when I saw what Susan did with it, I was thrilled and proud. My wife liked it even better than the movie. Its critical reception did not share my enthusiasm, however, and it only ran a half year. Sartre said, "Hell is other people." I would just like to change that to, "Hell is other people's taste."

And while I'm on the subject of the Broadway theater, I was asked to be in a TV version of *The Sunshine Boys*, the Neil Simon comedy. The movie version with George Burns and Walter Matthau was Herb Ross's best picture, and of course his two leads were superb. The TV redo fell to me and Peter Falk, a very gifted actor who was always fun to talk to and drove the director a little crazy with his many demands and quirks while I was as usual, an angel. No backtalk, no questions, knew my lines, tell me where to stand, tell me what you want, I'll do my best. Sarah Jessica Parker, then not the big deal she became but no less talented, played the female lead beautifully. There was lots of coverage, which necessitated shooting each scene over and over from every angle, with every possible field size.

By now you probably guessed, as a filmmaker I am an imperfectionist. I have no patience to shoot scenes over and over and get coverage from various angles, however invaluable it is later when editing. I like to shoot a scene, go on to the next, finish up, and get the hell out of there. I want to go home, fondle Soon-Yi, dandle the kids, eat my supper, and watch the ball game. I really don't like to bother with a profile shot, an extra close-up, yet another take of the stars arguing because maybe they'll do it better. I like making movies, but I lack the dedication of a Spielberg or Scorsese, not to mention their other gifts. I just can't get interested enough in the movie to shoot long days and maybe miss the tip off or putting my daughters to bed.

In a film, however, and most films made by responsible adults, they do coverage so later on in the cutting room the poor editor is not writhing on the floor, unable to make the story coherent. Some directors turn their footage over to an editor who puts it together, and the director comes in only then to participate. Some directors like the editor to cut the footage as it comes in so if something is missing or a new idea comes up the company is still together and hasn't dissipated all over the globe. I like to work as follows: no editing till the shooting ends. Then the editor and I sit down together before the AVID (the editing machine with its TV-sized screen) and we both begin at the beginning and cut our way through the movie.

I've always worked with bright and talented editors. After Ralph Rosenblum, I worked for years with Sandy Morse, who solved a lot of unsolvable editing problems with me. After Sandy is my current editor, Alisa Lepselter, whom I've worked with for twenty years. Gamely, she collaborates with me on the putting together of the film, sometimes agreeing, sometimes saving my life by fighting me, but both of us always with the same goal, to realize the original vision and make the best movie possible given the footage we have to work with. Lots of times we stick in music from records in our good-sized record collection. Because of the way I shoot, carelessly and irresponsibly, we are always facing problems, but I find being forced to come up with spontaneous solutions often leads to creative inspiration. I never would have put those title cards throughout *Hannah and Her Sisters* except I needed one title card to get me out of a cutting jam and to have just one title card in the film was awkward, so I went back and put in about six and gave the movie a stylized bit of panache.

I never saw *The Sunshine Boys*, but I got a lovely note of praise from Neil Simon, whom I've always looked up to and liked personally, and I admired his work very much. In fact I think for all his success he's underrated because writing laughs seemed to come so easily to him. The funny lines just flow and they're damn funny. Still, I doubted the note of praise as I couldn't imagine that, having seen his play done by George Burns and Walter Matthau, he could do anything but wince at me and Peter Falk doing it, but I pretended to be moved by his kind words and sent a thank-you card.

I remember the first time I saw Peter Falk. It was in Jose Quintero's brilliant production of *The Iceman Cometh* downtown. I took Harlene, my bride to be. I was stunned by the greatness of the play and the production, and who was this guy Jason Robards? He's off the charts with brilliance. Peter Falk played the bartender and he stood out to me in a much smaller part as a very gifted actor. I raved about him to Bob Dishy, an actor who was friendly with him, and I told Dishy, "Falk had a slight speech defect." Dishy said, "That's what you noticed about him? He'll kill himself." I also noticed how wonderful he was as an actor, so it wasn't all nit-picking. Years later, when I worked with Emma Stone, one of the best, most beautiful, most charming actresses I ever met, I noticed she had a speech thing, too. She didn't sound like Peter Falk, it was more like Sylvester Pussycat, but I heard it the minute she spoke, and on her it was endearing.

So I knocked off *The Sunshine Boys*, took home a buxom check for a gig which allowed me once again to sleep in my own bed and moved on to do my first dirty movie, *Mighty Aphrodite*. What interested me was doing a Greek style setting complete with chorus and deux ex machina. I acted with the very bright and talented Mira Sorvino. I loved working with Mira. If she had any fault it was that she couldn't appreciate how gifted and attractive she was. I think she even won an Oscar for herself. I used to laugh at her because when we'd do a scene together, we'd be standing there waiting for the assistant director to yell action, and because she wanted to hit the ground running and be in her character immediately, she'd begin little imaginary improvisations before the action call. Fine. But she'd expect me to join her, and I just thought she was nuts talking to herself.

Of course on action, she was beautiful. We filmed in New York and Sicily. In the background was Mount Etna. I was told not to worry unless the volcano smoked. It smoked. I worried. Couldn't wait to get home. The beautiful choreography work was done by Graciela Daniele, and I did get to work with Helena Bonham Carter, a wonderful and beautiful actress who was smart and charming. I visited her home in London, where she lived with her parents, and her mother was a very bright shrink and it was a really nice experience. In retrospect, *Mighty Aphrodite* is too dirty for my taste. I'd like to do it over and clean it up a bit, but all my films could profit by a do-over. I'd like to have a second chance with some of the women I took out in my life, too, but alas, the boat sailed. I do not think they will sing to me.

And speaking of singing (and heavy-handed segues), I had always dreamed of doing a musical; a musical for people who could sing no better than we all do in the shower. When I cast *Everyone Says I Love You*, I didn't bother to ask if the actor or actress could sing. I assumed they'd do the best they could. I wasn't looking to make a slick musical or break any new ground. I just wanted a group of New Yorkers to go through four seasons on the Upper East Side and sing some old sweet standards when the spirit moved them. When I told Goldie Hawn, who is a major, major talent—that's two majors—to please not sing so great as she was doing, she was put off a bit. Edward Norton, a flawless actor, had no idea he'd been hired to sing. Actors and actresses who couldn't carry a tune sang, and all I cared about was the feeling.

Only Drew Barrymore absolutely refused, and since I was such a huge fan of hers I gave in, rather than make

330

her unhappy or tense. We got a school friend of Soon-Yi's, Olivia Hayman, to dub her and it worked out fine. What can one say about making a movie where I get to work in Venice, to work in Paris, to work in Manhattan, and to kiss Julia Roberts? It was a treat from start to finish. John Lahr wrote a lovely piece about it for the *New Yorker*, but others did not wax so enthusiastically and criticized the fact that many in the cast couldn't sing. This, of course, was the whole point of the movie, but I'd guessed wrong. Not as many people found that notion as charming as I did. The film did so-so in America but was a hit in Europe, particularly in France.

Still I had the pleasure of working in cities I loved so much and of showing Manhattan in all four seasons, each one a treat to photograph. That's why I say the fun of the movie business for me comes only in the making of the film. It's the act of working, rising early, shooting, enjoying the company of gifted men and women, solving problems that are not fatal if you fail to solve them, working with great fashions, great music. When it all ends and the film is done, I always judge it for myself by asking, Did I come close to realizing, to fulfilling, that dream I had when I was laying across my bed and furiously creating characters and situations? Did I get 50 percent of my idea? Did I strike out altogether? I always move on after a film. I never think about it again, see it again, keep souvenirs, photos, even own video copies. When Turner Classic Movies put together a group to screen and discuss *Annie Hall* and asked me to be a guest on their talk panel—and I love TCM—I said no because I'm not interested in sitting there and dwelling in the past.

People ask me do I ever fear I'll wake up one morning

and not be funny. The answer is no because being funny is not something you put on like a shirt when you wake up so suddenly you can't find the shirt. You simply are funny or you're not. If you are, you are, and it's not a thing or a temporary madness you can lose. If I woke up and was not funny, I wouldn't be me. This does not mean you can't wake up in a bad mood, hating the world, angry at people's stupidity, raging at the empty universe, which I confess I do on schedule every morning, but it serves to bring out my humor, not erase it. Like Bertrand Russell, I feel a great sadness for the human race. Unlike Bertrand Russell, I can't do long division. And maybe I can't transmute my suffering into great art or great philosophy, but I can write good one-liners, which distract momentarily and gives brief relief against the irresponsible consequences of the Big Bang.

I never thought having biological children was doing them any favor, bringing kids into this world. Sophocles said to never have been born may be the greatest boon of all. Of course I'm not sure he would've said that if he ever heard Bud Powell play "Polka Dots and Moonbeams." Soon-Yi and I chose adoption to try and make life better for a couple of orphans already marooned on this orbiting psychiatric ward. And that we accomplished. I'm a very affectionate father who enjoys kids. I always think that Soon-Yi is too strict with the girls and she thinks I'm too liberal, but Soon-Yi knows the ropes of survival better than me. She's more practical. For instance, I couldn't last a week in a concentration camp without my Buf-Puf. Soon-Yi, on the other hand, after two days would have the Gestapo bringing her breakfast in bed.

And so all the important things; the kids' education,

summer camp, summer jobs, trips, doctors, tutors, lessons, and sleepovers, she does with Prussian efficiency. All that's missing is the dueling scar. I basically hug them, ply them with money, never say no, and only worry one day they will kill Soon-Yi and myself while we sleep due to some genetic psychosis. Soon-Yi attends every single school meeting or event, where I find them boring. I go out of a show of parental duty, but as the teacher drones on, my mind is far off devising fresh excuses to avoid jury duty. I mean, let us say the discussion is about what the upcoming term will cover for Manzie or Bechet. Like it's really important I know she'll be reading *Silas Marner* or dissecting a frog. I sit dutifully fighting vainly the old ennui as the teachers rant on, and then when it's all over and I'm champing at the bit to hit Chinatown and vacuum up some Ants Climb a Tree, there's always parents you want to strangle who ask questions and prolong me getting to my major munch. "Is science class only teaching one version of reproduction, or will there be equal credence given to the stork?" "Will the children be required to read and write to graduate?" "My daughter wants to be a suicide bomber, must she take a musical instrument?" Of course you haven't lived till you've seen your child perform at a handbell concert. But it's worth it because they're so cute.

So in answer to the question you never asked, I never woke up panicked thinking I'll lose my sense of humor, nor have I ever suffered from writer's block. But Harry Block, the lead character in *Deconstructing Harry*, was suffering from writer's block. I liked that movie, and if you check out the cast list it reads like an all-star team of gifted actors and actresses, some of whom I'd worked with before and some whom I had the privilege of directing for the first time. I recall that before we shot Mariel Hemingway came by my cutting room and told me she wanted to get back into acting; she had become single and the high point of her life had been the movie *Manhattan*. I didn't have anything comparable for her at the moment, but there was a part still uncast if she didn't mind a small role. She didn't mind and I cast her, and she did her usual excellent job. It was great seeing her again, and we met again years later for dinner at Cipriani's.

She was very much into healthy living both for herself and helping other people. I thought back to when she invited me to Ketchum, Idaho, the mountains and snow, and I remember looking out the window at her while she was bouncing up and down on a big trampoline in the freezing yard, and she was this six-foot, beautiful, healthy, gifted, athletic blond goddess and I kept thinking, If only Leni Riefenstahl could be here. Then my mind turned to her grandfather, who only a short distance away woke up one morning, took his shotgun, put it to his head, and pulled the trigger, and how Louise and I used it as an excuse to meet and talk and were blindly in love and how Louise was now my ex-wife, and here I was visiting Mariel and sharing a bathroom with Ernest's son and I don't want to share a bathroom with a guy no matter how many fine and brave bulls his father's seen die and I don't know where this thought is going except that life is too ironic to get a grip on.

In *Deconstructing Harry* I got to work with Judy Davis yet again. I'd worked with Judy on *Husbands and Wives* and found it an unnerving experience. Why unnerving? Because it was clear she was such a great actress that I was always intimidated by her. I never wanted to say anything to her and give away the truth: that I'm extremely uninteresting, shallow, and disappointing when you get to know me. Consequently I never spoke to her, and she, instinctively sensing I had nothing of value to say, never spoke to me. So we did several pictures where I'd nod hello to her at the wardrobe tests, a weak smile on my lips, and then not see her again till she'd show up on the set. Action would be called, she'd act, always wonderful, always exciting, sexy, unpredictable. Cut. I'd say, Great, let's move on. She'd exit the premises and I'd see her again on the set later that day or the next or the next week with the same silence between us. Hire great ones, is my motto, and get out of their way.

It has been written that I am a Renaissance man. Of course, they were not referring to the Italian Renaissance, but the Renaissance in Govind Ghat when the indigenous mountain yaks returned to the icy slopes in vast herds. Still, in keeping with that cultural image, I decided to take our jazz band on a European tour. As a devoted amateur, my style was modeled after (read stolen from) the great New Orleans clarinetists like George Lewis, Johnny Dodds, Albert Burbank, Sidney Bechet. My problem wasn't just that I played with no feeling, ear, or rhythm, it was that I had no humility and played out fearlessly as if I actually had something to say. And yet audiences showed up and when Eddie Davis, our true leader and first-rate banjo player, suggested we go on a concert tour of Europe, I, like a fatuous dunce who didn't realize how bad I was, jumped right in with the confidence of a true know-nothing. I practiced and practiced, experimenting with mouthpieces and reeds, never grasping it wasn't the equipment that made me sound like a rooster on amphetamines. It was decided, I believe by Jean Doumanian, we would document this tour. Jean hired one of filmdom's finest documentarians, Barbara Kopple, to stay with the tour and capture us on- and offstage for a time capsule should the Smithsonian demand one.

The result was *Wild Man Blues*, and predictably, despite my playing, Kopple made a really good documentary. I saw it and I found it sharp, funny, accurate. I guess I'm prejudiced because I personally didn't come off totally hideous. I was, as I am in life, innocuous but mildly amusing, and as for my playing, Barbara carefully winnowed out the wheat from the chaff, parlaying the small amount of wheat into a passable few licks.

As any student of Heisenberg knows, with a camera following one around every second and being only human, one acts differently, and it's impossible not to sometimes lose one's poise and get caught behaving like an inept buffoon. Fortunately, through the miracle of editing, my boorishness was kept to a minimum. Soon-Yi comes off nicely, and in a piece about the film in the *New York Times* the reporter dispels the notion that I, being older and more well-known, am presumably the one who sets the tone in our relationship, but it is really Soon-Yi who, in the reporter's words, comes off like a dominatrix. It's true Soon-Yi has a very large and strong personality and does all the deciding on matters that impact our lives like where we live, how many children, what friends we see, how we spend our money, but I'm still the boss regarding any decisions about space travel.

The jazz tour itself was a smashing success. We sold out every venue. And they were huge and beautiful: opera houses, concert halls. Mobs gathered outside my hotel and, after checking to make sure the group hadn't brought any tar and feathers, I greeted them all personally. We did many encores every show. Once in Milan, when there was a power failure and the lights went out and we played on in the black, we were much applauded. I received a plaque the following night from the local fire department as if I had done a brave thing. Of course, I played the hero in perfect Bob Hope fashion and said as the fire chief handed me the plaque, "I wonder what the cowards are doing tonight?" No laugh, but I'm sure it was the language difference.

Seeing the New York skyline is always thrilling, and I got right into casting with Juliet when I returned. I titled the film *Celebrity* and shot it in black and white. All the suits hemorrhage when you say you're shooting in black-and-white, but then you point to *Raging Bull*, *Schindler's List*, *Manhattan*, just to name a few. Audiences somehow feel that black-and-white means a cut-rate product, but it's really an artistic decision. It costs as much. The shooting of *Celebrity* went off smoothly, and I remember the last day or so when Melanie Griffith, a gifted actress, had to sit in a movie house with the man playing her husband. The husband only sat next to her for a few seconds and didn't have any lines and didn't appear in the movie anywhere else. We filled out the movie house and picked an appropriate extra to sit next to her as her husband. But when it came time to shoot, she didn't like our choice. She said she'd never marry a guy like that (I didn't tell him). I explained she wouldn't have to really marry him and live the rest of her life with him, but she couldn't see it. I thought it was very sweet and so typical of how actors get so into their characters. So we switched him and gave her a different extra to marry, and they lived happily ever after. Kenneth Branagh was a privilege to work with, and I finally got to work with Joe Mantegna, whom I had seen and loved in Mamet's play, *Glengarry Glen Ross*. Judy Davis was of course great, and since we had now done several films together, I was determined to say hello, but I lost my nerve when she couldn't remember who I was.

Okay, so for years Sean Penn was always sending back messages about how much he'd like to work with me, and every time I'd ask him he'd turn me down. Then one day, I send him a script about this virtuoso jazz guitarist with a complicated personality, and finally he likes it. Samantha Morton plays the little mute girl who Sean falls in love with, and Sean gets his first, long-overdue Oscar nomination. *Sweet and Lowdown* was the movie Santo had to make look like we shot all over the country except I never left Manhattan. It's not that I mind sleeping away from home in a hotel, provided of course the sheets are of the softest gossamer-like cotton and upon retiring, my wife presses her full complement of cells against me in a position Saul Bellow once brilliantly described as spoons. Since Soon-Yi and I became a couple; from the first day she moved in with me, we've never spent a single night apart in twenty-five years. Nor have we had many meals apart. We eat breakfast, lunch, and dinner together almost every day. You'd think we'd have long run out of things to say, but as the weather changes all the time, we are never at a loss for conversation.

Dinners were almost always with the kids or friends at some restaurant where Soon-Yi orders, ignoring all advice from the Surgeon General. I, on the other hand, for health purposes am careful not to eat anything pleasurable. Then it's home, a bedside prayer where I beg God to prove he's out there by giving me some sign like two or three winners at the track. Soon-Yi is of course in her bathroom, doing her nocturnal ablutions, a ritual involving a large jar with some eye of newt. Finally, it's lights out as I embrace her and fall asleep smiling, thinking about how different things might have been if I had been born six thousand years earlier in the Arctic and liked whale meat.

In my lifetime I had written gags for nightclub comics, written for radio, written a nightclub act for myself and done it, written for television, played clubs and concerts and TV, wrote and directed movies, wrote and directed in the theater, starred on Broadway, directed an opera. I've done it all from boxing a kangaroo on TV to staging Puccini. It's enabled me to dine at the White House, to play ball with major leaguers at Dodger Stadium, to play jazz in parades and at Preservation Hall in New Orleans, to travel all over America and Europe, to meet heads of state and meet all kinds of gifted men and women, witty guys, enchanting actresses. I've had my books published. If I died right now I couldn't complain—and neither would a lot of other people.

The only other occupation that ever interested me was a life of crime, a gambler, a hustler, a con man and I got to play a petty criminal in my movie comedy, *Small Time Crooks*.

Small Time Crooks gave me a chance to play opposite Tracey Ullman, a huge comic talent who I'm sure you know without me gushing about her. Also with a group of mugs that included some truly hilarious humans. Look who was doing my material: Michael Rapaport, one of my favorite actors, plus Jon Lovitz, and of course Elaine May. I've known Elaine since she and Mike Nichols came to New York. We had the same manager, Jack Rollins. I wanted to write for them before I became a comedian, but they didn't need me to. When I did my first film, *Take the Money and Run*, I asked Elaine to be in it and she brushed me by saying, "I can't, I'm wearing a neck brace." Our paths crossed many times over the years, and we both worked in the theater together, contributing one-act plays to an evening of one-acters with David Mamet and years later with Ethan Coen. Anyway, she agreed to be in *Small Time Crooks*, and we've since worked together on a TV thing I did. My point is, she is one of the very few people who is authentically funny.

What I mean is there are many who make their living doing comedy. Many who are amusing. Some who are thought of as geniuses when they are far from it. Some of the alleged geniuses aren't even good. Then, there are the authentically funny. A matter of taste, to be sure, and we all decide for ourselves. I have no interest in inflicting who I find truly funny on others. Nor am I interested in hearing who they find funny. Let us each enjoy our favorite comic performers unsullied by superfluous conflict. For the written record in this personal document, let me simply say to me, Groucho Marx, W. C. Fields, and Elaine May are indisputably funny, with S.J. Perelman the funniest human of my time on earth. Oh, and don't forget *Pogo*. Walt Kelly's comic strip was touched by genius. There are others, but let me move on.

Anyhow, the bad guy in *Small Time Crooks* was played by

Hugh Grant superbly. He was so elegantly smarmy, calculating, so debonair, a perfectly charming villain. The film did all right. My crime stories seemed to please the public.

Somewhere in what Tennessee Williams called "this dark march" I got a call from Jeff Katzenberg, who asked me if I would do the voice of the lead ant in an animated film called *Antz*. Years ago I had played a sperm and somehow when discussing who'd be right for an insect, my name came up. Jeffrey told me it would be the easiest job I ever had and fun to boot. All I had to do was read in a studio while they recorded me. I had always liked Jeffrey and was happy to do him a favor. As it turned out, it was not easy and I didn't have fun. It was hard and tedious and I was bored, and when it was over I vowed I wouldn't do it again and I never did. Much as I liked Jeffrey, I passed when he came 'round with another offer to be the voice of yet another garden pest. By then I feared being typecast.

I have done favors for people and appeared in cameos or tiny roles when they felt I could be of help. I did a cameo for Stanley Tucci, one for my friend Douglas McGrath, another for a total stranger. Some French girl in Paris needed me to play myself in a French film she was directing, and as it was her first movie and the whole appearance took an hour, I scooted over to her set when I was in Paris and did as instructed. I don't like to see myself in movies, so I never saw any of these films, and I never saw a full movie I appeared in called *Picking Up the Pieces*, which I could tell would win an Oscar for Most Unbelievable Waste of Celluloid for 2000.

Interesting I got to act with Sharon Stone in that film. Sharon had a minuscule moment in *Stardust Memories*, and would be in John Turturro's film *Fading Gigolo*, in which I'd play a big role. I was in three movies with Sharon Stone, but she'd be the first to tell you we were never romantically involved. I always found her a fine actress and very beautiful, and I wondered why whenever she heard I'd be in the movie she came to work with that ten-foot pole. I enjoyed being directed by John Turturro because he's a wonderful actor, he knew how to direct actors, and I felt in good hands. I saw that picture. I had to. Turturro insisted and was sitting in the screening room next to me. When the lights went on I gave him well-deserved words of encouragement.

Trying to cast *Curse of the Jade Scorpion*, was very hard and every actor I offered the lead to turned it down. I was forced to play it myself, and consequently I am the weak link in the movie. The cast was brilliant. Dan Aykroyd and Helen Hunt had big roles and were predictably wonderful. And Charlize Theron is a force of nature with wonderful acting range. But then there was me. It needed Jack Nicholson, or Tom Hanks would've been another way to go, but try as I did, I was not right for the part. The picture was a modest success despite my crippling presence. But what's interesting is that in different countries, one's films are received often very differently, and in Spain, it was a very big hit. It's fascinating how various cultures respond to the same material. One movie will do great in Argentina but not great in England. Another is big in Germany but death in Australia. One scores in Japan but dies in Brazil. It's observations like these that have kept my dinner invitations to a minimum. So *Jade Scorpion*, for whatever reason, rang a loud bell with Spaniards.

To me, my most disappointing film was *Hollywood*

Ending. I felt that movie was funny and it did not do well. The premise was funny, I executed it well, my leading lady Téa Leoni was wonderful, the supporting cast came through, the idea was fraught with potential. A film director goes psychosomatically blind and, unwilling to lose a chance to direct a comeback film, fakes his way through, pretending he can see. In Chaplin's hands or Buster Keaton's, it would've been a masterpiece. Even in mine, it was funny— or so I keep telling people.

On that movie, I fired Haskell Wexler. I always thought he was a genius cameraman but I found him infantile, annoying like a pestering child, and I realized early if we had to have a Talmudic disagreement before and after every shot, I'd run months over schedule. I was sorry to do it, as I had looked forward to working with such a gifted man, but the chemistry was bad.

And so, folks, after all these years, it turns out I was still writing about Louise. *Anything Else* was the title of the flick, and Christina Ricci played the obscure object of desire, and she was plenty desirable. Jason Biggs played a version of young me very charmingly, and I played an exaggerated version of David Panich, the writer I spent a few summers with at Tamiment. Panich was that brilliant influence on me who worked there, and we spent time ruminating about life, love, art, death; two sensitive poets, too fragile for the Sturm und Drang rife on this doleful orb, two lost souls looking for answers or a philosophy that worked and finding some measure of distraction thanks to the muse Thalia, moments sadly too short-lived to stanch the bleeding of our perpetual psychological hemorrhaging. (I'm starting to carry on like Young Werther.) But here we were, two misguided nudniks scrambling for purchase, one having already spent time in a straitjacket, the other conceivably heading for one but rescued by coarser genes.

I could see life as tragic or comic depending on my blood sugar level but always saw it as meaningless. I felt I was a tragedian locked in the body of a stand-up comic. A mute, inglorious Milton. But only if you meant Milton Berle.

Meanwhile, *Anything Else* did not do much in the box office, and I moved on to make the movie *Melinda and Melinda*, hoping to examine a story and some characters from two perspectives, comic and tragic. The movie was okay, not great, not terrible. Meanwhile, I was running out of backing for my films because they weren't very profitable yet I remained as demanding regarding control as if I were Toscanini. Studios, even ones who wanted to work with me, were put off. We're not a bank, they'd say, we want some input. What's the story? Who do you see in it? At least hear our ideas out. But no, I wouldn't think of it. I'd rather not make movies. The studio guys, the business heads, know less than nothing about creating. This is no sin. Those of us who make movies know almost nothing. It's not an exact science, and every film is a new experience with unique problems. You use your brain, you use your experience to the degree it means anything, mostly you use your instinct.

But at least the artists are full of insecurity and know they know nothing. Most of the money guys know nothing, have no instinct, but often fancy themselves guys who do know, even better than the artist. They maul and mangle the work in progress, floundering to please by any means necessary, and the end result is often ten times worse than if they let the artist alone. Let him sink or swim on his own. Once in a great while by sheer chance, which is later paraded as wisdom, does a business executive make a better choice than the artist and the project succeeds lucratively. This is rare, and more often projects are ruined by the interference of the "suits."

I am talking here about the general commercial cinema. If the filmmaker is an artist, a Bergman, a Fellini, for example, input from any source save the artist's soul is so out of the question; even the suits sense this and back off. Unearned as it was, I always operated like I was in a class with artistic moviemakers, and though it was a false comparison, my uncompromising demands won me respect more fitting for actual maestros. Nevertheless, I insisted, if you wanted to invest in my movies, you put the cash in a brown paper bag, go away, and I'd show up with a finished film which you then had the right to distribute as you saw fit. But Hollywood was changing and my track record, though solid, was not in keeping with the surging blockbuster mentality. So here I was, with the script of *Match Point* set in New York, the Hamptons, and Palm Beach, and no takers who had cash and a brown paper bag.

Then I got a call from London. Certain blighters said they would put up the scratch for my next opus if it would shoot in London. Unlike American moguls, they professed no knowledge of filmmaking and were not ashamed to be considered bankers. In a trice, I put pen to paper, and soon New York became London, The Hamptons were the Cotswolds, all the hoods on the cars became bonnets, and folks were no longer ordering Big Macs but Spotted Dick.

I cast Kate Winslet in the lead role opposite Jonathan Rhys Meyers. A week before shooting Kate called and said she couldn't do it. Too much time away from her kids, fatigued, needed some family space. I understood her priorities and hoped we'd work together again one day, which we did. Suddenly we were scrambling for a last-minute replacement, and somebody mentioned this young girl named Scarlett Johanssen was available. I had seen her be wonderful in Terry Zwigoff's excellent movie *Ghost World* and sent her a script. Within twenty-four hours, she was in. She was only nineteen when she did *Match Point* but it was all there: an exciting actress, a natural movie star, real intelligence, quick and funny, and when you meet her you have to fight your way through the pheromones. Not only was she gifted and beautiful, but sexually she was radioactive. You got the feeling any second she's about to take your hand, smile, and say, If you really want us to try that, I can arrange it. I used her in a few movies where she was terrific and only hope I get to work with her again before I die or senility sets in and I'm drooling, but not over her.

Making movies in London is like student filmmaking in the best sense. Everyone pitches in and helps. The guy dishing out food will move a chair and nobody calls a strike. If you need an extra few minutes without going into overtime it's not the end of the world; the makeup lady can quickly do a walk-on without belonging to a guild. And the weather. Those fabulous gray skies, so perfect for photography. I couldn't ruin *Match Point* if I tried. I needed a last-minute replacement for Kate Winslet, who do I get? Scarlett. I needed rainy weather, I got it. If I needed a sunny day, I got sun. It was like the gods of cinema were trying to make up for the many times they've screwed me.

And I'll never forget the day prior to shooting when I

went into a studio to record Jonathan Rhys Meyers do the opening off-camera speech. I'm listening to him read with my assistant Sarah Allentuch and I asked her, "Did I write those words?" I mean his Irish voice was so beautiful it made me sound like I was a writer, and not just any writer. I'm talking Dylan Thomas or James Joyce. At home, I tried reading my lines with that same sonerous lyric lilt, but Soon-Yi said I sounded like Elmer Fudd. I also got to work with Emily Mortimer, who took a part that in other hands would have been a quiet one, but she made it sing. It was amazing how in *Match Point*, every actor and actress in every small part made a real contribution. That movie was a joy for me. It was one of the only films I ever made that exceeded my ambitions.

So much so I returned to London three more summers to make *Scoop* with Scarlett and *Cassandra's Dream* with Ewan McGregor and Colin Farrell, and it was where I first discovered Sally Hawkins. I say *discovered* because she was included in a video highlighting a different actress we were considering but all I could think was, Who is that other one? She's great. Working with the exciting Hugh Jackman and Scarlett on *Scoop* was fun, and she and I both decided to make her look silly and unglamorous. When you're as beautiful as she is, you're not insecure about presenting yourself as a bespectacled goofball. I played the hero, but the real hero was the journalist played by Ian McShane. I always had a soft spot for journalists. Along with cowboy, jazz musician, FBI agent, private eye, gambler, and magician, I entertained the fantasy of being a newspaperman, a hard-hitting reporter on the crime beat whose relentless digging came up with the story that blew the lid off the corruption at city hall, or saved an innocent man from the gallows. It was either that or a sportswriter where I could document the poetry of athletics much the same as my idol, Jimmy Cannon.

Alas, fate had other plans for me, but one of the nicest memories I have is the night I made the Broadway rounds with the journalist Leonard Lyons. Lyons was a New York columnist who didn't rely on handouts from press agents but covered the city's nightlife himself and accumulated hundreds of great anecdotes about the town's celebrities. He and his wife had me to dinner one night at their apartment in the Beresford when I was an upcoming comedian. Around 10 p.m., his workday began. He kissed his wife good-bye, and we descended to the nighttime streets of Manhattan. He took me to Sardi's, to the Oak Room of the Plaza, to Toots Shor's, then to the Waldorf and Lindy's, all the while he chatted and listened to authors and actors, actresses and producers. I had a night I could only have dreamed about when I grew up on Avenue J in Brooklyn. At times, when I'm lying in bed at night unable to sleep and I have a rare break from picturing my death, crushed in a car press or swallowed by a python, I think nostalgically of that night on the town with Leonard Lyons.

A vanished era, when Broadway took the curtain up at eight forty. The first nighters dressed in black tie, scintillating theatregoers filled the Music Box and the Broadhurst and the Longacre, and the Booth. The shows began at a civilized time so you could dine first and maybe hit a supper club after the eleven o'clock climax. This was the city before middle-class New Yorkers fled, and turned Times Square over to the tourists. When fat yellow cabs had jump seats, before that god-awful pedestrian mall, and before the bike infestation. (If you read the Passover story carefully, in the part about the ten plagues, right after locusts, frogs, and boils, they mention bikes.) New York is a walking town. But that was a time when for two hundred bucks you could get a new suit *and* an orchestra seat to a show, not just the seat. Leonard Lyons, by the way, was the first and only columnist who had the nerve to print the joke when Philip Roth's book *Portnoy's Complaint* was bought for a movie and everyone asked incredulously, How can they make that book into a film? and some wit said, "With a handheld camera." It was a prissy time, but Leonard Lyons couldn't resist and I don't blame him.

After *Cassandra's Dream*, I took a hiatus from London before returning to film *You Will Meet a Tall Dark Stranger*, where I got a chance to work with Josh Brolin, who I'd seen be great in several movies, and Gemma Jones and Naomi Watts. Naomi is a truly wonderful actress. I had never met nor spoken a word to her. She showed up the morning we needed her to film somewhere in the middle of our shooting schedule. The first thing she had to do was her hardest scene, very emotional. She came in, no nerves, no fear, a bundle of justified self-confidence. A quick hello, we shook hands, and she simply knocked off her difficult scene quickly and perfectly. She ran through a full gamut of intense emotions. Then it was cut, print, and she smiled and bounded off to lunch. I have to say Naomi is not only a terrific movie star and very beautiful, but she has the sexiest two upper front teeth in show business.

Before I shot that fourth film in London I had made two other movies. (I know, I'm jumping around. But try and stay with me.) I spent a summer in Spain and made *Vicky Cristina Barcelona* with Scarlett, Penelope Cruz, Rebecca Hall, Patricia Clarkson, Chris Messina, and Kevin Dunn. Not to mention Javier Bardem, one of the finest actors in motion pictures. Quite a cast. Barring a mental breakdown where I hear voices telling me to conquer the English at Orleans, I'm going to look good. Apart from being a fine and complicated acting talent, Penelope is one of the sexiest humans on the face of the earth, and coupling her with Scarlett caused each woman's erotic valence to cube itself. Deservedly, Penelope won an Academy Award for her work. We wanted an R rating on the film, but the board only gave us a PG because they said the sex between the two women was so tastefully handled. The one time in my life I'm accused of good taste it hurts our box office.

My family and I had a great summer in Barcelona and had the pleasure of eating at Ca L'Isidre as many times as humanly possible, and that alone made the experience a joy. We shot a few scenes in Oviedo, a small town with London-like weather and a delight. I first visited Oviedo when I was notified I had been selected for a Prince of Asturias Award. I passed on it, first, because I have no interest in awards, and second, because while I never like to insult anyone who is nice enough to want to give me an award, I never accept any award the bestowing of which is contingent upon my presence.

A few years later the Golden Globes wanted to give me a lifetime achievement award, but it meant I had to show up to receive it. I passed. Two days later they said they'd give it to me and I wouldn't have to go. Then it was fine with me. I never watch any of those awards shows, and if

I don't have to go or watch it and they want to give me an award, I certainly am not going to rudely make an issue of it. Diane Keaton picked it up for me. Emma Stone was nice enough to introduce her. I never saw the show, but as they are both flawless in life, I'm sure they were both flawless at the event. So originally I passed on the Prince of Asturias Award. I never heard of Oviedo and I wasn't going to go and please leave me alone, there's a ball game on. Suddenly I get a panic-stricken phone call from our movie distributor in Spain. I cannot refuse this. This is the highest award in Spain, huge in all of Europe. The prince and queen give it out. It is their Nobel. Now I figure there's been a clerical error. Some poor, ink-stained wretch is going to catch hell for mistakenly putting my name on the recipients list.

But no; upon further investigation it's not a mistake. Cut to the future and I'm in a tux being honored alongside guys who invent the internet or write economic theories and in the arts, Daniel Barenboim, this classical music icon, and Arthur Miller. Yes, I'm going to get the same honor as the author of *Death of a Salesman*. This has got to be a mistake. What's wrong with this picture? My family meets the queen, also the prince of Spain, who would later come over to our house for dinner in New York. What am I doing with these people? I'm out of my depth. There are cars in front of our house on East Ninety-Second Street, and secret service are checking our basement, our roof, our garden. After all the prince, eventually to be the king of Spain, is coming for dinner. But that was later.

Meanwhile I was in Oviedo, and Arthur Miller proposed we have lunch, just the two of us so we could spend some hours just talking. Suddenly I'm having lunch with the author, who along with Tennessee Williams shared the exclusive shrine in my Brooklyn apartment. And folks, as if life were not unfair enough, I got the same award for artistic achievement that he got. A lunch with Arthur Miller was something I could have only fantasized about as a boy, as a young man, even the week before. I asked a million questions, and I recall quite vividly that he confirmed for me that life was indeed meaningless. I told him how I felt about mortality. I likened it to when you're used to waking regularly at a certain hour each morning, let's say eight, and on a particular day you have a seven o'clock appointment which necessitates waking at six to get ready and get there on time. So all night I don't sleep well knowing I have to get up early and the alarm will go off at six. It totally ruins my night's sleep, if I can even get to sleep. So it is that my life is ruined, spoiled, by the knowledge that the alarm will be going off one day and I must go, and this knowledge kills my peace of mind and makes me toss and turn through all the days of my existence waiting for the hour to strike. I explained this to the great playwright, whose mind had long since wandered to his profiteroles as I spun my metaphor. I recalled that years ago he had asked me if I would direct Vanessa Redgrave in his TV play, *Playing for Time*. My exclusive contract with UA forbade it. But he liked my work. I've been very lucky that pretty much all the ones I idolized seemed to enjoy what I did: Groucho, Perelman, Ingmar, Tennessee Williams, Miller, Kazan, Truffaut, Fellini, García Márquez, Wisława Szymborska, to name a few. Unless it's some kind of a joke they're all in on. Hmm. Like when the people of Oviedo erected a statue of me in their town square. They never asked me, told me, merely put up a statue in my honor. I had the feeling it was like in *The Hunchback of Notre Dame*, where they have some kind of fool's wedding and they make fun of some sad creature by celebrating him publicly, and that year guess who the creature was.

If I sound cynical, pessimistic, misanthropic, I worked next with a master of the cynical apercu, Larry David. On the set of *Whatever Works*, we talked a little about stand-up comics. When I think of the years I worked nightclubs, I'd have to say today's funny men and women leave me far behind. The only criticisms I have are that, one, many are gratuitously dirty. Remember, I'm saying *gratuitously*. I don't mind dirty when it contributes to the funny routine, but since language was liberated in the sixties, it's embarrassing to hear acts punctuate their material with the old so-called dirty words. Apparently, the comics believe it gives them a sense of hipness or sharpness, of outrageousness, or freedom when in fact they could do the same material and speak plainly without so obviously laboring to try and achieve what they think talking dirty does for them. It's often so forced and heavy-handed. Then there's the new cliché of presentation. When I was younger the clichés were that the comics came out and said—Good evening, ladies and gentlemen. They were mostly men and they often wore a tux. They were slick, cuff-shooting guys who did jokes they bought and may have even ended with a song. "That's why I say—When you're smiling..."

Today's clichéd comics come out, take the microphone off the stand so they can prowl around the stage screaming their lines, and God help us, going to a chair or table that's been placed center stage with bottled water on it, allowing the comic to drink now and then. Where did all these thirsty comics come from? I never knew a monologist to keel over from dehydration. Actors play hours of Shakespeare without Hamlet or Lear sneaking behind a drape for a belt of Poland Spring water. But on TV you find some funny guy marching up and back saying, "You know what bugs me— did you ever go on one of those fucking Caribbean cruises? They're the fucking worst." Now he needs to get some water somehow or his desiccated remains will be found onstage like a skeleton in the desert. Waiting for him to slake his parched tonsils, I always switch the dial to something more compelling, like the Invicta Watch channel.

I had to do stand-up recently, having been roped into appearing on an American Film Institute tribute to Diane Keaton. "You're coming," she said. "I'll send congratulations on tape," I pleaded. "Nope, buster, you're coming. Not only that, you're giving me the award." "But..." I fumfered. "Sorry. Get your soup and fish out of mothballs." And so I went and did a few jokes and got my laughs, and I could see that if I ever did stand-up again I wouldn't make the mistake I made when I began, like settling for many unworthy jokes, rushing to get off, cutesy fidgeting. I was such a weasel. But, since I'm not doing stand-up anymore, what the hell are we talking about?

After a few films made abroad succeeded, various countries started calling and inviting me to make a film in their country which they'd back with no questions asked. I was only too happy to work that way, and my wife loved the chance to live with the kids abroad and really absorb the different cultures. All fine, provided the host city was one I could live in decently for the three or four months it took to film there. London was a treat, Barcelona a dream. If I had gotten an offer from say, Thiruvananthapuram, it'd be a definite pass. When Paris beckoned, promising to make filming there easy with full cooperation, you can imagine how fast I pulled a contract from my back pocket and signed up.

The result was *Midnight in Paris*, which meant four months in a big suite at the Bristol and nothing but croissants, truffles, and those streets and rooftops. I wrote the part for an eastern intellectual, but when the chance to cast Owen Wilson came I rewrote it to fit him. I got a chance to work with yet another great actress, Marion Cotillard. I don't think she loved the experience, but I did. She was very sweet, clearly never appreciating how terrific she was. She was the only actress I ever worked with who wept on the set but I could never figure out why. Everything she did was superb. Maybe I didn't speak to her much, but that would only be because there was nothing to tell her; she got everything right. But somehow she was not satisfied with herself. And as for me, I'm very nice on the set, a sweet guy, in awe of her talent, on board with her performance all the way. Anyhow, it was a privilege to work with her, and I couldn't ask for better.

Owen was also wonderful and a pleasure to direct. He'd sit around swigging from a brackish concoction, green in color and I guess meant to extend his life span, but if you have to keep drinking that verdant ichor, who wants to live longer? I managed to get Adrien Brody to play young Salvador Dali, which was one of the high points of the picture, as was Corey Stoll's Ernest Hemingway. Then there was Rachel McAdams, an actress who makes every line real and looks like a million bucks from any angle playing Owen's not-so-nice fiancée. And the cherry on the cake for me was Léa Seydoux. I had never heard of her, and midmovie we realized we needed a quick hire for a small but critical part. I was sent a tape with lots of actresses on it to choose from and I had one of those "Who is that?" moments. Léa was magnetic. She was clearly a first-rate actress who has, over the years, proved it by playing a wide variety of roles to deserve her acclaim. We quickly hired her, and when I first met her I just kept staring. It wasn't only that she was beautiful, which she was a ten plus, but she was so exceptionally beautiful in a totally arresting way. Her personality, which was so charming, illuminated her face as if Renoir and Raphael had collaborated. While we were shooting late at night, standing outside for hours in the freezing cold, her nose started to run and she was still one of the most beautiful women I'd ever seen. Over the years, I've followed her work and almost cast her in another movie, but her French accent was too strong for the American character. Maybe if I'm lucky there'll be a role she's perfect for in one of my films, like maybe she could play a love-starved lonely housewife and I could play her personal trainer.

I loved shooting cities. The hustle and bustle and street life. And in the rain, they're so moody. I was able to begin with a montage of Paris accompanied by Sidney Bechet, who caught the French spirit on his horn so perfectly. I'd be happy just doing montages of cities with my favorite music in support. To work in Paris. To live in Paris. Why didn't I stay when *Pussycat* was over? What a different life I would have had. Couldn't have been a stand-up comic. Never would have met Soon-Yi. Paid a big price for loving Soon-Yi. All worth it. Pretty, sexy, bright, funny, a perfect wife. If only she remembers to have me cremated. While doing preproduction for *Midnight in Paris*, we were invited to meet President Nicolas Sarkozy and his wife, Carla Bruni. We brunched at the Élysée Palace. I was so nervous I forgot to bring my Joy Buzzer. And so we all chatted for a while and finally, because Carla Bruni was delightful and fascinating and I knew she had done some show business work singing, I got up the nerve to ask if she'd be willing to do a stint in the movie. She looked at her husband for a signal about how he felt about getting involved with a grubby commoner, and he said nothing wrong in it, so she agreed. From the press you'd have thought a spaceship had landed. All over Europe it was front-page news. When it came time to shoot she was totally professional. She came on time, did her acting and did it well, impressing all of us. She knew her lines, performed beautifully, and could make quick switches and add or cut lines on the spur of the moment. They should all be so good to work with, as Mom might have put it.

Naturally, her husband, President Sarkozy, came to watch our shoot one night, and you can imagine how the French crew was excited and on best behavior lest some clumsy grip accidentally drop something and get guillotined. The movie was very successful. I had the idea many years prior since every time I ran into Swifty Lazar—he told me Cary Grant was dying to work with me, and did I have an idea for him. In my original thoughts, a car pulls up in contemporary New York at midnight and Cary Grant says get in. I get in and we go to a party back in New York of the 1920s with gangsters and showgirls, theater icons. When Paris loomed invitingly, it was an easy jump on the typewriter keys from Sutton Place to the Place Vendôme.

Owen Wilson and Cary Grant could have made a great duo. At one time I had actually asked Cary Grant to do it, but Swifty Lazar had of course been lying about Cary wanting to work with me, and when we asked Cary if we could send him the script he said, "Are you kidding? I'm retired." Garson Kanin told me later, If Swifty tells you something you can count on it, it's a lie.

I must say I had reason to believe I might get Cary Grant for my movie, as he was a big fan of mine. I don't mean to boast but I can't tell this story without first telling you that fact. Grant has to be a fan or else the story doesn't work. So before any of this script stuff, Cary Grant, *the* Cary Grant, came to see me play jazz at Michael's Pub in New York. He came alone. He sat alone at a table fairly close. He brought with him all my books. He had me inscribe them to him. I sat with him for an hour between sets. He insisted on staying to hear our second set. Naturally, we talked movies. He knew mine well. Now, here's the amazing thing. He was there for hours, the room was packed, and not a single person ever came up to him to say hello, to ask, Are you Cary Grant?, to ask for an autograph. At the end of the evening, we said good-bye and I got a little hug. A few years later, when Swifty Lazar told me he was dying to work with me, you can't blame me for believing it. But he was retired, and warm and flattering as he was, he was also famously frugal, and it occurred to me he could have had me autograph my books so he could sell them on eBay.

To Rome with Love is a bad title. The original title was *Nero Fiddled*, but the guys who put up the loot in Rome were apoplectic. They begged me to change it at least for

Rome. After all, Berlusconi might get the wrong idea. At first I kept the original in America, but it wasn't a battle worth fighting. I could've pulled rank and insisted, but the Italian backers were nice men, and if I could keep them off Berlusconi's hit list with a small title change, why make their lives miserable?

So now I'm working with Penelope Cruz again and Judy Davis in Rome. Judy and I still don't speak, but now it's in Italian. I get to work with Alec Baldwin, always a privilege, and Ellen Page and Greta Gerwig, who went on to direct a wonderful movie herself. Both Ellen and Greta would later denounce me and say they regret having worked with me, and I'll get to that, but I loved working with both of them and thought they were terrific. Half the movie was in Italian, and I got two big thrills. The first was, I was directing an Italian movie. Me, who grew up on De Sica, Fellini, Antonioni, was directing Italian actors in Italian with subtitles. I knew it would cut down on the box office, as many Americans don't like to see a movie with subtitles, but this was only half with subtitles. Second, I had the honor of directing the great Roberto Benigni, who I can't say enough about. He didn't speak English and I didn't speak Italian, so I couldn't ruin him with my direction. If you see the movie you'll see what I'm raving about. I was very impressed. Incidentally, you don't have to know the language to recognize good acting from bad. It's in the air, the body movements, the facial expressions, the tone of voice. I bought Benigni a rare book as a good-bye gift when it was over, because he likes that stuff. I think it was the *Satyricon*. I'm not sure. It was in Italian.

OK, so now I'll let you in on a secret. An obvious

one. I always wanted to be Tennessee Williams. The other great American playwright of my youth, Arthur Miller, was always social, very involved in politics and ethics and moral choice, although *Death of a Salesman* wasn't only that, and *All My Sons* had some of the poetry I liked. *A View from the Bridge* was only great when Liev Schreiber played the lead and Scarlett was the object ball, and I had seen four different productions of it, including the original. The movie was also quite solid but it had Maureen Stapleton and was directed by a director I love, Sidney Lumet.

But Tennessee Williams. Let us pause so I can wax euphoric. I grew up idolizing Tennessee Williams. Abe Burrows asked me when I was eighteen if there was anyone I wanted to meet to discuss my interest in writing with. I said Tennessee Williams. He said Tennessee's not the kind of guy whom one can easily sit and chat with. I read all his plays, all his books. Two of my proudest possessions when I was that age were handsome hardcover copies of *One Arm* and *Hard Candy*. I've seen his plays many times. I have my favorite plays and productions. As I gushed earlier, the movie of *Streetcar* is for me total artistic perfection. With the exception of the bullshit end moment, bowing to what D. H. Lawrence called "the censor-moron." It's the most perfect confluence of script, performance, and direction I've ever seen. I agree with Richard Schickel, who calls the play perfect. The characters are so perfectly written, every nuance, every instinct, every line of dialogue is the best choice of all those available in the known universe. All the performances are sensational. Vivien Leigh is incomparable, more real and vivid than real people I know. And Marlon Brando was a living poem. He was an actor who came on the scene and changed the history of acting. The magic, the setting, New Orleans, the French Quarter, the rainy humid afternoons, the poker night. Artistic genius, no holds barred.

OK—now we cut to me, a purveyor of chuckles, of parking space jokes, a second rater risen inexplicably to the ranks of moviemaker, the product of hard work, amazing luck, the right place at the right time. So I experience a fair amount of success. So what does it mean if you long to create alongside Aeschylus, O'Neill, Strindberg, Tennessee Williams. My first attempt at drama is influenced by Bergman. Bergman is my cinema idol. I long to make *The Seventh Seal* and *Wild Strawberries*. Instead I bumble along with *Sleeper, Love and Death, Annie Hall*. Amusing, perhaps, but not where I want to be. *Interiors*. OK, nice try. Not a sell-out film, but I'm clearly not ready for prime time. This futile attempt to create in direct opposition to my natural flair happens again and again. *September, Another Woman*. And every time I'm parked before Turner Classic Movies and *Streetcar* plays I say to myself, Hey—I can do that. So I try but I can't, which brings us to *Blue Jasmine*. Nice try but no cigar. Blessed with a very great actress, Cate Blanchett, I do my level best to create a situation for her that will have dramatic power. The idea came from my wife and it's a good idea. But it leans too heavily on Tennessee Williams. One will see it again later in *Wonder Wheel*, my best yet, but I have to get out from under the southern influence.

Anyhow, *Blue Jasmine* was a success and Cate got her best actress Oscar. Oh, and Kate Winslet was as strong in *Wonder Wheel* but was hurt opening into the gale force of the second wave of the hideous false molestation accusation, which we're coming to. Meanwhile, suffice it to say, I'm not

Tennessee Williams, never could come close, and while I'm sure you've noticed, I just wanted to fess up to it and assure you, you haven't been wrong.

Sidebar: I'm at Elaine's one night paying my check on the way out when I'm stopped by who? Yes—Tennessee Williams. He is eating there with friends. He has had a few drinks and stops me on my way out to tell me that I was an artist. I looked around to see if there was an actual artist standing behind me, but no, he meant me. I wondered who he was mistaking me for. Pinter? Christo? I flushed crimson, mumbled a few incoherent obsequies and backed toward the door, bowing over and over like a Chinese eunuch. I wrote his compliment off to too many mint juleps, mistaken identity, routine show business insincerity. Cut to years later when someone did a book on him and stayed with him for months, taking copious notes of their conversations. After Williams's death, the writer was incredibly kind to send me these notes on what Tennessee Williams said about me. I am too shy to quote from them, and for all I know, the writer made it all up as a practical joke, but like belief that one's spouse is faithful, I would prefer not to look too deeply. I have the notes at home. I read them over like Moss Hart with his reviews of *Once in a Lifetime*, put them away, and never looked at them again.

On the plus side, between Bergman's influence and Williams's, I've written many parts for women including some reasonably juicy ones. Actually, for a guy who's taken his share of heat from #MeToo zealots, my record with the opposite sex is not bad at all.

My press representative, Leslee Dart, once pointed out to me that in fifty years of making films, working with hundreds of actresses, I've provided 106 leading female roles with sixty-two award nominations for the actresses, and never a single hint of impropriety with any one of them. Or any of the extras. Or any of the stand-ins. Plus, since being independent from studios, I have employed 230 women as leading crewmembers behind the camera, not to mention female editors, producers, and everyone always paid exactly equally to the men on my films.

Incidentally, Leslee Dart, a press agent at the top of her profession, handled my publicity for decades. She didn't know what she was signing on for when she threw her lot in with me, thinking it would be all setting up interviews and promoting my films. She hadn't counted on me falling in love with a woman thirty-five years younger who happened to be my girlfriend's daughter. It's kept her on her toes from the moment the happy news hit the fan, and she recently made a comment to friends about the privilege of handling my press and something about an early grave.

Anyhow, *Blue Jasmine* came and went, and I got to work with Alec Baldwin again, Sally Hawkins, and the first of the two great Cates or Kates. My life is going forward, Soon-Yi remained a constant delight, my kids keep growing up, and while I try and help them with their homework, I remind them I got a ninety-eight in algebra only if you add three of my test scores together. So summer comes and I take the Allen family to the South of France and experience for the first time the magic of Emma Stone.

Put simply, Emma has it all. She's not just beautiful, she's beautiful in an interesting way, which makes her fun to look at, which makes her a true movie star. Plus not only can she act but she can work the whole spectrum. She's authentically funny and a fine dramatic actress. She's one of the only people I spent a lot of time talking to around the set. And that's because she's extra charming and we had a lot of laughs together. She taught me to text, and after the movie ended we texted a lot back and forth. I was always teasing her, she was always topping me. When people ask about moviemaking and I try to make clear it's not the money, it's not the acclaim, the notices, the awards; all dross, or make that chaff. I constantly reiterate it's only the making of the movie that counts. You create, you bring your creation to life, and I wake up early in the morning in the South of France and there to greet me and work with me all day is someone like Emma Stone. It does wonders for your metabolism. And Colin Firth was so urbane and gifted, and Eileen Atkins, Simon McBurney, and the hilarious Jacki Weaver.

It was another film of mine that had magic in the plot. A perceptive critic wrote a book many years ago on the recurring theme of magic in my films. History has since borne her out. It seems to me the only hope for mankind lies in magic. I have always hated reality, but it's the only place you can get good chicken wings. Because the South of France was so sunny and rough on photography, we shot early morning, waited all day, and resumed at about six at night. The picture took longer to complete and it cost more, but the investors don't mind as long as I'm artistically fulfilled—and if you believe that, I have this bridge you may want to buy.

My next movie was a movie about philosophy. *Irrational Man*, which I shot in Rhode Island, didn't make much at the box office. Don't know why. It seemed an interesting commercial murder story, and Emma Stone was her delightful self opposite the brilliant Joaquin Phoenix. Joaquin is a lovely guy with, shall we say, an offbeat personality. He's very professional, very likable, and all you have to do is check out his movies over the years to know he's an amazing actor. To Emma's credit, in the most dramatic scenes, she matches him passion for passion. I was surprised at the small turnout to see it. One good thing about a movie is that it's a tangible hunk of celluloid that exists and always has a chance to be seen by those who missed it. It can someday be embraced as a neglected or misunderstood masterpiece. Naturally, this has never happened to me. Movies of mine that opened and I felt were misunderstood or neglected remained so, although one or two successes might've been reevaluated and deemed overpraised. An added pleasure in making *Irrational Man* was I got to spend a summer in Newport, as delightful a spot as one could imagine. My family lived in a huge rented house, and Soon-Yi cooked several dinners for people working on the film, taking advantage of the big kitchen and good food available. I carp when I called her cooking a hate crime, as there are certain dishes she can handle. Let me put it this way: If you like spaghetti with a can of tomato sauce poured over it three times a day, she can be your chef. The weather was delightful, given it was summer and I could see why all the turn-of-the-century nabobs chose Newport to park their yachts.

In thinking back over two movies with Emma and how our frequent texting waned to pretty much zero contact, I wondered if it was the soft-boiled eggs affair that cooled her on me. We had been chatting, and somehow the subject had gotten 'round to soft-boiled eggs. I told Emma I took mine this way: I filled an ordinary coffee cup halfway with Rice Krispies. Next I boiled two eggs for three and a half minutes, removed them from the pot and cracked them, depositing the contents into the cup of krispies. I added salt and stirred till it formed a thick though not too thick mixture. Then I ate it with a teaspoon while it was hot. Emma couldn't believe her ears and found it absurd I should regard such a concoction fit for human consumption. Relations between us cooled rather rapidly after that, and while out of politeness she reluctantly agreed to give it a try, my guess is she never did.

Eventually the texting between us stopped. Years later when I ran into a mutual friend and wondered if Emma had said anything, the person laughed and said, "Oh poor boy, don't you know it was the soft-boiled egg business. It's a touchy area within her life." Pity. I have only fond memories of her.

One weekend in the South of France, Soon-Yi and I had lunch with our friend Larry Gagosian. Soon-Yi used to work at Larry's gallery, after she'd just gotten out of school. Anyhow, we're chatting and Larry happens to mention that he spoke recently with Roman Polanski, who is planning a film next year in Prague. Larry and Roman are very good friends, and do I know him? Yes, I know him, but I haven't seen him in forty years. The last social moments I spent with him were when he and Sharon Tate and me and Charlie Joffe and Vic Lownes went to the prize fights in London to see Muhammad Ali batter a game Henry Cooper. Larry says, We're leaving France today but we'll be back in several weeks. Why don't we have dinner with Roman Polanski? Fine, I say, confident that like all social plans I agree to, the day will never come and as much as I like the people involved, I invariably will want to stay home at the moment of truth. We finish our dessert, say good-bye. Now cut to three weeks later. Gagosian sails back to town and calls. Would Soon-Yi and I like to come to a little dinner at Roman's house? Soon-Yi, eager as always to attend a social event, is already laying out her wardrobe ensemble. Okay, I figure, I haven't seen Roman in decades, he's a wonderful filmmaker, we can talk about movies, reminisce about our times in London in the sixties, what could be bad? Only that the day comes and I'm instantly socially ill at ease, but I suck it up. Naturally, as a director, I feel inferior to Roman and that doesn't help. Now we drive up to his house in Cap d'Antibes, and I must admit it's a knockout. Large, beautiful, majestically imposing on lush grounds overlooking the Mediterranean. Soon-Yi says to me as servants surrounded our car, "Just how strong were the grosses on *Rosemary's Baby*?" This type of spread couldn't have just come from a big box office, I assured her, he must've invested shrewdly. Soon-Yi gets me through my entering phobia, and presently a very beautiful woman comes to greet us.

"Hi," she says, "I'm Roman's wife." Now, I saw the movie where they met, so I remembered her as very beautiful. "Roman will be right down," she says, "Champagne?" Fighting my natural awkwardness, I overcompensate and take the stage too aggressively, launching into a stream of nervous babble. "I go back a long time with Roman," I say (all I needed was a cigar). "Really?" the sexy wife says. "Yes, we have some shared memories in London that I wouldn't trade for anything," I bombinate, ass that I am. Now we are joined by a few others and I wasn't sure from my erratic hearing aids, tremulous ganglia, and genetic stupidity, but I thought I heard the name Roman. Soon-Yi, who never met him, didn't know what he looked like and extended her hand and said, "How do you do?" The conversation among the group turned to some other topic like yachts or private aircraft. Meanwhile, the distaff side is nudging me and giving me the sotto voce wise-up, "That's Roman Polanski, you're being creepy to an old friend." "That's not Roman Polanski," I inform her out of the side of my mouth like a racetrack tout. "Yes it is," she says, giving me the patented wife-husband covert pinch. "Don't tell me, I've known Roman fifty years." "His wife just introduced him. You didn't catch it because you're deaf as Beethoven." "That's not Roman Polanski," I assured her. "Don't embarrass me," she says.

Meanwhile, they're calling him Roman. It turns out it's Roman Abramovich, the Russian oligarch gazillionaire, which explains the pricey digs. Christ, the gardening bill looked more costly than the ticket sales of *Rosemary's Baby*. When Gagosian shows up and we relate the story to him, he can't seem to figure out how we could possibly misunderstand. I explain to him we discussed Roman Polanski, agreed to see him for dinner the next time Larry would be in town. So now, you come to town, you call, and say, "Shall we go to Roman's for dinner?" How could I know you meant Roman Abramovich? I don't know Roman Abramovich from Adam. What would you have thought, dear reader? Guaranteed you would've thought what I thought. You might've caught on quicker, as you don't have my defective hearing, but it was a natural mistake. Anyhow, the story spread like cholera, and I was the rube of the Cote d'Azur social set, not to mention I get the horse laugh from all my enemies in show business, whose numbers are legion. Soon-Yi and I never lived that story down. Was it the worst thing that ever happened to me? No. The worst thing was getting stomach flu, or having to sit through *The Flying Dutchman* without my Adderall. Anyhow—onward.

I always wanted to do a movie that took place in New York in the late thirties, and in *Café Society* I got the chance. I worked with Kristin Stewart, Jesse Eisenberg, and Steve Carell in the main roles. Santo reproduced Manhattan and Hollywood in 1939, and I finally got to work with Vittorio Storaro, yet another genius cameraman. I'm so lucky. I've been made to look good starting with Davy Walsh, and then Gordon Willis, Sven Nykvist, Zhao Fei, Vilmos Zsigmond, Harris Savides, Carlo Di Palma, Javier Aguirresarobe, Remi Adefarasin, and Vittorio Storaro. If you know anything about cinematography, it's like I just listed the 1927 Yankees. I liked *Café Society*. I was trying to make a movie with the form of a novel. The original title was *Dorfman: The Novel*. For some reason we couldn't use it.

I changed the title of my next film, too. It was not originally called *Wonder Wheel*. It was then the trouble started again. With the making of *Wonder Wheel*, I was back in Tennessee Williams territory, but thanks to the cast and Vittorio and Santo, I did a better job. Raised not far from Coney Island, I had enough of my own self in there along with gangsters and a maladjusted kid who hated school. We also decided to use the color poetically and that Vittorio would change the lighting in the middle of scenes to underscore the emotions and stylize the drama. Still, despite a lot of original creative work, I had one toe or full foot in the French Quarter. The movie, and particularly Kate and Vittorio (although I think the whole cast), got a raw deal because of circumstances, which I'll now get into. But first, you should know the original title was *Coney Island Whitefish*. For those unfamiliar with the origin of that local nomenclature, it refers to the ubiquity of sex in the night under the boardwalk. The condoms were then thrown into the Atlantic, only to float back ashore with the incoming tide, and they were referred to as Coney Island Whitefish. The scene explicating this bit of ichthyology was cut from the movie, and Alisa, the editor, saved the day with the title *Wonder Wheel*.

And now, unfortunately, at this point, I am forced to return to the tedious subject of the false accusation. Not my fault, people. Who knew she was so vindictive? This time, the main victims were the hugely gifted cast of the movie and its genius photographer. I do not include myself, as I had the great pleasure of making the film, was handsomely paid, was inured to tabloid press and scurrilous accusations, and resigned to the fact that no amount of evidence or common sense was ever going to move the needle in the direction of reality. The plot had now taken an unexpected twist because Dylan was no longer seven but a grown woman of thirty-plus. Mind you, I have not been allowed to see her, speak to her, or correspond with her for twenty-three years. Everything she has heard about me since barely turning seven has been taught to her by Mia.

Meanwhile, as Moses poignantly describes, Mia makes her rage against Soon-Yi and me the center of everyone in the household's life, nurturing that fury and constantly reinforcing the idea to Dylan that I had abused her. I'd always hoped when Dylan grew up she would somehow realize how her mother had used her, taking full advantage of her age and vulnerability to deprive her of her father, knowing it was the surest vengeance toward me. I had hoped Dylan would reach out to me as her brother Moses had done. I thought for sure she would remember how much I loved her, how much I doted on her, how aggressively I fought to visit her or just to speak to her, and she would want to see me. She would at least want to discuss all that happened and put it in perspective. I felt sooner or later it would become clearer the abuse story was something she might at least be willing to examine. I hoped perhaps with the support or just the curiosity of her husband she might want to hear another side and take a moment to see if any of it made sense. What drawback could there be, I thought, if a conversation took place with Dylan and her husband present, or with her shrink if she has one. Anything to just review the version her mother has taught her versus the results of all the contradictory findings of every investigation. Now, I realize the oddsmakers in Vegas would make that meeting a million-to-one shot. Not only that but it will always be sold as: Dylan is free to do what she likes. She's a grown woman. She chooses not to see her father as it would be too traumatic for her.

Mia might even say she's actually encouraged Dylan to see me, but one can imagine what the encouragement or freedom of choice accorded Dylan sounds like. When Moses, at thirty, told his mother he wanted to reach out to me, there was hell for him to pay and he was banished from the family.

"My brother is dead to me," said Dylan, and one is reminded of Mia going around her house in a frenzy with scissors cutting Soon-Yi's head out of every wall-hung family photo so they looked weirdly surreal. Fortunately, Moses defied the bullying and Mia's insistence that even though I was his father and he had feelings for me, he must forever shun me. Mia made it clear any contact would constitute betrayal. Her intransigence caused Moses to experience encroaching thoughts of being yet another adopted child suicide; finally, on the advice of his therapist, he called me to reconnect. Predictably, he instantly became a nonperson in his mother's eyes, and of course the blacklisting became required family policy. Hence, "My brother is dead to me." This will give you some idea of the cult-like obedience demanded of the children. Anyhow, imagine my sadness when not only did Dylan not want to see me but instead wrote an "open letter" saying I molested her. The "openness" is important, as the strategy behind going public is not to resolve anything but to smear me, her mother's goal. With the emergence of the #MeToo era, the letter could then be fobbed off as "speaking out" and taking advantage of a legitimate movement. The fact that pushing a false accusation exploits genuinely abused and harassed women does not seem to matter.

For a long time, Soon-Yi was urged to speak up and tell her story but she was too busy raising a family, and she did not want to sink to responding to a mother who called her retarded, spread lies that she had been raped by the husband she loved, and fabricated a tale that her birth mother was a prostitute. Soon-Yi did finally speak up, as we will see. Sidebar: Despite all of Mia's faked outrage over alleged rape with an underage girl, she flew to London to testify on behalf of Roman Polanski who had actually admitted to and been jailed for sex with an underage girl. (A genuine victim, the woman is now grown up and forgives Roman but sees Mia for what she is. When Mia tweeted an apology to her for testifying on Polanski's behalf, the woman wrote, "I didn't need her apology and didn't want it. I felt used by someone pushing their own vendetta against Woody Allen.") Ronan Farrow always publicly urged women to speak out, but when Soon-Yi did tell her story, he did not like what he heard. He is fine with women speaking the truth as long as it's Mom's version of the truth.

Anyhow, an appearance on TV by Dylan weeping had great weight with the press and public. Remember, please, what Moses wrote, how he described the way Mia would rehearse him over and over to lie. Remember also when Judy Hollister, the woman who worked as housekeeper in the country house, asked Dylan why she was crying and Dylan said, "Because Mommy wants me to lie." It also struck me as interesting that no one cared that the detailed investigations made at the time concluded unequivocally Dylan had not been molested. For some reason, this fact has always remained an inconvenient truth. I found it fascinating that so many people chose to ignore the facts and preferred to buy into the molestation claim, almost eagerly. Why was it so important that I would be thought of as a child molester? Why, given my unsullied life and the sheer illogic of the allegation, would it not be met with more skepticism?

New to the story was a fresh, creative touch, something that never came up a single time during all the months of investigation in any of Dylan's numerous interviews. That is, Dylan suddenly claiming she was molested while she stared at the electric trains in the attic going round and round. As if I told her to stare at the toy trains circling like it was a hypnodisc. Moses writes, "There *was* no electric train set in that attic. There was, in fact, no way for kids to play up there, even if we had wanted to. It was an unfinished crawl space, under a steeply-angled gabled roof, with exposed nails and floorboards, billows of fiberglass insulation, filled with mousetraps and droppings and stinking of mothballs, and crammed with trunks full of hand-me-down clothes and my mother's old wardrobe. The idea that the space could possibly have accommodated a functioning electric train set, circling around the attic, is ridiculous." Obviously, this plot twist was added later to try and give the fabrication a dash of particularity in hopes a detail would make it seem more credible.

Having just weeks before turned seven, Dylan might've been realistically bribed at receiving a new doll or her favorite, a My Little Pony, for participation in the ugly slander afoot. But if the story Mia came up with doesn't stretch credulity to the breaking point, I give up. I mean, the notion of me offering Dylan a trip to Paris and a role in a film. My God, only weeks ago she was six years old. What does she know or care about Paris? Yes, Paris and an acting job might occur to Mia as a juicy inducement, but this poor little exploited girl certainly was not longing for Europe and pursuing a career in motion pictures.

And don't imagine for a second when Dylan recites her narrative of abuse or watching the train go 'round, that I'm accusing her of deliberately lying. Like several doctors I have spoken to about this awful story, I am convinced she believes what was suggested to her and drummed into her for so many years. She and her brother Satchel were innocent kids, with Dylan particularly vulnerable. As one former prosecutor stated, doing this to her is the real crime. When I told these various psychiatrists that Dylan was married with a child, so was it possible she was unharmed by the implanting, they all said it would assuredly take its toll.

Meanwhile, not only was the press more convinced by Dylan's TV appearance, but actors and actresses, having no real idea of whether I had abused her or not, rose up to support her and denounce me, saying they regretted working in my movies and they would never do it again. Some even donated their checks to a cause rather than accept the tainted salary. This is not as heroic a gesture as it seems, as we can only afford to pay the union minimum, and my guess is if we paid more usual movie money, which often runs quite high, the actors might have righteously declared they'd never work with me but would possibly leave out the part about donating their salary. The fact these actors and actresses never looked into the details of the case (they couldn't have and come to their conclusion with such certainty) did not stop them from speaking out publicly with dogged conviction. Some said it was now their policy to always believe the woman. I would hope most thinking people reject such simple-mindedness. I mean, tell it to the Scottsboro Boys.

Well-meaning citizens, brimming with moral indignation, were only too happy to nobly take a stand on an issue they had absolutely no knowledge of. For all these crusaders knew, I could be a victim on a par with Alfred Dreyfus or a serial killer. They wouldn't know the difference. (Even Mia's own lawyer publicly said she didn't know if the molestation took place or Dylan imagined it.) Still, that didn't stop actors and actresses from rushing to outdo one another in profiles of courage. By God, they were against child molestation and were not afraid to say it, particularly with these new scientific discoveries in physics that the woman is always right.

An interesting point to think about here is that through all of this, the Farrow contingent were busy not helping the victims of the sexual abuse her brother was in the hoosegow for, but making phone calls and pressing actors and actresses to blacklist me under threat of being publicly shamed. I must say, it amazed me how many in my profession caved in like dominoes. Perhaps it was personal conviction or perhaps out of fear or a chance to grab a moment to bask in what seems like the safe, no-risk stand of a politically correct issue. I had appeared in a film, *The Front*, about the McCarthy era and was very aware of what Lillian Hellman referred to as "scoundrel time," when so many frightened or opportunistic men and women behaved badly. I bring that up only because any number of actors and showpeople said to me and various friends of mine privately how appalled they were by the clearly unjust, disgusting publicity I was receiving and that they were solidly on my side, but when asked why they didn't speak out and say something, they all admitted they feared professional repercussions. I thought it was ironic as that was the exact reason women gave for not speaking up over the years against their various harassers: that their careers would suffer. For some the details of the whole affair were vague and not all that interesting, as showpeople have their own lives and problems, but they heard that not working with me had become the thing to do—like everyone suddenly being into kale.

Meanwhile, the press lumped me in with any number of men who were charged, convicted, or admitted to sex crimes or harassment of large numbers of women on numerous occasions, despite the fact the accusation against me had repeatedly been found not to have occurred. Not only did my fellow actors boycott me, Amazon breached my contract and didn't want to work with me. Schools stopped giving courses on my films. I was cut out of a documentary about the Carlyle Hotel. I was cut out of a series on poetry by PBS. My completed film, *A Rainy Day in New York*, lay around undistributed in America, though, mercifully, the rest of the world was not so nuts. When I stepped back, I must say it was very amusing to view all of these people running helter-skelter to help a nutsy woman carry out a vengeful plan. So fascinating and, as I say, not a bad idea for satire.

Unlike many poor souls who were wrecked by blacklisting during the McCarthy era, I was less fragile. For one thing, I was not in danger of starving, and as a writer I generated my own projects. Through it all, I must confess, given as I am to romantic daydreaming in which I usually star, I was now the real-life protagonist of a drama about an innocent person, wrongly accused. The malicious predicament appealed to my movie hero fantasies and I saw myself a maligned soul certain to triumph in the last reel. Of course, unlike Hollywood, no Jimmy Stewart or Henry Fonda emerged suddenly to take my case and right the wrongs. But in real life, some rose and were fearless enough to take a principled stand.

Alec Baldwin was one of the very few with the courage to speak out bravely and clearly on my behalf. Javier Bardem was also very outspoken and angered by what he called a public lynching. Blake Lively defended me, risking abuse from social media. Scarlett Johansson defended me in no uncertain terms, but she's always been courageous on issues of injustice. On TV, Joy Behar backed Scarlett and staunchly defended me. Wally Shawn was someone who saw what was going on early and wrote about it passionately and bravely at a time when it invited abuse. The fact that despite the fears of flack from social media, there was zero penalty paid by anybody for taking my side. The women in my life all stood by me. My first wife, Harlene, Keaton of course, Louise, Stacey. You have to figure knowing me intimately and even living with me over the years, they would have some inkling if I were capable of or interested in abusing an infant. I must say I was disappointed by the reaction of the *New York Times*. I guess because I grew up loving the paper, looking forward to reading it over breakfast every morning, and being proud of their rational humane courage.

Anyhow, the *Times* was very much against me, clearly buying into the notion that I had abused my daughter. It was one thing when silly actors and actresses would pop up and mindlessly trumpet that they regretted working with me, but the *Times*, I felt, consisting of serious men and women very much on the right side of issues I cared about, certainly surprised me. And yet, over and over they printed articles that implied or assumed I had done a bad thing, always writing that I had been accused of molesting my daughter and sometimes adding that I denied it or even that I was never charged. What they never mentioned, although they knew, is that I had been thoroughly investigated and totally cleared of the accusation by both separate major investigations. And so only the accusation was left in the news story to hang as if my innocence had never been resolved, when indeed it had been. I mean, what is that—he denies it? Al Capone denied it. So did the defendants at Nuremberg. If I had done it, I'd have denied it, too. And as I said, they knew that highly responsible investigations had determined no molestation had ever occurred. The *Times* had allowed me a response years ago, but since then there had been numerous attacks, and barring a more recent single piece in my favor by Bret Stephens, they had no interest in accepting anything written supporting me. But back to the question: Why were so many people in the press and in my profession so willing, so determined, to hurt me? I could only think that over the years I must have rubbed people the wrong way more than I realized and they were expressing pent-up anger or irritation. Else why not give me the benefit of the doubt over a highly questionable accusation that defies common sense? I couldn't figure exactly how I had accumulated this bad will, but then a dog does not see its own tail.

And before I leave the subject of principled stands, a special word about Bob Weide. While Alec Baldwin and Javier Bardem look like heroes and play them in films, Weide resembles the nearsighted Czech patriot in an old war movie who is dragged off by the Nazis and shot as he natters away about the eventual triumph of democracy. In actual fact, he is a producer and director on *Curb Your Enthusiasm*, and I met him for the first time when he interviewed me briefly for a documentary he was doing on Groucho. I never saw or spoke to him again till years later when he filmed an *American Masters* documentary on me for PBS. For whatever reason, Weide saw the dishonesty and ugliness of my plight right off and spoke out courageously from the start with nothing to gain, as his PBS documentary had come and gone successfully. Along with the great support his writing on the subject has received, there has been also vulgar abuse and even death threats from cranks, but that's who's out there. In doing the documentary, Weide had carefully researched my life and looked into the case deeply. He had read all the transcripts and was outraged by the injustice.

He wrote about the situation, exposing with cool, well-documented facts the sham that was being perpetrated. As he was not Zola, few people listened, and he was denied venues to answer scurrilous and smearing articles. Reduced to his own blog, he hung in and persisted with no payoff other than the knowledge he was pursuing a just cause. As we were not close or social friends, it was not like he was coming to a buddy's aid. Still, the satisfaction of righting a wrong obsessed him. It was an act of good citizenship, of conscience, of simple decency versus the hailstorm of a mob, willing and seemingly anxious to believe a lie. If the truth ever sinks in—and notice I don't say becomes known, because it has been known for years—Weide will at least have the personal good feeling of having been on the right side of a nasty issue, unlike a great number of people he had tried vainly to persuade who will no doubt be awash in assorted creative rationalizations. If it turns out there is a heaven, I believe Weide will have a good table—in the nonsmoking section.

In writing about this whole affair I've tried to document whatever I could so the facts would not be simply my version but the on-the-record words of the investigators, the experiences Moses had witnessed and Soon-Yi had lived through that corroborated him. I've quoted the Yale and New York investigations word for word plus the court-appointed monitors exactly as the appellate judge recorded their testimony. There were appalling incidents attested to by two separate women who worked in Mia's house and witnessed a number of encounters firsthand. They also corroborate Moses. But even without all of that, I appealed to people's simple common sense. And yet I have no illusions that any of it will change minds. I believe if Dylan and Mia recanted today and said the whole thing was one big practical joke, there would still be many who would cling to the notion that I abused Dylan. People believe what is important for them to believe, and each person has his or her own reason, sometimes not even known to them. Therefore, when I write about this case, which personifies what Alan Dershowitz calls in his book "guilt by accusation," it is only because in writing about my life it played such a dramatic part. Hopefully it will give some confidence to the very decent people who spoke out on the right side of the issue. They made the correct choice.

And how have I taken all of this? And why is it when attacked I rarely spoke out or seemed overly upset? Well, given the malignant chaos of a purposeless universe, what's one little false allegation in the scheme of things? Second, being a misanthropist has its saving grace—people can never disappoint you.

Finally, there's a very different perspective one has when you view something as an innocent person rather than what a guilty man must go through. You relish the close looks and investigations rather than fear them, because you have nothing to hide. You're eager to take the lie detector test rather than ducking it. It's like sitting at a poker game and holding a royal flush. You can't wait till all the bets are in and the hands are shown. But what if I never get a chance to play my cards? What if I'm gone before I scoop up the chips? Well, as someone who's never had any interest in a legacy, what can I say? I'm eighty-four; my life is almost half over. At my age, I'm playing with house money. Not believing in a hereafter, I really can't see any practical difference if people remember me as a film director or a pedophile or at all. All that I ask is my ashes be scattered close to a pharmacy.

A crazy question: Is there any humor to be falsely accused of a crime? A sex crime, yet? There was a funny sidebar, and that was the flap with Louis C.K. Louis is a very nice man whom I worked with briefly on *Blue Jasmine*. I always wanted to do a screen comedy, both of us acting together. With the right script I thought we'd be funny playing off each other. He agreed. We both wracked our brains to come up with an idea. I spent a lot of time to no satisfactory avail. He tried as well, but nothing emerged as the one to work on. Now a few years pass, and he contacts me saying he has a script he wrote and wants me in it; has a great part for me. So I read it and I'm appalled. Not that it was a bad story—it was a good one—but I'd be playing an iconic film director who once either molested a child or was accused of it, and the director has a too close relationship with his daughter.

I say, "Louis, I can't play this." "Why not?" he says. "Because I'm always fighting this false accusation and people are always writing things and making remarks and this just plays right into the hands of the yahoos." "It'll be good for you," he tells me. What is he thinking? "It'll help your image." Now I like Louis a lot and I know he thinks he means to help me, but what is he smoking? I wished him luck and passed. I would never say, Don't do this, it's going to hurt me, because the guy spent months writing it and has a chance to direct it, and who am I to try and torpedo another guy's project because of personal discomfort? Naturally when the film is seen by the press prior to the opening, my situation with Dylan is the main focus of everything, and it's used as fodder to malign me left and right. Then, as fate would have it, poor Louis suddenly has real harassment problems of his own, and his film is pulled from release. He's taking flack and dealing with an onslaught of problems. The mind boggles at what O. Henry could've done with a twist like that, and if not O. Henry, certainly Monty Python.

Despite all the smears and terrible PR, there are a few actual upsides to being a pariah. For one thing, you're not always asked to sit on some dais, blurb a book, save any whales, or give a commencement speech—not that a guy whose knowledge of the Constitution is limited to the Twenty-First Amendment is a good choice to inspire students. Hillary Clinton wouldn't even accept Soon-Yi's and my donation to her campaign for president, and we couldn't help wondering if another fifty-four hundred to spend would've enabled her to carry Pennsylvania, Michigan, or Ohio.

The great Moss Hart in his enchanting autobiography, *Act One*, writes of the difference between a playwright having first-act trouble versus last-act problems. First-act problems are much easier to deal with. Last-act problems, endings, wrap-ups, and climaxes are what separate the men from the prepubescents. And so it is, having scribbled down the trivia that has sketched in my life, I find myself with last-act trouble. My golden years. The Roach in Winter.

As usual, I continue to work. I made a movie called

A Rainy Day in New York. I always wanted to shoot Manhattan in the rain, do a whole story that takes place on one rainy day. I don't know what it is with me and rain. When I wake up in the morning and open the blinds and it's raining or gray and drizzly or at least overcast, I get a good feeling. When it's sunny I feel depressed. And the city is so beautiful in the rain, under cloudy skies. Don't know why. It's been suggested that it's the objective correlative of my inner state. My soul is overcast.

So I hired Elle Fanning, Selena Gomez, Timothée Chalamet, Liev Schreiber, Diego Luna, Jude Law, and the fabulous Cherry Jones and made this romantic improbable tale. It's about two college seniors in New York on a weekend and the romance between them.

Naturally since the movie is *A Rainy Day in New York*, the sun was out every day when we needed gray skies and rain, and all the rain in the movie was supplied by our own rain towers and water tanks. Seeing that this is all coordinated falls to Helen Robin, who makes the whole picture happen from budgeting it to getting a crew, negotiating deals for locations, making nice with the unions, getting everybody fed, and attending to all the postproduction work that needs to get done: the editing, music, prints, rating. She even types my scripts and has been doing it for forty years. It's truly a 24/7/365-days-a-year job filled with nothing but crises and aggravation, but if she didn't have aggravation, she couldn't worry. And if she couldn't worry, her enjoyment of life would vanish. Before her, for years Bobby Greenhut did it and also did it well, and I recall he was always riddled with anxiety about the budget and about going over schedule and about reshoots. If it wasn't for his anxiety, he'd get no aerobics at all.

All the three leads in *Rainy Day* were excellent and a pleasure to work with. Timothée afterward publicly stated he regretted working with me and was giving the money to charity, but he swore to my sister he needed to do that as he was up for an Oscar for *Call Me by Your Name*, and he and his agent felt he had a better chance of winning if he denounced me, so he did. Anyhow, I didn't regret working with him and I'm not giving any of my money back. Selena was adorable. She had all the hard stuff to do, and she knocked it off beautifully. Elle is simply a great natural talent like Keaton. When reporters pressured her, trying hard to get her to say she regretted working with me, she told them she wasn't even born when the allegation was made and has no opinion. An honest reply. More people should have said, I really don't know all the facts so I have to withhold my judgment. God forbid anyone should say, "This accusation has been thoroughly investigated and found to be untrue." Although I'm told Joy Behar did make that point on TV. I should mention others who I've been made aware had come out publicly in my defense. Ray Liotta, Catherine Deneuve, Charlotte Rampling, Jude Law, Isabelle Huppert, Pedro Almodóvar, Alan Alda, and I'm sure there are more that I just don't know of. At least I hope. But thanks to all, because it was very nice of them to speak out, and I assure them it's not something they will ever be embarrassed having done.

As of now, unless some American distributor puts it out here, *A Rainy Day in New York* will not be seen in the USA. Fortunately, the rest of the world remains sane, and it has opened all over and is quite successful. It's funny to think of me doing films that are shown in every country but not

America. Look at it this way: If the film I make is a bad one the public cannot be suckered into blowing their hard-earned cash on a turkey. On the other hand, if the film is one they'd enjoy, they miss it. Either way, they'll live. I can't deny that it plays into my poetic fantasies to be an artist whose work isn't seen in his own country and is forced, because of injustice, to have his public abroad. Henry Miller comes to mind. D.H. Lawrence. James Joyce. I see myself standing amongst them defiantly. It's about at that point my wife wakes me up and says, You're snoring.

After *Rainy Day*, I embarked on my next film and I found it was hard to cast. One after the other, actors and actresses refused to work with me. Some I'm sure sincerely believed I was a predator. (I still can't figure out how they could be so utterly convinced.) Clearly, a number of actors thought they were doing a noble thing rejecting offers to appear in my film. Their gesture might've been meaningful if indeed I were guilty of something, but since I was not, they were just persecuting an innocent man and helping to confirm Dylan's implanted memory. Unwittingly, they had become Mia's enablers. Then there were a number of actors who assured me privately they had followed the case more closely and said they realized I was getting a very raw deal. They railed against a criminal blood libel, invoking Medea, the McMartin school, Sacco and Vanzetti—all that was missing were the Moscow show trials. Yet as unconscionable as they said my pickle was, they could not work with me, as the backlash would cause them to wind up on line E at the unemployment office. A few said, "I waited my whole life for this phone call and now I can't take the job." I felt for them, as they sincerely believed they risked blacklisting. In reality, as those who did speak out could tell them, they risked nothing. Off the record, I had envisioned a little more peer support, nothing overwhelming, perhaps a few organized protests, maybe some irate colleagues marching arms linked, a little rioting, perhaps a few burned cars. After all, I had been a member in good standing of the creative community and was certain my predicament would infuriate my union brethren and fellow artists. A carefully planned demonstration on my behalf by hundreds of individual citizens failed to materialize due to the day's fine beach weather. When Juliet Taylor mentioned the name Wally Shawn a bell went off. I always loved Wally as an actor, found him very real and funny, poignant, and with just the right intellectual vibe for the lead character in the movie I was preparing in Spain.

Even under ideal circumstances, making a decent film is an endless series of land mines. When presented with additional obstacles, the goal posts are pushed way, way back. Apart from my usual small budget, there was, as I described, a paucity of actors willing to throw their lot in with a toxic personality. Fortunately, Wally was not among them. Still, I was filming in Spain, and the Spanish tax laws required me to use a large percentage of actors from the EU. While so many of them are wonderful, few speak good enough English to nail the one-liners like the guys at Lindy's. Then there was the fact I was up to my neck in a lawsuit against Amazon, plus the press was constantly writing about me as though I was actually guilty of something. To quote the usually reasonable and level-headed *New York Times*, I was "a monster." Somewhere, Kafka was smiling. Anyhow, with so many bars in the saddle, can a decent race be run?

Meaning, can a maligned, distracted director, no Bergman to begin with, with so much stacked against him, turn out an enjoyable movie? Suddenly, the challenge of making the film became more exciting. So how will *Rifkin's Festival*, my project in Spain, turn out? Who knows? But I do know it was fun to do and great to hear Wally say my lines. The lesson here, I suppose, is that some men can thrive under pressure. I, of course, am not one of them, and if the movie turns out well, it will be a miracle.

And will the films of my "golden years" now play everywhere but the nation in which I am an honest, upright, tax-evading citizen? Who knows? Who cares? Not I and certainly not audiences with plenty of other fine movies to entertain them.

And so summer came, and I went with my jazz band all over Europe and played to lovely audiences everywhere. The turnouts were huge. Don't ask me why because I have no answer. It's New Orleans music, and over the years I haven't improved. Still thousands come to hear us night after night, and we can't get offstage. If anyone had told me, one day I'd be standing before eight thousand fans playing the "Muskrat Ramble," I would have doubted their sanity. Then I moved on to Milan where I directed an opera, or should I say, I restaged the Puccini work I had done successfully for the Los Angeles Opera. Again, if anyone had told me when I was hitting a Spaldeen two sewers in Flatbush that I'd be at La Scala taking a bow having staged Puccini, I would have put him in the same hat factory as the guy who told me I'd be playing "Muskrat Ramble." Next day it was off to San Sebastian for a few months to make a movie, and work in that mini paradise with Wally, Gina Gershon,

Elena Anaya, and Louis Garrel till Labor Day. Both of my daughters worked on the film, and Soon-Yi went hiking and sightseeing all over, every day, in temperatures that average seventy-two degrees all summer. Meanwhile *Rainy Day* has opened quite successfully all over Europe and South America, soon to play the Far East and spurring a demand for the movie in the United States as intense as when the Edsel was unveiled. Soon-Yi, the kids, and I flew back to the delightful Bristol Hotel in Paris and hit those rues and boulevards like Americans in a musical. Actually, my loved ones hit the rues. I stayed in the hotel doing publicity for *Rainy Day*.

So what else can I say about writing this book? A book as essential to the reading public as Amanda McKittrick Ros's masterpiece *Irene Iddesleigh* or Stoker's *The Lair of the White Worm*. I regret I had to devote so much space to the false accusation against me, but the whole situation was grist for the writers' mill and added a fascinating element of drama to a life otherwise pretty routine. To a guy whose high point of the day is his walk on the Upper East Side, a lurid tabloid scandal certainly gets the adrenaline going. I agree with what Francine du Plessix Gray wrote when she interviewed me years ago: "There are no great Woody Allen stories."

To me, the best parts upon proofreading the galleys were my romantic adventures and writing about the wonderful women I was passionately smitten with. I have included all that was of interest about my career, which ran too smoothly to produce many sparkling anecdotes. I did not include technical details about my filmmaking because I find them a bore and don't know any more about lighting and photography now than when I started, as I was never curious enough to learn. I do know you have to remove the lens cap from the camera before you film something, but there my technical expertise ends. When I direct, I know what I want, or more important, I know what I don't want.

For students of cinema, I have nothing of value to offer. My filming habits are lazy, undisciplined, the technique of a failed, ejected film major. As for writing, for those interested, I rise and after breakfast, work in longhand on yellow pads lying across my bed. I work all day and usually work at least part of every day of the week. This is not because I'm a workaholic but because work keeps me from facing the world, one of my least favorite venues. I go to my drawer to fish out notes I've accumulated throughout the year with ideas. If none of these ideas pan out after I think them through, then I force myself to think of a story to write, even if it takes weeks. It's the worst part of the process as it entails me sitting or pacing in my room alone day after day, trying to focus my concentration and not get sidetracked thinking of sex and death. Eventually, an inspiration comes, or more likely I settle for some workable premise, figuring I better shape up because baby needs a new pair of shoes.

I like writing more than shooting because shooting is hard, physical work in hot and cold weather at ungodly hours and requires a million decisions on subjects I know little about. Suddenly, I have to call the shots on camera angles and tempos and women's fashions and hairstyles and house furnishings and automobiles and music and colors. Not to mention that the meter is always running once filming begins, and at approximately a hundred or a hundred fifty thou a day, so if you fall behind a week, you've dropped a half million bucks. When the shooting finally ends, people you've worked day and night with intensely for months instantly go off in all directions, feeling sad and empty and vowing unending love and the desire to work together again. I usually say good-bye to the cast by shaking hands rather than the flashier kiss on the cheek or pretentious foreign double-cheek kiss. By the next morning, all the emotion and closeness has evaporated, and ones are already bad-mouthing certain others.

I enjoy sitting with my editor and gluing the cuts together, and mostly I enjoy picking out records from the collection and dropping them in, allowing the music to make the film look so much better than it really is. I like making movies, but if I never made another one it would not bother me. I'm happy to write plays. If no one would produce them, I'm happy to write books. If no one would publish them, I'm happy to write for myself, confident that if the writing is good, it will someday be discovered and read by people, and if it is bad writing, better no one sees it. Whatever happens to my work when I'm gone is totally irrelevant to me. After I'm dead, I suspect very little will get on my nerves, even that annoying noise the neighbors make with their leaf blower. The fun for me was always in the doing, and I was well paid and worked around gifted, charismatic men and gifted, beautiful women. I was lucky to have a sense of humor, or I would've wound up in some odd occupation like Fake Mourner or Circus Geek. I consider myself primarily a writer and that's a blessing, as a writer is never dependent on being hired to work but generates his own work and chooses his hours. Sometimes I think it would be fun to get up onstage and do stand-up comedy again, but then the thought of it fades.

Meanwhile, I go about my middle-class life. I practice

my horn (or as my mother used to say, "Oy, I have such a headache from him sitting in the bedroom, tweeting on his fife"). I turn out the pages, dote on Soon-Yi, and peel off twenties so my kids can go see movies that are not as good as ones I saw for twelve cents. How would I sum up my life? Lucky. Many stupid mistakes bailed out by luck. My biggest regret? Only that I've been given millions to make movies, total artistic control, and I never made a great film. If I could trade my talent for any other person's, living or dead, who would it be? No contest—Bud Powell. Though Fred Astaire's right up there. Who in history do I most admire? Shane, but he's fictional. Any women? There have been so many I've admired, from standards like Eleanor Roosevelt and Harriet Tubman to Mae West and my cousin Rita. I'll finally say, Soon-Yi. Not because if I don't, she'll kneecap me with the rolling pin, but because she hit the cruel streets alone at five to try for a better life, and despite dreadful obstacles made one for herself. The thing I most envy? Writing *Streetcar*. The thing I least envy? Frolicking in a meadow. If I had my life to do over, would I do anything different? I would not purchase that miracle vegetable slicer the guy advertised on TV. And really, no interest in a legacy? I've been quoted before on this, and I'll leave it this way: Rather than live on in the hearts and mind of the public, I prefer to live on in my apartment.